Students

SRHE and Open University Press Imprint
General Editor: Heather Eggins

Current titles include:

Mike Abramson et al.: *Further and Higher Education Partnerships*
Catherine Bargh, Peter Scott and David Smith: *Governing Universities*
Ronald Barnett: *Improving Higher Education*
Ronald Barnett: *Limits of Competence*
Ronald Barnett: *The Idea of Higher Education*
Tony Becher: *Governments and Professional Education*
Robert Bell and Malcolm Tight: *Open Universities: A British Tradition?*
Hazel Bines and David Watson: *Developing Professional Education*
John Bird: *Black Students and Higher Education*
Jean Bocock and David Watson: *Managing the Curriculum*
David Boud et al.: *Using Experience for Learning*
Angela Brew: *Directions in Staff Development*
Rob Cuthbert: *Working in Higher Education*
Roger Ellis: *Quality Assurance for University Teaching*
Maureen Farish et al.: *Equal Opportunities in Colleges and Universities*
Shirley Fisher: *Stress in Academic Life*
Sinclair Goodlad: *The Quest for Quality*
Diana Green: *What is Quality in Higher Education?*
Susanne Haselgrove: *The Student Experience*
Robin Middlehurst: *Leading Academics*
Henry Miller: *The Management of Change in Universities*
Jennifer Nias: *The Human Nature of Learning: Selections from the Work of M.L.J. Abercrombie*
Keith Noble: *Changing Doctoral Degrees*
Gillian Pascall and Roger Cox: *Women Returning to Higher Education*
Graham Peeke: *Mission and Change*
Moira Peelo: *Helping Students with Study Problems*
Tom Schuller: *The Changing University?*
Peter Scott: *The Meanings of Mass Higher Education*
Michael Shattock: *The UGC and the Management of British Universities*
Harold Silver and Pamela Silver: *Students*
John Smyth: *Academic Work*
Geoffrey Squires: *First Degree*
Kim Thomas: *Gender and Subject in Higher Education*
David Warner and Charles Leonard: *The Income Generation Handbook*
David Warner and David Palfreyman: *Higher Education Management*
David Warner and Elaine Crosthwaite: *Human Resource Management in Higher and Further Education*
Graham Webb: *Understanding Staff Development*
Sue Wheeler and Jan Birtle: *A Handbook for Personal Tutors*
Thomas G. Whiston and Roger L. Geiger: *Research and Higher Education*
John Wyatt: *Commitment to Higher Education*

Students

Changing Roles, Changing Lives

Harold and Pamela Silver

Society for Research into Higher Education
& Open University Press

Published by SRHE and
Open University Press
Celtic Court
22 Ballmoor
Buckingham
MK18 1XW

and 1900 Frost Road, Suite 101
Bristol, PA 19007, USA

First Published 1997

A catalogue record of this book is available from the British Library

ISBN 0 335 19558 X (pb) 0 335 19559 8 (hb)

Library of Congress Cataloging-in-Publication Data
Silver, Harold.
    Students: changing roles, changing lives / Harold and Pamela
Silver.
      p. cm.
    Includes bibliographical references (p.) and index.
    ISBN 0–335–19559–8 (hardcover). — ISBN 0–335–19558–X (pbk.)
    1. College students—Great Britain—Social conditions. 2. College
students—Great Britain—Conduct of life. 3. College students—
United States—Social conditions. 4. College students—United
States—Conduct of life. I. Silver, Pamela. II. Title.
LC208.8.S55 1996
378.1'98—dc20   96–25916
                                                                            CIP

Typeset by Graphicraft Typesetters Limited, Hong Kong
Printed in Great Britain by St Edmundsbury Press Ltd, Bury St Edmunds, Suffolk

Contents

Preface

The Introduction to our book suggests that previous research on 'students' has in fact focused principally on their learning and attainment, and on statistics. It was against this background that this book was planned in order to encourage what we hope will be a more systematic interest in the wider experience of the greater number and diversity of students, in their changing economic, social and cultural contexts, as well as in sources emanating from students themselves. It is some of the threads in the changing contexts and the changing lives and roles of the students that are the subjects of our discussion. The limits we have placed on the investigation arise from our central concern with students in the recent past, and the roots of important changes since the 1960s. Generally speaking, we have not been able to explore the experience of postgraduate or further education students, or – as we explain in the text – of Open University students. There are aspects of students' lives and roles to which we have had to pay only cursory attention, again for reasons which we hope the text will make clear. Over the time we have spent working on this book, with each of the visits we have made, with each archive or interview, we have realized more clearly the limits on the range of topics with which we could deal. Our picture and analysis may not be that of any one student, students' union, university or college, but we hope the features will be recognizable enough to prompt further interest in what we have, and have not, considered.

With the exception of a grant to help us visit the United States, the project has not had outside funding, and within the time-scale and resources it has not been possible for us to sample student cohorts over this period by interview or questionnaire, or to spend as long on some campuses as we would have wished. Our research has included core visits to 11 British and two American institutions for discussions and/or to consult records, and several others more briefly for specific purposes.

On our main visits we have consulted university or college records, either in archives or through the administration, including the minutes of senate or academic board, other senior committees or other bodies concerned with student affairs or welfare. This also included files of publications and other collections where they existed (for example, newspaper cuttings). We interviewed any available academic or administrative staff with long experience of the campus. At these institutions and others we examined students' union executive and general meeting records, other union documentation and files of student publications. Handbooks, leaflets, annual reports and other documentation by students' unions and other student bodies were crucial to the study. One difficulty is the relatively haphazard way in which students' unions keep or fail to keep their records, though in all cases we saw enough to contribute effectively to our research. We interviewed students' union presidents and a small number of other students and union staff. We were able to talk informally with other students, but these did not constitute formal interviews. Students' union officers and staff were unfailingly helpful in trying to locate documentation and in discussing their experience and impressions.

In addition to university and college libraries, we had access to the library of the National Union of Students and that of the Center for Studies in Higher Education at Pennsylvania State University.

We have listed in Appendices I and II details of the places visited or which provided material, the resources used, and the individuals interviewed, and we extend our warmest thanks to them all for their unfailing readiness to help. Some people played a particularly important role in helping to arrange our visits or in suggesting and establishing contacts. In the United Kingdom this applied: at the University of Durham to Ian Stewart, Deputy Secretary, and Victor Watts, Master of Grey College; at the University of Teesside to Mark White, Head of Academic and Administrative Performance; at Queen Margaret College, Edinburgh, to Tom Begg, Lecturer in Applied Consumer Studies; at the University of Plymouth to Christopher Sparrow, Academic Registrar; at the University of Glasgow to Forbes Munro, Clerk of Senate, Lawrence Reynolds, Assistant Clerk of Senate, and Lesley Richmond, Deputy Archivist; at the University of Strathclyde to Mike Day, Students' Association Membership Services Manager; at the University of Liverpool to Adrian Allen, University Archivist; at Nene College, Northampton, to Howard Parkinson, Students Union General Manager; at the University of East Anglia to Bill Rhodes, Union of Students Central Services Manager; at the Swansea Institute of Higher Education to Ken Reid, Academic Secretary and Registrar; at the National Union of Students to Sofija Opacic, Research Officer. In the United States this applied particularly at the University of Pennsylvania to Linda Koons, Executive Assistant to the Provost, and Mark Lloyd, Director, University Archives and Records Center; at Pennsylvania State University to Lee Upcraft, formerly Assistant Vice-President for Counseling Services and Program Assessment, and Leon Stout, University Archivist.

We offer our thanks for help of different kinds to the following: the Nuffield Foundation, for a grant towards the cost of our visit to the United States; Grey College, University of Durham, for a one-term Visiting Fellowship for Harold Silver which enabled this project to make a start; the Faculty of Arts and Education of the University of Plymouth for a part-time

Visiting Professorship for Harold Silver which helped in a number of much appreciated ways.

Some of the ideas in the book were tested out with students and staff in an inaugural lecture at the University of Plymouth, a public lecture at Nene College, and seminars at Grey College, Durham, the Centre for Applied Educational Research at the University of East Anglia, and a seminar at the National Union of Students annual summer conference for sabbatical officers held at Liverpool John Moores University.

We dedicate the book to students, especially those who have had, are having and will no doubt have to grapple with those problems that have been identified particularly with the 1980s and 1990s.

Harold Silver
Pamela Silver

Abbreviations

AAU	Academic Audit Unit (of the Committee of Vice-Chancellors and Principals)
AAUP	American Association of University Professors
ACE	American Council on Education
AGM	Annual General Meeting
AUT	Association of University Teachers
CCP	Center for Community Partnerships (University of Pennsylvania)
CHE	Committee on Higher Education (Robbins Committee)
CNAA	Council for National Academic Awards
CND	Campaign for Nuclear Disarmament
CSA	College Students' Association (Queen Margaret College)
CVCP	Committee of Vice-Chancellors and Principals
DES	Department of Education and Science
DFE	Department for Education
DSU	Durham Students' Union
EGM	Extraordinary General Meeting
EHE	Enterprise in Higher Education
EU	European Union
GUU	Glasgow University Union
HEQC	Higher Education Quality Council
JCR	Junior Common Room
MSA	Mature Students' Association
NBHS	National Bureau for Handicapped Students
NUS	National Union of Students
OGM	Ordinary General Meeting
PCAS	Polytechnics Central Admissions System
PSU	Pennsylvania State University
SA	Students' Association
SCA	Student Community Action
SCADU	Student Community Action Development Unit
SCANC	Student Community Action National Committee

SCANUS	Student Community Action in the National Union of Students
SCUE	Student Committee on the Undergraduate Experience (University of Pennsylvania)
SRC	Students' Representative Council (Durham)
SSLC	Staff/Student Liaison Committee (Teesside)
SU	Students' Union
SUS	Scottish Union of Students
SUSU	Sheffield University Students Union
THES	*Times Higher Education Supplement*
UA	University Assembly (University of Pennsylvania)
UCL	University College London
UEA	University of East Anglia
UGC	University Grants Committee
UPSU	University of Plymouth Students Union
USG	Undergraduate Student Government
USSU	University of Sussex Students Union
UWUS	University of Warwick Union of Students
VSU	Voluntary Service Unit

Notes

The references in square brackets are to the archival material in Appendix II. UPA, USG and similar references indicate the files of the relevant archives in Appendix II.

References to Penn are to the University of Pennsylvania, in Philadelphia. References to Penn State are to Pennsylvania State University in central Pennsylvania.

'Students' union' is used with an apostrophe except when used without in their title by specific organizations.

Introduction: Students as a Subject of Research

Our interest is in recent changes in significant aspects of students' lives and roles on campuses of higher education. What we mean by 'recent', 'lives' and 'roles' and the limitations we place on these and related terms will be explored as we proceed. First, let us clarify what this book is *not* about, by outlining what the interests of other researchers concerned with students have been.

The story of research about students in recent years says at least as much about researchers as it does about students. Who does the research? What are their motives? What do they want to know? For what purposes? Who else wants to know it? When does it become important to find out, and what do researchers ignore? A great deal of research that sounds as though it is about students is not about students at all. It is about statistics, totals, percentages, based on race or sex or age or social class. This literature answers questions about where students come from – geographically and socially, how many there are in what categories (for example, part-time or full-time), who obtains what degrees, and some of the reasons. Useful as the information is, the end product of the analysis is about higher education and social policy, opportunity and access, and its importance is as data for national and institutional policy-making. It is, with one important exception, not concerned with students themselves. The exception is the strong tradition of research into academic success and failure, with the distribution of classes of degree, with the teaching and learning and assessment of students. Books and articles with titles concerning *student learning, success* and *failure* form the largest part of the literature for the past half century or so. A survey of research on British students 20 years ago was concerned primarily with the effect of measurable factors on test scores and degree performance, and argued that this kind of classification was necessary in order to 'increase the utility of the research' (Biggs 1976: 87–8).

Interest in the causes of success and failure has at different times focused on the effects of family background, type of schooling, physical and mental health, social and sexual relationships, type of accommodation, and whatever seems to affect students' motivation. Most of this concentrates not on the experience itself but on how it influences academic outcomes. Again, this is important, given that the purpose of higher education has to be defined at least partly in terms of such outcomes, though it can also be defined in other ways. The purpose of such research, however, is not simply to know and understand students, it is most often to help to shape policy, to provide services, to improve institutional and teaching behaviours. Given the purposes (and often the sources of funding) of the research, it generally addresses only a severely limited range of students' experience, particularly given the rapidly increasing differences, internationally, in who students are, what they want and expect from higher education, and how they judge the experience.

The strange aspect of the story, therefore, is how little research exists on students as 'real people'. All research on human communities is complex, difficult and controversial, but that does not prevent researchers from doing it. The student 'community' seems a major exception. One study of student traditions as a field of research in the United States in 1935 did suggest that college life had special features which made the campus an 'experimental laboratory comparable to that of the biologist with his white rats, guinea pigs and drosophila flies' (Cowley and Waller 1979: 377). This was and remains nonsense. The campus is not that sort of laboratory, and students are not an object of study in that sense. They are, of course, an active, influential, participative force within the total campus and wider community, and they have become less and less homogeneous as a community themselves: their backgrounds and profiles make them an extremely diverse constituency – within a diversity of contexts. Are students in fact somehow 'different', or are they – as one American commentator suggested in 1962 – just the age group in a different place, a form of expensive youth culture (Millett 1962: 133)? That suggestion, of course, no longer applies when 'youth' describes – as in the British case – a minority of students.

Given the diversity of students and their life experience, why does anyone undertake the research, and for what purpose? An American anthropologist spent two years living among students at Rutgers University in order to explore what students make of this 'odd mixture of higher learning and youth culture', what kind of a life they lead and what they think about things (Moffatt 1991: 44–61). Such a research effort is unusual, however. Institutions which research student opinions about their courses, facilities and services – referred to blandly as 'feedback' or 'student satisfaction' surveys – do so with the intention of *using* the information in some way. One American study to find out about students' 'college involvement', for example, aimed at providing administrators of student services with data for planning purposes, as was a study of how roommates get on with one another – 'the level of rapport and compatibility', particularly 'peak alert time' – since information about students' daily period of 'maximal energy and alertness' would be a helpful 'matching factor' in placing students in shared rooms (Abrahamowicz 1988: 233; Carey *et al.* 1988: 239).

Such approaches to research can be categorized in broad outline through recent decades, and though the focus here is on British research, it is necessarily concerned also with the American research, given its greater scale and often its international influence.

What little British research on students there was in the 1950s focused on student success and failure, on students' backgrounds and the health and psychological factors affecting them. Nicholas Malleson, in charge of a student health unit at University College London, did most to establish this field of work, addressing the relationship of study techniques and academic performance to family and school background, sex, lodgings and other factors. He looked, for example, at the performance of what he called 'unioneers' and 'social isolates' (concluding that the union activists obtained fewer first-class and the isolates fewer poor degrees), and of those who lived in different types of accommodation. It was unusual for students in the 1950s in most institutions to be married at entry or to marry while students, and Malleson's conclusion was that 'a good many students get engaged, and some get married during their course. Some university teachers deprecate this, feeling it must be a diversion of energies from academic channels. There is nothing . . . to suggest this was so' (Malleson 1960b: 61; 1959–60: *passim*). Researchers in health and psychiatric services at the University of Leeds and the London School of Economics were concerned with 'the state of mental health of students', to which attention had been 'repeatedly called' since the war – depression, schizophrenia, suicide and factors which might impair the capacity to study, including family history, personality and love affairs (Still 1954: 32–5).

At a time when a very small proportion of the age group entered higher education, the interest in this field of research was predominantly in students' work habits and performance, and what might prevent them from completing their studies or succeeding in them. Researchers at UCL in the 1960s looked back over how little 'systematic enquiry into university "wastage" of students' there had been in Britain, and the vocabulary of their study of 'Mental health and student wastage' encompassed 'vulnerable' and 'emotionally disturbed' students, 'emotional ill-health', 'students under psychiatric care', 'character disorders', 'delayed students', 'wasted students' and evidence of some or marked disturbance, emphasizing 'the very variable relationship between mental health and capacity to sustain study' (Lucas *et al.* 1966: 277–82). The Provost of the College was moved to write a prefatory note suggesting that there were 'reasons for thinking that the picture may be changing for the better' (*ibid.*: 277). A 1954 symposium on 'health and the student' focused on the emergence of health services for students and some vivid portraits of the need. One commentary, urging improvement of human relations in universities, suggested cautiously that in doing so the university, 'while not responsible for predisposing its members to break down, will fulfil its duty to see that its social structure and climate do not bring the predisposed nearer to illness' (Still 1954: 38). A researcher from the Institute of Psychiatry at the University of London explained that:

With the psychiatric needs of the defective, the delinquent and the mentally severely ill making such obvious claims on our attention, it is easy to lose sight of the amount that can be done for the psychological health of those who are able and willing to take their place in the normal ranks of the community . . . the adolescents and young adults who make up the undergraduate population of our universities are at a stage in their development both personal and social which makes them peculiarly vulnerable and without the resources to fend for themselves.

Increased access to grants for higher education, and therefore the diversification of the student population, had also 'increased the financial and cultural difficulties incurred in becoming an undergraduate' (Read 1954: 39).

The meagre crop of research expanded in the 1960s, continuing to focus on what in Britain was unfailingly termed 'wastage' and its causes. One researcher found a higher failure rate among students who spent more than three hours a day in the students' union, or preferred to live at home, or did less than ten hours' studying a week. She also found more good degrees obtained by students who attended church regularly (Maclay 1968). But some of these attempts to establish correlations or cause and effect rested on uncertain foundations and were controversial. The research on the effects of different types of accommodation, for example, focused on the study habits and factors affecting them among students in halls of residence and other kinds of accommodation. Researchers probed what kinds of books students had read, what kind of conversations they had and with whom, their visits to cinemas and other forms of entertainment (see, for example, Mann and Mills 1961; Albrow 1966). The research was often tentative and the conclusions unreliable. There were different perceptions of different types of accommodation by men and women, but there was an emerging consensus about the social and academic value of halls of residence and their 'distinctive culture'.

Much was changing, however, in the 1960s. The cultural and social attitudes of students, and the emergence of student activism internationally as a significant feature of campus life, increased research interest in the social and psychological characteristics of students, together with those of the age group in general. A major interest therefore emerged in the concept of adolescence, and the particular nature of the student population, at a period of their lives seen by psychologists as no longer entirely one of the dependency of childhood or of the independence of adulthood.

Not until 1967 did a Lord Chancellor's Committee, the Latey Committee, recommend that the age of majority be lowered from 21 to 18, a measure accepted by the government and implemented by Parliament in the Law Reform Act of 1969. Until then students under the age of 21 were legally still 'children', and, like others in the age group, could not marry or take out a hire purchase agreement for a refrigerator or a guitar without parental consent. The pressures for change were strong, and the researchers were interested in the anomalous position of students whose 'social responsibilities of adulthood are postponed' but who were preparing for greater responsibilities than others in the age group already in employment (Abercrombie 1966: 13). The great majority of students at that time came straight from school at 18, and one study concluded that their position was one of a mixture of late adolescence and young adulthood, and that universities seemed to make 'deliberate attempts to extend this period of uncertainty and to delay full adulthood' (Oxtoby 1968: 444). The Latey Committee said clearly of young people in general that it felt 'extremely strongly that to keep responsibility from those who are ready and able to take it on is much more likely to make them irresponsible than to help them' (Lord Chancellor's Office 1967: 27). Researchers were concluding that students were in a period of 'role transition' and the associated stress (Miller 1968: 459) and of an 'abrupt alteration in status', resulting in what the title of one book called *Student Casualties* (Ryle 1969). The legacy in the 1960s was one of institutions shaping their provision to take care of what a character in an Anthony Powell novel had described as 'those uneasy, stranded beings, no longer a boy and hardly yet a man' (Powell 1951: 72). How that discussion might apply to women was not yet seriously on the agenda. Nor were other changes. This was the beginning of a period of higher education expansion, bringing in new student constituencies, the results of which were of only limited interest for research.

A good deal of this kind of research was paralleled in the United States, in terms of students 'experimenting with maturity' (Millett 1962: 110–11), the reasons for what Americans were investigating extensively as students' 'persistence' or 'non-persistence' or 'attrition' (Yonge 1965), the reasons for their disappointment and dropping out. Until the late 1960s there was little acceptance (although increasing student pressure) in the United States, as in Britain, of a role for students in the government, decision-making or 'political system' of the institutions. Neither in research nor in policy and public perceptions was there a perception of students living through a stage of life or a form of experience which merited such an involvement. A report by the influential Carnegie Corporation, published in 1960, talked of the need for American universities to find 'improved ways of enlisting all members of the enterprise – trustees, academic and administrative officers, faculty members, librarians, and maintenance employees – in a dynamically improving collaborative effort'. The exclusion of students was deliberate. Elsewhere the report lists students, together with alumni, professional associations and state governments, as an 'external group' (quoted in Foote *et al.* 1968: 75). The fact that student activism triggered many campus changes is a reminder of a different sort of research. In 1968–9 a House of Commons Select Committee studied and reported on the topic of 'student relations' in the wake of national and international events. That report and its six volumes of evidence (collected in writing, in committee interviews, and in visits not always welcomed by students) are both research and a major source for it – not least the evidence submitted by the National Union of Students and the Scottish Union of Students (House of Commons 1969a; 1969b; 1969c).

At the end of the 1960s Sir Eric Ashby was widely arguing the case for treating students as 'members' of a corporation (Ashby 1970: 2–3; Ashby and Anderson 1970: ix–x). The inquiry of the Select Committee and Ashby's views (which were discussed by the Committee with NUS representatives) are indications of the range of perceptions of students and their roles that had emerged in the second half of the 1960s. In the 1970s the research entered somewhat puzzling territory. Important changes in realities and perceptions had taken place. The lowering of the age of majority in Britain, followed in 1971 in the United States by the 26th Amendment which did the same thing, had implications for student representation and participation. What in this century had been known in both countries as *in loco parentis*, with institutions assuming the same roles of surveillance as parents, had now – at least formally – been abandoned. Although there was a considerable literature on youth and youth culture, the changes one might have expected in research on students in the 1970s were limited. Some researchers, particularly in the United States, further explored who were the activists and the causes of their activism (see, for example, Lipset 1972; Searle 1971), and there was some interest in Britain in what constituted 'campus culture', including the special role of residence (Wilson [1970]; Brothers and Hatch 1971), and the beginnings of an interest in the new constituencies of students in the expanded system, notably in the polytechnics (Whitburn *et al.* 1976), but the research basically continued along familiar channels.

Student 'wastage', personality problems, success and failure, and study methods, remained the core of research, though with a marginal interest also in the balance of student participation in the organized and informal life of the institution (Entwistle and Wilson 1977: 77–9). 'Wastage' had become a burgeoning activity. A report on the subject in 1971 listed work on this and related topics at 30 British and Irish universities, London University colleges and medical schools, and colleges of advanced technology, as well as in the United States and Australia. These were investigations 'into the causes of success and failure in academic performance', and the wastage recorded in this way indicated 'the efficiency of an educational process, and of the individual's reaction to that process. It can give a measure of the productivity of the system' (Heywood 1971: 230–7, 190–1). Health-related analyses continued in the tradition pioneered by Malleson. Some research related to the new contexts of higher education did begin to appear, looking at student perceptions of their education, including its vocational aspects (Brennan and Percy 1976), and aspects of student choice in the context of institutional changes (Adelman and Gibbs 1979). The debates about student representation were accompanied by much advocacy but little research into the meaning or impact of student representation in the government of institutions (Startup 1974).

The British research of the 1970s does not, for example, consider the powers of students' unions, the growth of student community action organizations, students' ambitions and horizons, and what was happening to the broad picture of students' lives on campuses, given that these now included diversifying colleges of education, polytechnics and universities of various vintages. What it meant to be a student could have very different connotations for new or changed constituencies of students in new conditions. One project in Australia asked students in three universities what they thought it meant to be 'a good student', and it did so because of the lack of studies of 'how the student role is defined' (Katz and Arbib 1971). One American book with an international interest addressed the question of whether students were apprentices, wards, clients, customers or members (Ross 1976: 67). The implications of major changes in the system, in individual institutions, in relationships between staff and students, in the nature of the student body, and in students' expectations and behaviours remained for the most part outside the interests of researchers, operating in traditions already defined heavily in statistical, psychological and medical terms.

A graphic example of the focus of research on American student behaviours is a book entitled *Revolving College Doors: The Causes and Consequences of Dropping Out, Stopping Out, and Transferring*, published in 1975. The bibliography contains some 450 items, the titles of all of them containing this kind of phraseology – success and failure, drop-outs, persisters and non-persisting students, student persistence, student attrition, withdrawal, why students fail, retention (Cope and Hannah 1975). This was not an isolated example, but a feature of the dominant research paradigm. The phenomena were, of course, different in many respects in the United States than in Britain, where only a fraction of the age group attended higher education by comparison. But like the British research tradition, the American had more to say about what institutions wanted to know and why than about the students themselves.

A British development in the 1980s and 1990s was an interest in the obviously important new or greatly expanded student constituencies – including part-time and adult students (Bourner *et al.* 1991; Percy 1985). Again, research projects tended to be concerned with numerical trends, educational provision and demand (Tight 1982), with clearly defined policy interests for the higher education system and its component parts. American interest in the changing student population had attracted consistent analysis from the late 1960s (see, for example, Astin 1991). Student course feedback was of growing interest in Britain and internationally (McDowell 1991; Silver 1992; Richardson 1994). Dominant research themes in Britain and other countries remained 'approaches to learning and perceptions of the learning environment' – the title of a special issue of *Higher Education* in 1991.

How little has been the research conducted on students beyond this cluster of themes can be seen from the entry 'students' in the index to the British *Research into Higher Education Abstracts,* published three times a year. In 1984 there were a dozen entries about students, to do with selection, careers and employment, employers' perceptions of students, the provision of part-time courses, lecturers' materials for students, and a range of even less directly relevant entries – on student numbers and, above all, examination results. Ten years later, in 1994, a similar number of entries had to do with franchising, bias in marking, awarding credit, *teaching* study skills, support systems in distance learning, and so on. In neither case was there even a handful of entries to do with the students themselves.

A continuing American interest was in those aspects of student life, including residence, which impinged on the responsibilities of 'student life administrators' (Abrahamowicz 1988). One American study, published in 1990, considered how students spend their time, including doing classwork, using computers, and attending concerts or the theatre, and it concluded that the students' experience was in general 'a rather prosaic, uninvolved affair' (Baird 1990: 271–7). There was also some American research on the change in the 1980s to what was sometimes called the 'me-generation' (Levine and Wilson 1979: 633–9), the generation of 'getting ahead', materialism and occupationalism – the importance to students in the United States, as in Europe and elsewhere, of the prospective employment market. An important feature of the American research in the recent past has been the continued strength of the research into teaching and learning, and the late 1970s and 1980s saw an increase in research on a range of influences on student development and academic outcomes (for example, Tinto 1975; Terenzini *et al.* 1982; Terenzini and Pascarella 1984).

Across these decades there are evident continuities but recognizable distinctions. There are also extraordinary silences. In 1966 the American historian, Frederick Rudolph, talked about the major impact of students as the 'most creative and imaginative force' in the history of American higher education, and yet the students themselves 'flow rather aimlessly in and out of our picture of the past'. The protests of the 1960s, he contended, were simply a fresh reminder of the students' presence. We knew about the roles of professors and finance and administration, but students 'as human beings' tended not to appear in the story (Rudolph 1966: 47–58). The first American attempt to chart the 'changing styles in undergraduate life' pointed out similarly:

> There are hundreds of histories of American colleges and universities. Unfortunately most institutional histories do not give much treatment to student life. They usually cover such subjects as the presidents who lead their institutions, the increases in enrollment over the years, and the number of new buildings that have been built.
>
> (Lee 1970: 176)

More recently, the study of student life at Rutgers commented on the way 'outside-the-classroom life' has been ignored in the research (Moffatt 1991: 45). A study of American higher education published in 1993 emphasized that students, along with professors, 'are at the core of the educational equation. They play a profoundly important role in shaping the ethos, culture, and orientation of colleges and universities everywhere . . . they are the defining characteristic of higher education'. The literature of higher education, however, was 'far more extensive about the influence of higher education on students than about the influence of students on higher education . . . the overall influence of students on the academy has received considerably less attention' (Altbach 1993: 203).

The treatment of 'students', historically and in the present, has for the most part been conceived in narrow and often misleading terms in Britain and the United States. British conferences and publications apparently concerned with 'the student experience' have focused only on corners of what the 'experience' has been or is. A revealing American example is an account of 'Research on college students' – with that title – which begins: 'The study of *college students* is relatively old compared to such avenues of inquiry as environmental studies, computer science, or semiotics'. That may seem self-evident, but it continues: 'Indeed, research on college *student attrition* has appeared in published form for at least sixty-five years' (emphasis added). The shift from the study of *students* to *student attrition* heralds attention to 65 years of work on reasons for students dropping out of college and research which, again, has entirely to do with 'student success', 'college outcomes', 'failure rates', 'withdrawal' and 'retention' (Stage 1990: 249–58). This is not to question the value of such research, but in presenting a collection of essays in this way on 'the cutting edge of quantitative college student research' (*ibid.*: 249) the author is not at the same time leading us to what he began by describing as the study of *college students*.

This outline of research done since the 1950s suggests the nature of some of the significant silences. In Britain there has been no research on the impact of the reduction in the age of majority on the lives of students, or on the strengths and weaknesses of changes in student representation on academic or administrative bodies from the early 1970s. There has been no research on students' unions or on participation in clubs and societies. The interest in poverty and debt, or in the increase in part-time work, produced some limited research on their implications for academic performance, but not on the campus lives of students – for example, their willingness and ability to stand for union office. The reason for their unwillingness, more than one students' union president suggested to us, is that students are 'concentrating far more on their academic work', reluctant to be diverted from their commitment to the twin targets of obtaining a degree and 'having fun': they 'work hard and play hard' (e.g. R. Curley, Weinstein ints). We know about the numbers, problems and academic attainment of part-time and mature students, but only anecdotally about their campus involvement or lack of it.

There has been little interest in the meaning and implications – rather than the assertion – of changing definitions of students, ranging from ward, apprentice or junior partner to customer, client and consumer. An American comment 60 years ago suggested that 'to the average undergraduate student life constitutes the real life of the college' (Cowley and Waller 1979: 387), but we do not know to what extent this has been or remains true in Britain. An American research project has for the past quarter-century mapped national changes in the student constituency and has concluded that over this period the attitude with the strongest upward trend has been students' aspiration to be 'very well-off financially' (Astin 1991: 131). There is very little British research evidence to go on. Another example of silence (except within student organizations themselves) is the growth, since the late 1960s but particularly in recent years, of Student Community Action by British students, in parallel with American 'service' activity or 'volunteerism'.

Another, very different, example could begin with a book about and for women students in the United States published in 1960, coming out of what now reads like a remote world, of interest here though it is not based on what we would describe as 'research'. The college girl, it tells us, 'sees her residence hall as a place to catch a 30-minute snooze after breakfast, a place to hang the clothes her roommate likes to borrow, a site for late-evening popcorn parties'. There are impromptu parties: 'maybe it's a Coke-'n-cookie affair celebrating somebody's "A" in trigonometry . . . Pincurls and pajamas replace taffeta dresses and satin slippers'. Someone demonstrates a new dance step, across the hall four girls are playing bridge, and 'a home economics major with a mouthful of pins is altering a dress for her roommate'. The authors suggest that

> the untidy girl who leaves her bed unmade and clothing strewn may find herself with an unhappy roommate . . . College girls give one another advice on hair styles, grooming, what to do at fraternity dances, what to wear to a garden party, how to keep kid gloves clean . . . exchange confidences about life, love, religion . . . the chatter really reaches a peak on the night of a formal dance. Clouds of pink tulle and white satin float through the corridors. Perfume fills the air and fingers tug anxiously at long white gloves. Elegant corsages in cellophane boxes bring gasps and little cries of pleasure.
>
> (Muller and Muller 1960: 79–82)

One chapter is entitled 'Tips for dating'. This is not research, but it is – taken with much caution – evidence for the researcher. The two authors of the book, one a former member of staff of a state college for women and the other on the staff of a major university, do tell us something about the social composition, values, attitudes, behaviour and campus life, in this case the all-important 'dormitory life', of at least one kind of institution. They also tell us something about the 'between world' of the adolescent female student as perceived not many decades ago. The portrait has to be set, however, against what one British sociologist describes as the 'unpolitical revolt of youth in the 1950s, which was symbolized in the films, and the life, of James Dean', and from which the student political movement of the 1960s seemed a continuation (Bottomore 1968: 428). A study of whether this picture of college life was paralleled by the experience of any British women students several decades ago, and what has changed in their campus identities since then, would find little systematic evidence, on this as on other aspects of campus experience.

There is no readily available evidence of student interest in systematically exploring their campus lives. The limited and short-term research effort that the NUS is able to mount is inevitably geared to providing evidence for debate and policy purposes. Students themselves do not become involved in assignments on such topics, and local students' unions have only rarely surveyed their members – and the results have been either on too small a scale to seem important elsewhere, or they have not become public. Students' union records, however, as well as institutional records relating to students, student affairs and students' unions, often do contain clear indications of students' behaviour on and off campus, and tackle a variety of campus issues and students' concerns – the roles of bars, sports facilities or societies, political, social and moral attitudes, issues relating to mature or overseas students or students with special needs. They call attention to efforts to improve the course representation system or the efficiency of the students' union itself, as well as reluctance to stand for election to office – a Nene College student paper headline referred to the 'Collapse of Democracy', and a later issue appeared with a blank front page and announced 'This page cancelled due to lack of interest' [*Link*, February 1977, March 1978]. A research interest in the NUS, its functions and policies (Appleton [1987]; Rhodes 1990; Thorn 1991) has not been matched by any extensive interest in the operation of campus students' unions, though there is a small number of 'house histories' (for example, Bates and Ibbetson 1994; Warner 1985). There has been no consistent research interest in the clues the records can provide about continuity, development and change in attitudes and activities. In our experience few university and college libraries and archives attempt to preserve students' union records, or to persuade and help the students' unions themselves to do so. Executive, general meeting and other minutes and papers are treated as dispensable ephemera by more or less everyone concerned. No research advantage has been taken of student publications, or the experience of student officers or students generally, or of former students, contact with whom has become increasingly possible as a result of the growth of alumni organizations in Britain from the 1980s.

The reason, as we have suggested, is the strong influence on research of the demands and pressures of public policy, and in the case of higher education the institutions' own internal pressures to attract, keep and improve the academic performance of their students for accountability and funding reasons. This explains the *kind* of research that is common in the United States, where 'attrition' may often account for more than half of the entering students, where the data needs of student services and other personnel are paramount, alongside the salient concerns (now equally salient in Britain and elsewhere) with the elements of teaching, learning, assessment and student progress, and employment. We have seen what limits all this has placed on an interest in the students themselves, and what has been true in the United States has become increasingly true in Britain. What Rudolph wrote in his article on the 'Neglect of students as a historical tradition' still raises questions in both countries: 'College students constitute the most neglected, least understood element of the American academic community . . . Neglect of students as alive human beings is a venerable academic tradition, a tradition that deserves inspection and repudiation' (Rudolph 1966: 47, 58).

1

Students in Contexts

In some ways for all students, and in fundamental ways for most, their educational and wider worlds have changed. What it means to be a student is itself not what it was a quarter of a century, or a decade, ago. Universities which did not exist in the 1950s today have several thousand students and an established identity, having remodelled a somewhat different one. Students who would not have had the opportunity or the incentive to enter higher education in 1960 or 1970, or even 1980, are entering either from school or having rediscovered at a later stage a possible purpose and identity after failing to do so at school. They and their institutions vary. Many, in some institutions, have inherited but adapted the confidence of a tradition, while others have helped to create one. Not for all students is this an in-between time, a halting place between school and life. It is for many a time shared with jobs and families, one in which credit may be accumulated or transferred, one which may be an anxious prelude to the difficult employment market.

There are continuities. Students learn and are assessed, they make friends and allegiances, form ambitions, play sports and join societies, are concerned about finance, their sexual roles and experience, and succeed or fail academically. But their expectations are not now as those of students used to be – their expectations of academic or social life, relationships, leisure, access to jobs and security, independence and status. In many respects the vocabularies are unchanged – lectures, examinations, assignments, sport, sex, drink, and so on. Their world is not entirely new, but those who were there 30 or 20 or 10 years ago recognize the differences. We are concerned here not with the implications of all of these and related features, but with some of the aspirations and experiences of students outside the formal academic processes. We are engaging not just with student diversities but also with commonly held models and images. What it means to be a student is only in part a Durham question or a Plymouth question, a Scottish question or a Pennsylvania question: it is also a BBC, a *Guardian*, a *Daily Mail* question, a mature student and overseas student question, a matter of sudden change and long histories.

We shall explore the parameters of some of these images of what students are and what defines them. Historically the images have had less to do with the classroom than with students in the street and the inn, whoring and rowing, enjoying the privileges of the interval between school and 'life'. Images are almost always obsolete. That more than half of students no longer come straight from school is the kind of reality that takes a long time to affect the images. That students are almost by definition politically and in every other way radical, are promiscuous, riotous, alcoholic layabouts, has for more than seven centuries been the essence of the truth as seen by image makers and disseminators. The images, including the students' own images, have always reflected some reality, but rarely accurately reflected the dominant experience and roles of students in their learning and other environments.

The student experience is not, indeed, divided into unrelated 'academic' and 'other' categories, and it is important therefore to retain in the discussion a sense of how closely interrelated are the fragments of the student's experience. Attending lectures and visiting the library are not unrelated to the student's allocation of time, relations with peers, need for recreation, anxieties about the future. Students shape themselves in relation to the changing constituencies, activities and attitudes of their peers, traditional or innovative curricular structures, common or diverse uses of new technologies, old or new understandings of 'learning' and 'assessment', differences in institutional styles and cultures. All the partners in the higher education enterprise help to establish the presence of the outside world and the amalgam of experiences of it, its conflicts of values, its impacts on the present and future lives of students.

The 'experience' and 'roles' of students when not involved in lectures, laboratories, tutorials, writing essays, working in libraries or with information technology, are subject to influences along a variety of axes. Their activity and inactivity are influenced by institutional and personal factors, including where they are, what is expected of them by the institution and their peers, what they themselves expect, fashion, finance, and the anticipation of employment and unemployment. These are sociological and economic factors, but they are also historical, determined by the interaction of institutional and personal histories. Numbers are important – the scale of institutions and their residential accommodation, the numbers of fellow mature students, the sense of involvement or isolation deriving from the size of classes or the operation of the students' union: its bars, discos, clubs and societies, the effectiveness of student representation at course or other levels. Discussion of students in recent decades has to remain close to discussions of the scale and pattern of student recruitment, and the size, patterns and pressures of higher education itself.

In the mid-1990s there were roughly $1\frac{1}{2}$ million students in UK higher education, almost 1 million of whom were on full- or part-time first degree courses. In 1938–9 there were 50,000 students in UK universities (when 'higher education' in fact meant the universities). A rapid but painful process of postwar growth took numbers to nearly 80,000 in 1947, and 90,000 in 1956. A decade later the government target was 150,000, which was resisted by the universities for lack of resources (University Grants Committee 1948; 1953; 1958; Association of University Teachers [1963b]). Involved in this and later expansion was a degree of planning in response to pressures of various kinds – for more scientists and technologists, and more places for would-be students – and for all the reasons presented to the Robbins Committee on Higher Education appointed in 1960. A view from 1947 was that British higher education had grown up casually, never 'viewed, much less planned, as a whole. A cynic might give a book on the subject the title of "Drift"' (Livingstone 1948: 12–13). The story of the world entered by students from that time, however, was one of a strong mixture of drift and a growing element of planning. This was true of other countries, including the different 'system' of the United States, where the number of college students grew, for example, from 3.8 million to 8.5 million between 1960 and 1970, and then more slowly, levelling off at 12 million between 1980 and 1990 (Stadtman 1980: 16–17; Altbach 1993: 204–5). By the 1980s roughly a third of 18–24-year-olds in the United States were attending college, and between 1974 and 1988 the number of students over 24 grew from 3.2 to 5.1 million (American Council on Education 1984: 1; Andersen 1990: 1–2). Campuses of over 50,000 and classes of 1,000 were increasingly familiar (Lee 1970: 122–3). Pennsylvania State University, for example, had reached (at its main and branch campuses) 55,000 in 1973, 63,000 in 1983, and 68,500 in 1993. State-wide planning in some cases and private initiative in others resulted in a mixture different from the British position in many ways, but with similar elements of planning and drift. There are a number of entry points, important to our later discussions, through which to approach the issues and realities concealed by such aggregate numbers.

First, there are the student constituencies. In 1938–9, for example, the ratio of men to women among full-time British students was roughly four to one (UGC 1948: 13). After the postwar ex-service students had left the system the number of older undergraduates in the universities was minute. By the mid-1970s, however, the number of undergraduates over 21 on entry had risen to 17 per cent of the whole (30 per cent for full-time and sandwich students on the courses of the Council for National Academic Awards) (Jones and Williams 1979: 14).

Second, the comparatively small total numbers, compared with those of later decades, disguise the degree of strain involved at all stages of the expansion, in particular the economic difficulties of the immediate postwar period. The existing and planned increase was described by the University Grants Committee in 1948 as involving 'problems for the universities of the most profound importance' (UGC 1948: 32), given doubts at the time, especially among the vice-chancellors, about the reservoir of suitable students, and the lack of resources – which had 'imposed heavy strains on staff and students alike' (*ibid.*: 35). The UGC concluded in 1953 that 'no further substantial increase in student numbers could be expected in the immediate future without reducing university standards' (UGC 1953: 26). Expansion continued to be faced with the same problems and the same resistances. In the 1960s the Association of University Teachers and others were underlining the impossibility of targeting growth without adequate funding (AUT [1963b]). Voices sympathetic to expansion were pointing to overcrowding and its effect on the quality of life of staff and students: 'Many students are concerned that the university should be a community, and that it fails to be one. This lack of community may well be a function of size' (Gowenlock 1962: 65). Less sympathetic voices were decrying the continuing attempt to expand. Already in 1948 universities were described as seriously damaged by 'desperate overcrowding', the outcome of a fundamentally flawed assumption: 'the world is "explosive", therefore the universities should explode' (Oakeshott 1989: 111, 117). The underlying issues were to re-emerge at critical moments in the demographic and financial changes of the following decades.

The third crucial point in disaggregating the total figures for the past half century is the differential impact on institutions. Initially this meant demands on the existing universities and the remaining university colleges such as Hull and Southampton to meet the targets of overall growth. A Committee on the Future of the University College of Hull reported in 1950 that the plan for 1951–2 was to reach 1,000 students, and thought the optimum number for 1957 was 'probably not more than 1,250, or at the very most 1,500, but growth should not be forced even to the extent of the lower figure'. By 1963–4 Hull in fact had 2,250 students, a 208 per cent increase in less than ten years, when the average national increase across the same period was 54 per cent (CHE Appendix Two (A) 1963: 19). The main burden of growth was borne by the 'provincial universities', and Birmingham, for example, was planning to increase its numbers from 4,500 in 1961 to 7,000 in 1970 and 10,000 by 1980 (Gowenlock 1962: 65; AUT [1963b]). The University College of Swansea, with 1,700 full-time students in 1961–2, had almost doubled that number by 1967–8 (and was to have 8,300 full-time and 1,300 part-time students in 1994–5). From the early 1960s the pattern of growth within which students could declare choices included the new (to be nicknamed 'plateglass' or 'green fields') universities established before or as a result of the Robbins Report in 1963; the colleges of advanced technology, which in the middle of the decade were either given university charters or amalgamated into the federal universities of Wales or London; the development of the regional colleges under the National Council for Technological Awards from 1955; the creation of the CNAA in 1964, and the polytechnics from the end of the decade; the colleges of education and the creation of the colleges of higher education in the 1970s. It is important to pursue some final implications of these indicative numbers.

It was ultimately the polytechnics that were to have the strongest impact on the statistics and pattern of higher education as they attracted different student populations – including local, mature and part-time students. They offered a broadening range of courses for awards of the CNAA, and in the 1980s and 1990s expanded most rapidly and were incorporated into a single university sector in 1992. In 1971 Plymouth Polytechnic, for example, had under 1,000 full-time or sandwich course students. By 1978 it had over 3,000 full-time equivalents. It continued steadily or in leaps by amalgamation (with colleges of education, art and agriculture) to increase its numbers of full- and part-time students as Polytechnic South-West and then as the University of Plymouth. By 1992–3 its numbers exceeded 15,000, over 10,000 of whom were full-time or sandwich students, and 2,600 of whom were enrolled for its courses at partner institutions. Such patterns of growth, in some cases on a larger scale, were common features of the polytechnics, as was the pattern of recruitment, including greater numbers and proportions of mature and part-time students than was common in the older universities.

Expansion of the system and of individual institutions also had other repercussions for students, including the balance of residence and non-residence. It was the view of the UGC in the early 1960s that any new university should be able to plan for at least 3,000 students and have a minimum of 200 acres, and John Fulton, Vice-Chancellor of the University of Sussex at the time, thought that 3,000 students was 'a not unsatisfactory equilibrium' in which the university could make appropriate provision and students find their bearings (Fulton 1962: 54; UGC 1963: 94). This question of size dominated much of the discussion about new universities and about the student experience in the 1960s – in continental Europe and the United States, Australia and elsewhere, as well as in the United Kingdom. Fulton pointed out that predecessors of the new universities had not had to ask such questions as 'How big shall we be?', which had become crucial questions (*ibid.*: 48). Two years later, he again emphasized that creating a new institution in the new conditions meant confronting the questions of 'How big?' together with 'How soon?' and 'How fast?' Was it to be a university 'of 3,000 or 10,000 (Robbins's figure) or 25,000 (London University) or 100,000 (University of California) or what?' His answer remained that a desirable 'community of scholars' was 300–400 strong, and this translated into a total student population – undergraduate and graduate – of some 3,000 (Fulton 1964a: 6). The pressures to grow beyond these commonly accepted figures of the 1960s were those of what Martin Trow considered, on an international stage, to be the transition from elite to mass education. By the beginning of the 1970s the pressures in Britain and Europe had meant that 'growth has mainly been by expanding the elite university system. But the old institutions cannot expand indefinitely; they are limited by their traditions, organization, functions, and finance' (Trow 1972: 3).

The implications of growth were to be momentous in various ways, though for most of the half-century following the Second World War it would be misleading to talk of mass higher education in the United Kingdom. The creation of a 'binary' system of universities and polytechnics, followed by colleges of higher education, the increased scale of institutions, the impacts on organization and relations, and on the traditional sense of a university or college 'community', all contributed to the emergence of student activism in the second half of the 1960s, in Britain as in other countries. Questions of control and administration, discipline and regulations, 'participation' and 'representation', accommodation and student finance, access and equity, the teaching–learning relationship and assessment, and the very nature and purpose of a 'higher education' all came under new and often intense scrutiny and controversy. The tensions of a system moving, often slowly and jerkily, towards a 'more mass' higher education were those of reluctant change, of modelling at least some of the new on the long established – with elements of change in the curriculum, policy- and decision-making, and the student population.

One feature of the new universities of the early 1960s was the appearance of new curricular shapes or collegiate structures within which students were to find a 'home' different from that of conventional departments. This was particularly so in the case of four of the seven new universities, intending to provide students with 'a smaller and more intimate focus for academic and social life than that provided by a university which, within the foreseeable future might contain 6,000 or more students' (UGC 1963: 109). There were from the early 1960s attempts to adapt the increasingly large institutions to the British tradition of providing students with a sense of belonging in a community of manageable size. The staff–student ratio, relatively favourable by comparison with equivalent American and European institutions, the tutorial system, and attempts to provide a period of campus residence, were being sustained with difficulty. The Chaplain to the University of Edinburgh in 1961 described the 'unique pattern of a community of learning' at Oxford and Cambridge, where scholars submitted themselves to 'a well-defined academic, social and residential discipline'. He warned against the tendency 'to reproduce this discipline in institutions whose roots and presuppositions . . . are quite different' (Home Universities Conference 1961: 45). The problem of adaptation in the new conditions of increased scale was not confined to the United Kingdom. Some American campuses, for instance, experimented with 'collegiate' sub-structures, and there were European echoes. A view from the Catholic University of Louvain, Belgium, encapsulated the issues as seen in the 1970s:

> The problem of the student and mass higher education is partially a question of how to recapture the finer qualities of university life lost or threatened in the larger institutions and how to restore the confidence of the younger generation in its teachers.
>
> (de Jonghe 1973: 243)

Red Brick University and *Redbrick and These Vital Days* by Bruce Truscot (the pseudonym of Liverpool University professor, E. Allison Peers), published and widely discussed in 1943 and 1945, triggered discussions which continued long after the war about a range of features of what were also often called the 'civic' or 'provincial' universities. Truscot's strong message was of underfunded, underprivileged institutions, which were not understood, whose mission was not clearly understood by themselves, and whose students had few of the advantages of an Oxbridge education. Newly established or 'promoted' institutions of higher education, of course, had in the past had to overcome such problems of the quality of their facilities and to defend the standard of their courses. The same was to be true of further waves of entrants into the definition of university or higher education, with the exception of the purpose-built plateglass universities of the 1960s. The colleges of advanced technology, the colleges of education, the polytechnics and the colleges of higher education encountered various degrees of difficulty and prejudice. In 1968, for example, the University of Warwick Union of Students – at a university then only three years old – looked with some anxiety at 'the technical or polytechnical institutions'. The purpose of a university was to offer 'a whole education' and to engender a sense of responsibility. A university was 'a community of equals pursuing knowledge', it 'teaches one to think', rather than just providing vocational training – the latter by implication what the competitor institutions provided (UWUS 1968: I, 1–2). The CNAA, the polytechnics, and the latter when they were renamed universities in 1992, suffered the same problems of public perception as their predecessors had done.

What students wanted or expected from higher education was only partly governed by the particular kind of institution and its reputation, important though these were in terms of full- or part-time attendance at an institution, living at home or in lodgings or in a hall of residence, and by images of what constituted a 'real' university within the hierarchy established for them by teachers, parents and folklore. A small amount of research in a number of countries, particularly in the 1970s, suggested a degree of constancy across types of institution and time in students' reasons for applying for higher education. An Australian study in 1964 concluded that 70 per cent of students entered university for vocational reasons (Philip *et al.* 1964: 44). Another Australian report then found that student motivation in entering a university was based on 'quite definite occupational expectations'. Fewer than 10 per cent admitted 'to being uncertain or undecided about the occupation which they intended to enter', and there was consensus about a cluster of goals, including 'generalised vocational preparation' (Katz and Katz 1967: 8–11; 1968: 111–18). A project in Hawaii in 1960–3 found the majority of university students to be 'degree-bound, security-minded, and achievement-dominated' (Dole 1970: 375–7). British research pointed in similar directions. Grammar school aspirants for university or college (which at the time could include polytechnic and teacher education), as reported in 1970, considered the 'definite vocational purpose' to be important (71 per cent of university aspirants, 87 per cent of college aspirants) (Cohen 1970: 68–72). A report two years later on university students at Swansea concluded that '90 per cent of the students indicated that considerations to do with future occupation did contribute to their attempts to gain entrance to the university' (Startup 1972b: 319–30). Research in the mid-1970s suggested that the majority of sixth-formers 'had a particular career in mind – 52 per cent definitely and 28 per cent probably. Girls were more likely than boys to have a firm idea of what they wanted to do' (Gordon and

Williams 1977: 30). A study of the goals and aspirations of higher education students concluded that 'there is a sense in which vocational goals are relevant to all students in higher education' (Brennan and Percy 1976: 150).

As attention shifted in the 1980s and 1990s to such areas as graduate employment, employers' perceptions and needs, and the skills and competences required to enter and succeed in the employment market, this interest in student motivation weakened. However, these reminders of the 1960s and 1970s are important, despite other studies with more ambiguous findings, and some difficulty in interpreting the meanings of 'vocational' and 'occupation'. The dominance of other themes from the 1960s, notably the expansion and diversification of higher education, funding, autonomy and the state, and student militancy and passivity, has disguised this level of continuity in student expectations.

The 1960s were important in many respects in the history of higher education. Students found the contexts changing in obvious and sometimes perplexing ways, and the implications of these changes will be elements in our continuing discussion. Student life in the 1960s was conditioned by developments beyond higher education itself – not only in the political and international issues prominent from the 1960s, but also in more personal terms. The statutory grant for full-time university students had been introduced following the Anderson Committee's recommendations in *Grants to Students* in 1960 (Ministry of Education 1960b), and the level of grant was to be an increasing focus of concern and agitation as economic conditions changed from the late 1970s. The decline or uncertainty of graduate employment prospects affected students' attitudes towards their studies and campus activities, and also in many cases their choice of course and therefore the popularity of subjects and courses. The scale and nature of institutions, in some polytechnics in the 1970s and more widely across higher education from the 1980s, led to changes in students' opportunities for curriculum choice – notably through modular structures. Accompanying changes in examination practices directly affected new generations of students. In those institutions where the traditional final or end-of-year examinations were replaced by assessment within term- or semester-long modules, more continuous pressure was placed on students to succeed in modules which could count from the outset towards their degrees. Students could also be strongly affected by scale, as numbers at lectures and tutorials increased, while in some situations they could benefit from more participative teaching and learning strategies.

A major implication of expansion was continual concern about the provision and nature of residential accommodation. Student life in the traditions of Oxford and Cambridge overwhelmingly meant residence in college or hall, certainly for the first year (followed by residence in approved lodgings or other accommodation). In the 1950s and 1960s slightly over half the students at these universities lived in colleges or halls, and small English civic universities often matched this figure. The Robbins Committee reported that the figures for students in these kinds of residence were 51 per cent for Oxford, 55 per cent for Cambridge, 56 per cent for Reading, 52 per cent for Leicester, 42 per cent for Exeter, 68 per cent for Durham and 98 per cent for Keele. Most of the larger civic universities had between 10 and 25 per cent in residence, and the figure for Wales was slightly higher. In Scotland, with different traditions, numbers ranged (with the exception of St Andrews, which had 37 per cent) between 3 and 13 per cent, with Edinburgh at 13 per cent and Glasgow at 7 per cent. The national average, at 28 per cent, was slightly more than half that of Oxford and Cambridge (UGC 1953: 28; CHE Appendix Two (A) 1963: 176). The figures were generally higher for teacher education. Halls of residence were broadly accepted as the most desirable form of residence for the overwhelming majority of students – who, until over a quarter of a century later, were young school leavers. Truscot, during the Second World War, felt that the case for halls of residence, at least for one year of residence, had been won (Truscot 1945: 49), though winning the case – as the redbrick universities and then the polytechnics were to discover – was not the same as securing the finance and the amenities.

From the 1950s students in England were increasingly to attend universities away from home, though the polytechnics of the 1970s and 1980s, partly because of their sub-degree and part-time courses, had significant local and regional student clienteles. By 1960 Queen Mary College, London, had found that it was 'no longer a local East London institution in the sense that it once was', a fact which mirrored tendencies 'which are apparent both nationally and elsewhere in London University' (Kendall and McDonnell 1960: 29). By the late 1950s the UGC was recording, for the whole of the United Kingdom, a steady fall in the numbers attending a university within 30 miles of home. Between 1951–2 and 1956–7, for example, the numbers dropped from 44 to 38 per cent (UGC 1958: 25). Not until the 1990s was this trend to be halted. The position across these decades in Scotland was different. In 1961–2, when the average number of English students living at home at the larger civic universities was 18 per cent, at the smaller civic 4 per cent, and at London 26 per cent, the average in Scotland was 47 per cent – 70 per cent in Glasgow. The Scottish Union of Students, while emphasizing to the Robbins Committee its support for halls of residence, suggested in oral evidence that 'there has grown up in Scotland a pattern of applying to one university. If it cannot take you then you do not go to university' (CHE Evidence Pt 1, vol. C 1963: 898). Although the figures for home-based students declined in Scotland, in the 1990s the figure for Glasgow was still over 40 per cent, and for Strathclyde over 70 per cent. The Students' Association President interviewed at the latter, a law student, had spent all his four years living at home in Glasgow (McMonagle int.). Scotland's tradition of 'more local' universities colours some aspects of the Scottish student experience discussed in later chapters.

Halls of residence and university 'licensing' of lodgings relate to later discussions about the doctrine of *in loco parentis* and its abandonment, questions of discipline and codes of behaviour, and the interpretation by students and others of the nature of a community. In very many American institutions there was a strong attraction for non-residential or commuter students much earlier than in England, and a more persistent sense of the custodial function of halls and their pivotal role in the pattern of services provided by universities and colleges for residential students. In Britain, before the formal ending of *in loco parentis* following the report of the Latey Committee in 1967, there was indeed a strong regulatory basis for residence in hall, whether in Oxbridge, the civic universities or teacher education, but together with a pervasive sense of the cultural advantages involved. This was not just a question of following the Oxbridge model, but also a commitment to the major benefits for the increasing numbers of students from less advantaged backgrounds, a case which Truscot had made particularly powerfully in the 1940s. His analysis was based on the realities of students' attempts to study in inappropriate conditions, with long journeys, and inhospitable redbrick university conditions (Truscot 1951: 33–4). The UGC's argument was straightforward: the case for residential accommodation was reinforced 'by the presence in the universities of increased numbers of students who come from homes with little or no tradition of culture and whose undergraduate lives would be greatly enriched by a period of residence in hall' (UGC 1953: 28–9). The Committee on the Future of the University College of Hull in 1950 set out in full the purpose and virtues of halls of residence, views that were probably commonly held – at least until the expansion of the 1970s and after:

> One of the main difficulties with which the College is faced is the lack of background in many of its students. This raises problems of teaching but also leads us to a consideration of the ways in which the life of the College community can be so ordered as to compensate for deficiencies in earlier upbringing and education. Here the function of the Halls of Residence is one of the main matters to be considered. In our opinion the stress should be on the positive contribution which they should make to the development of our students rather than on the opportunity they give us for exercising a wider control.
>
> [Hull 1950: para. 4]

Halls of residence were not, however, to prove the only solution.

As the numbers of students increased so did the expectation of suitable accommodation, but also the interest in independent living. Institutions were under pressure to recruit, including students from overseas, and students were under new peer and social pressures to gain entry. From the beginning of the 1970s, as institutions faced the problems of increased recruitment without equivalent residential accommodation, the word 'crisis' began to appear at regular intervals in the internal reports of institutions, the pages of student newspapers and the local and national press. At the University of Liverpool, in the 1971–2 session 518 men were placed in approved lodgings – a type of accommodation previously used only for women students [Guild A. 032/45 1 February 1972]. At Glasgow in 1974 students squatted in unoccupied University premises, and in 1975 the Students Representative Council turned its offices into temporary accommodation because of the crisis [Glasgow cuttings 27 April 1975]. In 1976 Teesside Polytechnic was facing an accommodation crisis, and the local paper announced: 'a desperate lodgings crisis has forced Teesside Polytechnic to limit its student intake – for the first time ever'. Its first step had been to stop offering places to overseas students, producing a strong reaction from the Students' Union, which expressed its objection to what it saw as a racist decision [SU Council 13 September 1976, 7 October 1976, 19 October 1976]. The recurrence of crises was being reported nationally across the 1970s and into the 1980s. In October 1988 the Liverpool Guild Council described 'the present appalling accommodation crisis', and in October 1989 there were 400 new students without rooms, announced by the students' *Gazette* as 'New Term – Old Problem' [Council 13 October 1988; *Gazette* 19 October 1989]. As rapidly as institutions tried to build or acquire accommodation, the pressure of student numbers presented new and considerable difficulties. Across Britain in the 1970s and 1980s there were stories of new students being accommodated, if only on a temporary basis, in gymnasia or libraries, and one response of universities old and new in the 1990s was to raise capital on the finance market to build new halls of residence. The student experience was therefore often dominated by accommodation questions, including those of cost and alternatives, preference, dissatisfaction with the early new halls, and fluctuating interest in independent, off-campus living.

These are just some of the broad contexts within which students have been defined and have defined themselves, mainly those strands of postwar development which have influenced student perceptions and experience. Students have become increasingly diverse, as have their environments, though with continuities in both. We shall return to these and other features of students' lives which explain what it has meant and means to be a student presented with new choices, opportunities and pressures, in often unstable institutional and wider conditions. An important part of the discussion is inevitably concerned with the prevalent perceptions of students, which have continued to change with the moving picture of higher education in recent decades. One European commentator portrays what he calls the permanent image of students as young alcoholics, on which have been superimposed other images associated with the changing world of higher education since the Second World War. At the end of the war students were seen as hard-working, privileged, with values in common with their society. By the mid-1960s there was a diminution in student–society understanding, and students seemed uneasy but qualified. By the end of the decade they were alienated, prepared to act illegally, and contributing to an increasingly negative image of the university (Seidel 1979: 7–13). When the retired president of a Canadian university, also in the 1970s, questioned whether the role of the student was that of apprentice, ward, client, customer, or member and citizen of the university, or some combination of these, he emphasized that the role of the student had not become a burning question in the university until 1960 (Ross 1976: 67–8).

All attempts to define and portray students have had to come to terms with their association with the period of 'adolescence' (even as the proportions of older students have increased). In the 1980s one historian of higher education considered the most critical latent function of the university to have been, and to be, 'keeping adolescents out of trouble', though with decreasing efficacy. By the 1980s Oxbridge college gates were kept open, one writer describing how 'men and women live unsupervised side by side in the same colleges, and students are free to enter the pubs of the city. Provided they behave discreetly, no one bothers any more about how they conduct their private lives' (Stone 1983: 27). From the mid-1970s in the United States and then in Britain they became consumers, and then they could be seen as purchasers (El-Khawas 1977: 169; Higher Education Quality Council 1994c: 217–19). These and other definitions have been framed by government funding policies, changing conditions of graduate employment, the constituencies of students and their reasons for entering higher education, and the ways in which they and their contexts have determined their lives and roles. We are inevitably concerned with both the images and the realities.

2

The Students

Traditionally the 'student as adolescent' has been at the heart of the model, challenged increasingly by the accelerating changes in the once almost exclusive constituency of 'qualified school leavers'. Discussion has turned to the 'new students', their needs and identity. The changes have been not only in their social and educational backgrounds, but also in their mode of attendance. They are full-time, part-time, sandwich course or distance learning students, benefiting from access courses, the accreditation of prior learning, credit accumulation and transfer, accredited 'in-house' courses while in employment, or partnership programmes between employers and higher education. Women and 'mature' students are the most notable categories in the pattern of change.

Although the proportion of women students in higher education grew only slowly before and after the Second World War, from 23.3 per cent in 1938–9 to 25.4 per cent in 1961–2, these figures disguise not only an increase in numbers but also great variations in distribution. At the latter date, for example, the percentage of women at Oxford and Cambridge was 12, at Sheffield 22, at Exeter, Keele and Reading over 40, and at the new university of Sussex 67. Although the percentage of women students overall increased from 34 to 41.6 between 1973 and 1983, the figures remained constant in the arts, fell in education and more than doubled from a very small base in engineering (from 3.3 to 7.8 per cent) (*Times Higher Education Supplement* 22 November 1985: 12). In 1994–5, of the $1\frac{1}{2}$ million students in higher education 49.6 per cent were women. In Scotland the figure was 28 per cent in 1961–2, and 20 years later it was 43 per cent (CHE Appendix Two (A) 1963: 24; Woodley *et al.* 1992: 20; *Higher Education Digest* 1995b). The increase in the numbers of women in American universities followed a similar pattern, with a particularly marked increase in the case of adult women learners in the 1970s – a 45 per cent increase as against that of 18 per cent for men. Women college enrolments in the United States exceeded those of men for the first time in 1979 (Cross 1980: 137; Stadtman 1980: 18).

The presence and roles of women on campuses – for example, as officers of students' unions – changed markedly from the 1960s. Although in terms of their experience of higher education there remained difficulties, it is worth remembering that at the end of the nineteenth century 'reformers of both sexes thought about women, with some reservations about feminine endurance, as if they were almost men' (Soffer 1992: 193). It was only after the Second World War that women were admitted as full members of the University of Cambridge and to its degrees on a completely equal footing with men. The traditions of the segregation and minority status of women were to be confronted by the often difficult and controversial admission of women to the men's colleges of Oxford, Cambridge and Durham from the 1970s (as well as that of men to women's colleges), the ending of the single-sex status of colleges of education, and widespread campaigns for 'mixed' halls of residence. The implications of these and other developments were to be far-reaching for all aspects of the higher education experience of women.

The vocabulary of 'mature', 'older' or 'adult' students is difficult and often ridiculous, and the statistics, nationally and internationally, vary according to the threshold age chosen. The postwar awards system in Britain acted to prevent the entry of most would-be students not straight from school – with a limited number of state scholarships for those over 25. One commentator in 1954 drew attention to 'the chief reserve of highly intelligent potential entrants . . . to be found in the age-group between about 19 and 25, a group largely neglected at the moment' (Charlton 1954: 367), but from the late 1960s these and older students were to feature more prominently in higher education as the CNAA and the polytechnics encouraged them to enter as full-time and part-time students. In 1994 just over half of all home entrants to higher education in Britain (full- and part-time, undergraduate and postgraduate) were mature students (over 21 for undergraduate and 25 for postgraduate students). Their numbers had increased by 140 per cent since 1979 – twice as fast as the number of school leavers. Over half of mature entrants were studying part-time (Department for Education 1994: 4). Mature entrants were replacing the falling number of 18-year-olds, and the trend was similar in other countries. The Organization for Economic Co-operation and Development called this 'a major social phenomenon', though it might be too soon to speak of 'the greying of the campus' (*THES* 15 January 1988: 11). In Britain it was the expansion of the polytechnics that provoked the most fundamental change in this regard. In 1977 mature student entrants to first degree courses in universities in England and Wales (excluding the Open University) accounted for 17 per cent of all entrants, as against 30.3 per cent on full-time and sandwich courses for CNAA degrees, and 94.4 per cent on CNAA part-time degrees (Jones and Williams 1979: 14). In the university sector mature students had tended to be in particular institutions or parts of institutions, including Birkbeck College of the University of London and St Cuthbert's Society of the University of Durham. In the early 1990s, according to a report by its Students' Union, almost half of the undergraduates at the University of Sheffield were aged 21 or over [Gerrard 1993a: 7].

These categories of students, as well as overseas students, ethnic minorities and students with disabilities (this being the terminology in use for most of the period covered by this study) announced the presence on campuses of 'new students'. From the beginning of the 1960s conferences were debating the implications of this 'leap', actual and potential, in the university population, the arrival of students who (as reported by a 1960 conference session on 'The New Student'), would 'feel the pressure of the meritocracy more directly, perhaps, than any previous generation' (Hall 1961: 1953). A universities conference in 1961 held a session on 'problems of the maturity of students: their welfare and discipline', chaired by the President of the Association of University Teachers, who described the new student as one who 'has come because he has been carried on a sort of academic assembly line into the university without any positive act of volition on his own part'. Students, emphasized another speaker, were coming 'from homes with no academic background' (Home Universities Conference 1962: 40, 43). This was to be a continuing element in the analysis of higher education, its procedures and its students through to the 1990s. If, as an Oxford tutor put it, going to the university had become 'the done thing', it meant that large numbers of students were coming 'without intellectual interest or moral sense of direction' (Ogilvie 1962: 86).

This level of description and concern was also vigorously expressed in the United States. One analyst of American higher education posed the dilemma facing the large state universities, which recruited many able and motivated students, but whose students were now on average 'academically less able, less highly motivated, and in possession of less of the common coin of intellectual discourse, than are students on average in the selective private colleges and universities'. Some undergraduates 'are dull, many ill-educated and barely literate, others profoundly uninterested in their education apart from the cash value of the diploma'. The entry of such students into increasingly universal higher education had become 'involuntary', the result of 'coercions' of many kinds, including family and peer pressures: 'As more and more college-age youngsters go on to college, not to be or to have been a college student becomes increasingly a lasting stigma' (Trow 1966: 27; 1972: 8–9). Another version of the theme described the university as 'no longer the intellectual church . . . Every "kid next door" is going, and he is not ordinarily an ambassador of glamour and intellectual power' (Johnson 1971: 6–7). However described, the new students brought to the campus different backgrounds, experience and expectations.

As the presence of these new generations of students became an established fact of British higher education, attention turned to who they were, why they had chosen to come, their expectations and needs. The case of the large numbers of part-time students on CNAA courses was of particular interest, with part-time numbers in many institutions increasing at least as fast as those of full-time students. At Plymouth Polytechnic in the decade from 1970–1 part-time numbers increased from 1,642 to 3,500. By the late 1980s over 37 per cent of students in UK higher education were part-time

– nearly 65 per cent of whom (approaching quarter of a million) were in the polytechnics and colleges (Bourner *et al.* 1991: 3). The position was also beginning to change in some of the older, particularly the large urban, universities. Between 1988–9 and 1992–3 the percentage of part-time students at the University of Sheffield rose, according to a Students' Union report, from 8 to 11 (also reflecting an increased percentage of postgraduates in the student population) [Gerrard 1993a: 14–15]. In Britain, as in the United States, a large number of these and of full-time students were 'non-traditional', 'first generation' students, from the kinds of backgrounds begun to be described by researchers in the 1960s, but treated with more understanding than had initially been the case. Part-time students were in the 1980s the fastest-growing group of American students. They were often, in the words of the Carnegie Foundation for the Advancement of Teaching, 'not respected as citizens of the campus', with educators haunted by 'the specter of the "shopping mall" college' (Carnegie 1986: 49–53). The growth in student numbers and the problems of particular student populations continued to underline the often ambivalent concerns about student motivation and academic commitment (*ibid.*; Carnegie 1990: 9–11), as well as the inability of institutions to understand and address the needs of diverse student constituencies, including the large numbers of commuter students (Jacoby 1989).

Although students from diverse backgrounds were entering increasingly diverse institutions, and the number of 18-year-olds entering higher education had begun to decline, the image of students remained rooted in their share in the youth culture, their identification as adolescents. Part of the decline in public respect for or confidence in higher education also stemmed from high-profile student activity, together with what one American called 'the all-pervasive concern about youth. The defects and dangers associated with youth and youthful action are in turn linked with the universities' (Johnson 1971: 8; Silver 1987). If young people were rejecting the authority, culture and values of their elders, for many students it was their own teachers who were first in line. The nature of the confrontation helped in some respects to confirm the view of students as adolescents, while declaring that they were and wished to be treated as adults. The late 1960s and 1970s were a turning point in addressing and relinquishing some implications of the 'adolescent image'.

This image was strengthened by the emergence in the 1950s and 1960s of the youth culture with which the concept of 'student' was inevitably associated. The higher education institutions were seen as simply housing one category of difficult and dangerous youth, even more so when coupled with the declining disciplinary authority of the institutions. Students' activism from the mid-1960s was directed essentially at establishing their adult status and rights, expressed in campaigns and protests on and off campus. Not all students saw it that way. The *Alternative Prospectus* produced in 1982 by the University of East Anglia Union of Students made the interesting comment that a university campus 'is a very unnatural and artificial environment.

It brings together a fairly large group of individuals, of approximately the same age, all of high "intelligence", and many in the end stages of puberty and adolescence' [UEA 1982: n.p.]. The most profound changes in the ways in which students are perceived have resulted not only from changes in the constituencies but also from this tension between the 'end stages of adolescence' and confrontation with adulthood.

One of the characters in Trollope's novel, *Barchester Towers*, published in 1857, asks: 'What merit will there be to a young man to get through safely, if he be guarded and protected and restrained like a school-boy?' The effect was simply that 'the manhood of the man will be deferred from the age of twenty to that of twenty-four' (Trollope 1906: 302). Disregarding the precise ages, a concern about 'deferred' adulthood continued, and more than a century later psychologists were focusing on students, for whom there was an 'abrupt alteration of status' (Ryle 1969: 27) or perhaps even the deliberate delaying of 'full adulthood' by the nature of university arrangements and policies (Oxtoby 1968: 444). Malleson, including in his evidence to the Robbins Committee, and other writers during this period of crucial changes in the late 1960s, were exploring the impacts – in terms of stress and related conditions – of these 'student upheavals' on this 'role transition' in the adolescent and student years (Malleson 1963: 120; Miller 1968: 459). American students were similarly being described as 'beginning to experiment with maturity' (Millett 1962: 110) and the anomalies of their position were being similarly examined. By the 1970s the messages were more confused, partly as a result of the traumas of the main period of student radicalism, partly because – in both countries – the historical position of those under 21 being legally considered to be children had been abandoned.

The President of the Students Union at Nene College, Northampton, told new students: 'once you are eighteen, and out of the school environment . . . you are fully responsible for your actions' [Nene 1983–4: 9], and he was legally correct. The abandonment in Britain and the United States at roughly the same time of the doctrine of higher education institutions being *in loco parentis* was in the long run at least as influential as the student protest movements at the same period. Young people generally, as the Albermarle Report on the youth services emphasized in 1960, were inheriting a world 'more than usually different from that of their parents', and they were at the same time exposed to 'excessive public attention' (Ministry of Education 1960a: 31). The concept of the 'adolescent child' was rapidly disappearing. The political pressures to recognize the changes favoured treating 18-year-olds as adults, although there were some misgivings about their ability – notably that of students – to accept or significantly contribute to the responsibilities implied. In the case of students it was a widely held view that their role as 'learners' in fact debarred them from such a contribution. As one study of adolescence suggested, it was by virtue of this learner role that 'they are reminded that they are not ready for responsibility because they have not yet been trained' (Smith 1968: 21). Resistance to student involvement in institutional decision- and policy-making sprang perhaps mainly from such a view, and the combination of prominent, radical student action with a legal transition to adult status presented sympathizers and critics alike with degrees of ambivalence about new definitions of student roles.

The report of the Latey Committee on the Age of Majority in 1967 reflected the trend already strongly in place, and it helped permanently to shape student experience and attitudes. The report dealt for the most part indirectly with students, by focusing on the lowering of the age of majority from 21 to 18. It acknowledged, only to reject or bypass, current concerns which might be seen as obstacles to such a change. It was easy, it argued,

> for those not closely in touch with young people to get an entirely wrong idea of what they are like. The very word 'teenager' conjures up horror images of pop fans screaming at airports, gangs roaming the streets and long-haired rebels being rude to their headmasters.

The balance of evidence led the Committee to believe that

> the withholding of responsibility from people of a responsible age *could* be a factor in making them anti-social. It could *not* be a factor in making them significantly better behaved . . . we must not legislate merely for a fistful of felons, but for the vast majority of young people.

It felt 'extremely strongly', and italicized the fact, that '*to keep responsibility from those who are ready and able to take it on is much more likely to make them irresponsible than to help them*'. In recommending lowering the age of 'full legal capacity' to 18 it concluded:

> [t]hat the historical causes for 21 are not relevant to contemporary society; [t]hat most young people today mature earlier than in the past; [t]hat by 18 most young people are ready for these responsibilities and rights and would greatly profit by them as would the teaching authorities, the business community, the administration of justice, and the community as a whole.

With regard to students, the Committee emphasized how much broader an experience students now brought with them to college, and the resentment likely to be caused by attempts to control their private lives. It quoted evidence that students were being given greater freedom and responsibility, that in these cases it worked well, but that students considered the new freedom to be 'patchy, and that the isolated pockets of restriction cause immense resentment'. Colleges and students would benefit from the removal of 'the pseudo parental obligation' (Lord Chancellor's Office 1967: 25–7, 31, 40–2). The Latey Committee itself had clearly felt and responded to the pressures of change. From Roman times 14 had been generally accepted as the minimum age of marriage for males, subject to parental consent, in Europe. The emergence of 21 as an appropriate age, based on a variety of 'curious developments', became codified in Britain from the Marriage Act of 1753 (James 1960: 31–3). This was one of the relics of the past which the Committee rejected. The government accepted the recommendation to lower the age of majority, and it passed into law two years later.

The implications of such a change for higher education were the subject of only modest debate in the 1960s. A major contributor was Sir Eric, later Lord, Ashby, who in the 1960s repeatedly, if ambivalently, considered the position of students as mature 'members' of their universities. That students were dissatisfied with staff–student relations, he told the London School of Economics in 1964, was surprising 'unless one regards students as adults'. The *in loco parentis* positions of masters had been acceptable when students came to the universities at the age of 14, but this had persisted and created difficulties:

> paternalism in universities is now difficult to sustain, and in any case to fuss over boys of 18 runs counter to the spirit of the age, and to the freedom which their contemporaries outside universities enjoy. Twenty years ago we were prepared to trust boys of this age with guns and bombs; it seems hardly reasonable not to trust them today with liberty.
>
> (Ashby 1965: 10, 17)

Paradoxically, three years later in the United States, Ashby agreed that there were sharp differences of opinion about the need for the universities to stand *in loco parentis* towards their students, and expressed his opinion that 'this attitude to students is important and should be preserved', for a variety of complex reasons, but ones shaped by what he saw as contradictory attitudes among students in this period (Ashby 1968: 11). He subsequently revised his view of the extent of students' rights and the limitations, forms and stages of their admission to full membership of the guild of scholars, and he considered the pros and cons of the impact of the Latey Report on such areas as discipline, committee representation and student participation generally (Ashby 1970; Ashby and Anderson 1970: 118, ch. 6).

Latey and the abandonment of *in loco parentis* represented an important moment in the history of British students, to some extent lost in the noise of other battles. The government's decision to accept the Latey recommendation to lower the age of majority was welcomed in 1968 in a joint statement of the Committee of Vice-Chancellors and Principals and the National Union of Students, responding to student action, actual and planned. They agreed that men and women of student age were expected 'to bear the full responsibilities of adult life much earlier than would have been thought reasonable a generation ago', and that the change in the age of majority altered the universities' responsibilities in relation to student welfare. It was important therefore for universities to review with their student bodies the existing regulations: 'In general the criterion on which regulations should be based is the need to maintain the university as an ordered working community' (CVCP and NUS 1968: 3, 7). This was rapidly to be seen (including when this document was repudiated by a new generation of student activists) as open to widely different interpretations. The Federation of

Conservative Students told the Select Committee on Student Relations that it 'rejects the concept of "in loco parentis" and the old belief that authorities should act as "Platonic Guardians"' (House of Commons 1969b: 325). A view from the NUS was that universities were unable to sustain an active personal tutorial system and it was therefore difficult for them to provide *in loco parentis* advice, and simply imposed rules in halls of residence and lodgings which students would not encounter at home: 'to many students the concept of "in loco parentis" seems to bear little relationship to the attitudes of their own particular parents' (Fisk 1967: 129–30). Bryan Wilson, Reader in Sociology at the University of Oxford and soon to be author of a book on *The Youth Culture and the Universities,* spoke in 1968 for a different view from the universities. He bracketed the youth culture with 'the enemies of a received cultural tradition', in this case abetted by the communications media:

> Legislators have rushed forward to endorse the transfer of rights and status to the young, mistaking social change induced by publicity for change necessary to maintain harmony with economic and technical developments. The report of the Latey committee is an indication of the extent to which officials have been 'conned' into believing that 'the wind of change' is some sort of autonomous, real force . . . The growth of dissident entertainment values of the youth culture is part of the context of contemporary student troubles. Spockism in child-rearing; 'free expression' in early education; the permissive morality advocated by self-styled 'liberals', are other elements.

The important implication for students was that they were 'no longer a class apart from youth in general: the universities have lost their distinctiveness of culture and commitment' (Wilson 1968: 94–5). The simple point, as seen from within a Durham University college, was that students were now 'adults *vis-à-vis* the police'. The law said 'they're adults . . . and the Master of the College couldn't interfere' (Holgate int.).

Alongside the importance of student-organized action during this period, student roles and experience on campuses were to be influenced in a variety of ways by this symbolic and real change in their status. The effects were to be felt, for example, in attitudes to discipline in halls of residence, in the freedoms enjoyed by students in their campus activities, and in participation at various levels of university decision-making. The same is true, in somewhat different forms, of the United States, when the voting age was lowered to 18 in 1971 by the 26th Amendment. *In loco parentis,* however, had a different American history, and for students it was undermined not by Congress, and to only a limited extent by challenges in the courts to the 1913 ruling which had legitimized it, but primarily as a result of pressure to weaken and remove the doctrine in institutional practice. Among the varied American institutions of higher education there were many in the 1960s which were struggling with a loss of shared values, the willingness of students to go to law in defence of their rights, the influence of older students. The legacy of *in loco parentis* remained strong everywhere, for example in campus housing, and in regulations which attempted in different kinds of college and university to control behaviour and morals. In many cases colleges not only retained the authority of parents, but acted as 'surrogate for Mother Church' (Morrill and Mount 1986: 31), with traditions of compulsory chapel, dress codes and approved manners. Because of the haphazard way in which *in loco parentis* was undermined or abandoned it remained beyond the 1960s in many forms, and a researcher at the end of the 1970s could still classify American higher education by types of *in loco parentis* institution, based mainly on the philosophy and practice of their disciplinary rules (Rees 1979: ch. 4). Because of the strong residue, or in many cases dominance, of *in loco parentis* attitudes and structures, students were widely involved in the 1960s in asserting their opposition to the many procedures which invaded their private lives, as well as expressing their opposition to racial oppression or government policy. They were in search of forms of campus citizenship – in the 1970s having obtained political citizenship. They sought a role in influencing educational policy and practice, often including – like their British counterparts – curricular change and satisfactory teaching and faculty–student relations. As one account put it, what began as opposition to *in loco parentis* developed into opposition to faculty *in absentia* (Wilson 1966: 62). In protest and action students criticized or condemned their own institutions' governance and educational practices, power and authority, in which students were not able to share.

At the University of Pennsylvania, an Ivy League university in Philadelphia, in 1968 restrictions on visiting to men's and women's dormitories were being dismantled, and curfews on women were being lifted. Most members of the Council's Committee on Undergraduate Affairs agreed that 'the University should relinquish its "in loco parentis" attitude', and an article in the students' newspaper recorded what was happening in other Ivy League universities. Columbia had transferred responsibility for setting and enforcing dormitory regulations to a student committee, had abolished restrictions on visiting hours in men's dormitories, and had done away with women's curfews. At Harvard the regulations were not being strictly enforced. A curfew at Cornell applied only to first-year women students, and this was being gradually removed. At Princeton and Brown the same process was taking place [*Daily Pennsylvanian* 18 September 1968: 1; 27 November 1968: 1]. By the early 1970s Penn committees were discussing why there had historically been a policy of *in loco parentis*, and the fact that 'we have disavowed the policy . . . Its underlying philosophy was one of considering students charges of the university community rather than an integrated part of it' [*Almanac* 10 October 1972: 6]. At Pennsylvania State University, in the state's rural heartland, the local paper reported in 1965 that 'the hottest issue' on campus was not Vietnam or the way the University was run, but one which united left and right – 'the students' demand that the university let the coeds out more often'. They wanted the extension of curfew hours and permission for girls to live off campus: 'these "in loco parentis" policies of the university had come under sustained fire from the Ad Hoc Committee' on Student Freedom [PSU *Evening News* [1966]; Records, 'Women – Protests']. Limited relaxation of regulations by Senate proved unacceptable to students, and initially to the Trustees [*On Campus* 13 April 1970: 1], but by the beginning of the 1970s the rules had been dropped and the first mixed halls were being opened. Here, as elsewhere, students were finding new problems: the removal of *in loco parentis* left them responsible, for example, for their fraternities, and therefore open to police raids instead of university scrutiny.

A document produced by the Scottish students' associations (the most common term for what in England are unions) made the doubtful claim in 1985 that 'in 1967 *The Latey Report* made students adults' (Eight Scottish University Student Bodies 1985: 3). What this discussion of *in loco parentis* demonstrates is the path through uncertainty being trodden by students and institutions in Britain and the United States in the 1960s, with prolonged repercussions. The uncertainties related to who students were, what their relationship was with their institutions, and what roles they could expect or others could expect them to play. Two American academics pointed out that 'students are the only members of the academic community who are not paid for the work that they perform', and that something closer to a trade union consciousness was bound to emerge (Horowitz and Friedland 1970: 340). Lone cries for the financing of students to treat them unambiguously as adults, freed from dependence on grants and parental support, were heard in Britain. Interestingly, when the Anderson Committee reported on *Grants to Students* in 1960, it had set out and supported the case for abolishing the parental contribution, and did so in terms of a number of 'interests' that would be served: the public interest, the family interest, the university interest, and the administrative reasons. It did not include any reference to a 'student interest' (Ministry of Education 1960b: 49–55). One of the present authors proposed salaries for students in 1965,

> so as to make students more recognizably partners, however junior, in the university community of scholars . . . so as to release students from some of the arbitrary and haphazard aspects of their dependence on home and local authority . . . The student would become a wage-earner on the same terms as his school companion gone into employment or apprenticeship.

> (Silver 1965: 412)

An article in the *Sunday Telegraph* in 1970 came to a similar conclusion for a somewhat different reason:

> Merely from the point of view of efficiency, there is something to be said for considering students as national conscripts, to be paid a wage, by no means approaching the £17.17s now offered to army recruits, but a sum which, within the limits of educational choice, offers them

a material subsistence commensurate with the culture they are expected
to imbibe and impart.

(Andrews *et al.* 1970: 8)

The Director of Education for Brighton explored the nature of the student
status with similar questions in mind: was the student eligible for a grant as
a privileged member of the community, or as 'one whom we, as a community, recognise as having earned and earning a wage for the work he is
doing . . . ?' (Antcliffe 1972: 6). A former president of the National Union
of Students reported that there had been in the movement a demand for
a 'student wage' (Slipman 1979: 11). In 1971 an NUS conference, as reported by the Durham student delegation, had indeed adopted a report on
the subject: 'This report, very adequately, but also very academically, presented as an executive report, accepted the theory of a student wage in its
widest sense' [DSU Council 1970–1, report]. Any such calls, however, were
lost in other routes taken through the uncertainties of defining and expressing the student status. Through the 1970s and 1980s an integral feature of the journey was the struggle to maintain the level of the existing
grant, and into the 1990s it was accompanied by opposition to the introduction and extension of student loans, by which the government intended to
keep down the cost of student support, given greatly increased student
numbers and restrictions on public expenditure.

The reality of the campus was now predominantly its increased size and
diversity. *In loco parentis* affected those who had previously 'become adults'
at 21, but the student population now consisted, especially in the CNAA-
related institutions, of the mix of older and younger students, full-time,
part-time and sandwich students (who were also a significant feature of the
colleges of advanced technology, which had become universities following
the Robbins Report). However, there was still a research and institutional
interest in the related issues of the health and academic performance of
students. Malleson carried through into the 1970s the interest in the relationship between failure and personal problems. He and others were involved in reporting and extending the health services being developed to
help those in difficulties (Ryle 1971; Cauthery 1973; Malleson 1975). The
focal issues were those of the causes of stress and failure, psychic disturbances and illness, and in the 1980s particularly the difficulties faced by
mature students (Wallace 1987: 14), and the incidence of stressed conditions as a result of changing social and economic pressures. Research was
showing, for example, the rapid increase in stress during many students'
first term, and the response to continuing academic, financial and social
pressures, including especially the management of low income, and in some
cases the guilt of spending parents' contributions at a time of economic
hardship (Fisher 1988: 18).

One of the concerns consistently expressed since the 1960s has been the
'depersonalization' of higher education, the loneliness and homesickness
felt by many students in the new scale of the campus, together with new

curricular structures, the transition from grant to loan and debt, and residence possibly in a tower block – described on one occasion as 'Neurosis Hall' (Armstrong and McMurdo 1979: 15). One description of the first impact of the campus in 1995 used adjectives such as 'daunting' and 'unbearable' of the reaction of many students, ill prepared for the experience (Redwood 1995: 6–7). The personal tutor system had come under immense strain. In some cases modular structures left students with only a tenuous 'home' on the campus, a feeling of anonymity moving from module to module without a secure peer group of fellow students, a sense that 'no one cares about you'. As one students' union president put it: 'Loneliness is a big issue at this university' (Weinstein int.). Issues of mental breakdown and suicide (potential, attempted and actual) were increasingly reported and discussed in the 1980s and 1990s. A survey of suicides in the University of Oxford between 1976 and 1990 suggested that Oxford students were more likely to commit suicide than the same age group in the general population, with 11 suicides and 254 non-fatal suicide attempts by 216 students (*THES* 22 January 1993: 3). In 1995 the Professor of Social Work at the University of Southampton considered that:

> Students are at 'special risk' from stress-induced suicide because of fears over unemployment and subsequent 'failure' . . . The financial pressures facing today's students, combined with growing competition for graduate jobs, are creating anxiety which is responsible for an increasing number of suicides and dozens of attempted suicides every year.
>
> (Pritchard, reported in Tysome 1995: 6)

A British Medical Association survey at the same time found 'growing instances of panic attacks, chronic fatigue and depression among students trying to hold down part-time jobs while studying, or worrying about their employment prospects on completing their courses' (*ibid.*). Fear of failure had many dimensions.

From the 1950s, however, higher education institutions had attempted to match their concern to the increasing problems perceived on their campuses. Their solutions ranged from chaplaincies and a variety of health-related services to attempts to sustain a system of personal tutoring while finance and staffing failed to parallel the increase in student numbers. Campus health and counselling services regularly reported increased numbers of student visitors and sessions – the rate of increase frequently outstripping that of total numbers. The counselling literature from the 1960s is pervaded with the sense of difficulty in coping with the growing incidence of problems among different groups of students. In 1986 the Association for Student Counselling estimated that about 10 per cent of students at most institutions consulted the service each year (Boseley 1986: 23). Student counsellors were generally reporting significant increases in the number and percentage of students consulting their service. At the University of East Anglia the counselling service reported that in 1994–5 it had seen more people for more hours than at any time in its 22-year history (495 students for a total of 3,161 sessions, plus 42 clients in group counselling). The director of the service thought there was 'much more fear of failure and confusion' [UEA *Broad View* 2 November 1995: 2].

The students' unions also became involved in expanding their support services. The approach to student services on British and American campuses, as well as the student experience of residence, and the range of environments and activities in which students define their roles and satisfaction, are discussed in the next and subsequent chapters. Although the beginnings of many contemporary aspects of the student experience of higher education have been traced back to the 1960s, there are others which have since emerged to shape that experience in significant ways, and these are also threads through future chapters. The definition and self-definition of students have been strongly influenced by events and trends in their demographic, legal, economic and other contexts. These, and others, will remain part of our attempt to highlight aspects of the students themselves.

3

Living

In Liverpool there are more than 35,000 students in the three institutions of higher education, and a third or so of the students use the services of a jointly organized Liverpool Student Homes to find private sector housing. In Plymouth students have the choice – 'live in a hovel in the city, or upmarket property, or a hall of residence' (Gillett int.). In 1993 at Plymouth there were 35 students living in caravans and mobile homes who had come together to form a Travelling Students Welfare Society, and were pressing the University for an official, secure site with appropriate facilities. The University of East Anglia has 3,000 mainly single study bedrooms, with a student population of 7,200 full- and part-time undergraduates and 2,300 postgraduates. It can therefore guarantee accommodation in University residences to first year students, as can Glasgow and many other universities. UEA also guarantees such accommodation to students with disabilities and international students throughout their period at the University. The norm at collegiate universities is for students to live in for at least the first year. The University of Portsmouth has 1,400 places for first year home students and these other categories, and the first year intake is about 3,000. Institution and students' union accommodation offices, student handbooks, 'survival guides' and other publications, offer help on everything to do with accommodation, including university or college halls, local authority housing and recommended private addresses, how to apply, tenancy agreements, gas safety, legal advice, and shared flats and insurance. In 1982 the NUS estimated that about one-fifth of all UK full-time students were living in their parents' or their own homes. About 35 per cent were living in halls of residence and 44 per cent in private rented accommodation. At that time the polytechnics had little or no residential accommodation – North East London Polytechnic, for example, at that time had 7,500 full-time students and no college-owned accommodation (Baker 1982: 5–6). These are just some indications of the kaleidoscope of student accommodation, and within their financial limitations students have choices.

Accommodation crises persisted, notably during the rapid expansion of higher education from the late 1980s. In the summer of 1990 the *Times Higher Education Supplement* surveyed the position and found it equally as bad as the previous year when students were queuing 'for temporary homes in holiday camps, caravans, hotels, libraries and lecturers' front rooms'. Total admissions increased, especially in the polytechnics, by 6,000 in 1989 and 15,000 or so in 1990. Kingston Polytechnic was making preparations to double up on single rooms with camp beds, and Lancashire Polytechnic and Stirling University were booking short-term hotel or bed and breakfast accommodation. Large numbers of universities were making emergency arrangements. The director of accommodation at Glasgow described the expansion of student numbers as being like 'opening a new transatlantic air service with propeller planes' (Griffiths 1990: 9). Students' images of what constituted a higher education had to survive often extremely difficult initial experiences and the struggle for longer-term, suitable living arrangements.

All forms of accommodation have their problems – noise in halls, insufficient independence living with a family, the possibility of poor private lodgings ('a hovel in the city') and the uncertainties of sharing a house or a flat ('you don't know who's coming in . . . you've got to be on your guard'). Throughout the 1980s and 1990s there were not only crises of availability, but also ones connected with rent rises in university accommodation – Oxford, for example, had rent strikes in 1987–8 and 1995 (*THES*, 15 January 1988; *Guardian*, 30 May 1995). In the 1990s some cities – among them Luton, Middlesbrough and Oxford became building sites for halls of residence or other student housing. There was still, however, something in the conception of a university, as well as in the needs of students away from home, which retained elements of the long tradition. 'The residential community of scholars has been the archetype of our own approach to university development', wrote a sociologist in 1965, 'and American studies have indicated that living arrangements can have a powerful influence, for good or ill, upon students' personal and intellectual development' (Taylor 1965: 332–3). What remained of this 'powerful influence', and in what forms, in the greatly altered situation?

The crucial questions before and after the Second World War concerned how much and what kind of residence the new and slowly expanding universities could and should provide. Technical and other further education was not residence-based, and the teacher training colleges were for the most part based on complete residence. There were those, among them Sir William Beveridge, as he was when Director of the London School of Economics, who believed that 'a full University life did not depend upon living together in a medieval building' (Beveridge 1960: 33), but pressure for increased residential accommodation in parallel with expansion increased from the 1940s. The growth of urban university institutions produced other policies and visions. In 1951 Ashby queried whether the expense of hostels for *local* students could be justified, given that in the civic universities 55 per cent of students were living at home and 28 per cent were in lodgings. In principle, he thought it could, but as an alternative he suggested improving general university facilities so that students could sleep at home, but spend the rest of the time during term at the university, with laboratories and libraries, refectories and other amenities staying open late. Such arrangements might go a long way 'to bring[ing] the benefits of community life into a civic university', and emphasize to students that tertiary education was 'a full-time job, needing the student for all his waking hours' (Ashby 1951: 150–3, 177). Oakeshott, in 1948, commended the example of life in the university quarters of German towns, with the relief to students of '*not* belonging to a tightly organized community' (Oakeshott 1989: 124). At an urban university such as London, Bernard Williams saw students treated more as adults, though presented with a choice between the autonomy of lodgings, attics and loneliness, and organized university life where the senior tutor might be lurking behind the dustbin (Williams 1968: 4–5). Like Ashby, Hatch in 1971 thought that good university facilities narrowed the gap between resident and non-resident participation in student life (Hatch 1971: 186–7).

Student preferences over time have been difficult to gauge, as have their images of what constitutes university or college life. Residence on campus has at times been seen as the academically related ideal, whereas lodgings could be seen as more embedded in the mass society. Hall meant access to its sub-cultures and those of the institution itself, lodgings (if without an over-intrusive landlady) greater independence within the wider society. Non-resident students, particularly in their relatively local institutions as in Scotland (and in the large American commuter universities) could build, or continue, a dominant or parellel cultural and social life in the city. For four years at Glasgow, a girl who travelled daily from Paisley was 'immersed in Glasgow', enjoying some of the facilities of the campus, but 'the commuters stuck together' and with them and old school friends she felt herself rooted in the city (Mackay int.). Freedom of access to shared flats and new types of university or college housing, as well as the private market, meant new perceptions. Self-catering halls also altered the perception of life on campus, as the popularity of 'catering halls' declined. Collegiate life, in small institutions, and the collegiate structures of Oxford, Cambridge, Durham and some of the 1960s universities, could have different meanings for different students. In the 1990s, for example, an American judgement of Oxford was that its division into colleges 'achieves a real sense of community that is hard to find even at smaller American colleges. The college bar, the porter's lodge, the college library and the JCR serve as meeting places which tend to unify students and [give] each college its unique identity' (Rooney 1993: 25). At a Durham college, however, 'some found it claustrophobic, there were always people around, knocking on the door' (Tooke int.).

At the new University of Sussex and in surveys of other universities some 70 per cent of students did not want to live in lodgings (Hutt 1964: 45). At Sheffield at the beginning of the 1960s 44 per cent of unmarried male students gave a hall of residence as their first preference for accommodation, a long way ahead of the second choice – 17 per cent for university bedsitters with communal refectories. Female students' preferences were very different – 28 per cent for such bed-sitters, 26 per cent for bed-sitters with self-catering facilities, and only 20 per cent for halls of residence (Mann and Mills 1961: 31). The Warwick Union of Students study later in the 1960s rejected the style of hall construction at the University as:

> intolerably noisy, but also useless as communal units ... The long corridors are not only aesthetically unpleasing they are also socially divisive. The Common Rooms unfortunately resemble railway waiting rooms ... the whole hall of residence is a very poor compromise, that fails to attain the needs for which it was constructed.

It accepted lodgings reluctantly as a 'reasonable alternative' for first year students. The flat or house was excellent for second and third year undergraduates, especially for the latter as an adjustment back to 'normal' life in society (UWUS 1968: II, 1).

The NUS summarized the available evidence in 1982, arguing that:

> the vast majority of students ... prefer to live independently of their parents and, indeed, free of the restrictions of living in someone else's home. They wish to develop an independent life-style with as much personal freedom as possible; this will most usually be found in rented and shared accommodation. If students do live in college-owned property, they would prefer it to be of the self-catering type.

The report drew on a study at the University of Kent, which had examined student housing in Birmingham, Brighton, Edinburgh and Leicester, and which concluded that:

> students have a clear conception of their ideal type of accommodation. After the first year, when living in halls or houses provided by their institution enables them to settle down to independent study, make friends and generally cope with a new experience ... students reject the idea of a self-contained residential community and prefer to live in the open housing market in the wider community.
>
> (Baker 1982: 26)

Although halls of residence, well designed and varied, were crucial to students and to university development, preferences emerged for university-owned houses, and for different configurations of study bedrooms and common spaces in halls of residence. First year students, particularly school leavers, needed to establish themselves in the city or neighbourhood, but wanted the freedom to make other choices in later years. In all types of accommodation students wanted an acceptable degree of independence, and changes in the grant system enabled students in halls of residence to opt for or against full refectory catering. A small pilot study of Queen Mary College, London, and the University of Sussex in the mid-1960s found a decline during the students' three years in the proportion living in lodgings with evening meals, and a sharp rise in those in flats or lodgings without meals, as well as a marked fall in the proportion of women resident in hall (Kendall [1966]: 22–4). Students' unions frequently placed adequate housing for students as their main campaigning priority. The Guild of Students at the University of Liverpool, for example, in 1971 called on the University to take urgent steps so that within five years two-thirds of students would be housed in University-owned accommodation, to enable all first year students to be accommodated in hall if they so wished, to safeguard the interests of local people who might be affected by the expansion of student housing, and to strengthen the welfare and accommodation service and consider employing a legal expert to deal with housing problems [Guild Council 1 November 1971: 5]. The interests of local people were a regular theme in students' union policy in Britain and the United States from the 1960s, notably concerning building in disadvantaged areas. The legal aspects of private accommodation remain an area of prominent concern in student handbooks prepared by students' unions, institutions, or the two in collaboration.

The architecture of the new 'plateglass' universities of the 1960s was intended to provide, in some cases, an equivalent of the collegiate experience of Oxford and Cambridge, and in other cases a flexibility of 'academic interaction and flexibility . . . the relationship between academic and social life' (Cassidy 1964: 354). Later buildings or reconstructions took greater account of student opinion, sometimes expressed in satisfaction surveys, though other considerations were as or more prominent. As the manager of a Student Homes organization in Leeds put it: 'change has come about because of two important factors – increased managerialism within universities and the growing importance of the provision of accommodation as an incentive to recruitment' (Blakey 1994: 73). A development at Oxford Brookes University was a hall consisting of ten two-storey blocks, each with between eight and 18 flats, each flat designed to accommodate between five and eight students in single study bedrooms with shared kitchen and bathroom or shower (Wood 1994: 20). For students, the major changes in halls of residence which came out of the Latey Report and the activism of the 1960s were, however, those regarding regulations, and particularly in connection with mixed visiting, the 'curfew' questions we have mentioned, and mixed halls of residence.

After Latey and the 1969 Act the rate of change varied, often influenced by the nature of the student body and the roles of wardens and other management personnel concerned with halls of residence. At Liverpool one observer thought that 'after the end of *in loco parentis* students changed, as did the extent of experimentation on entry', although *in loco parentis* was not the only reason (Belton int.); and another thought that with regard to residence there was 'a slow process of change post-Latey, depending on the warden'. There was a 'slow shift' to mixed halls of residence (Lewis int.). There was certainly, with varying pressures and degrees of success, student opposition before and after Latey to the amount of control exercised in institution-owned property. Surveys early in the 1960s had shown student 'demands for less autocratic control and more independence' (Cassidy 1964: 358). A study of first year students at the University of Reading, however, interpreted hall culture as 'a favourable response to university authority rather than of rebellion against it'. Students living in hall were more prominent than those in lodgings in mentioning 'freedom and independence' as benefits appreciated at university. Students at that time, it was underlined, were not allowed to live in private lodgings until they were 23 (Albrow 1966: 407–14).

An important element in student hostility to 'autocratic control' throughout and beyond the 1960s related to institutional attitudes to relations between the sexes. Colleges and universities, with their segregated accommodation, imposed on their halls of residence narrow limits for mixed visiting, and active student campaigns for the removal of these rules and for establishing mixed halls of residence preceded the period of student militancy on other issues. The relaxation of rules only brought demands for their complete abolition, but institutions were nervous about how far they should go in this direction, particularly in the face of parental and public opinion. The NUS issued a leaflet on *Mixed Visiting* in 1967. NUS Council had expressed the belief in 1962 that 'it is desirable to encourage intermixing between men and women students'. It instructed the Executive to approach those higher education institutions and local authorities (in the case of colleges of education) which 'prohibit or severely restrict students entertaining colleagues of the opposite sex in their own rooms and to express its disapproval of this restriction'. An NUS survey reported the following year that most institutions allowed such visiting: 'an "average" situation was one in which afternoon visiting was permitted each day, and evening visiting on two days a week, usually Saturday and Sunday'. Two women's halls required chaperons for students other than third years after 7 p.m., while another insisted that, in a strictly controlled period of visiting, 'no doors may be locked and no curtains may be drawn'. The usual time for the end of visiting was 10.30 or 11 p.m., and the NUS thought that this 'could not be considered to be unreasonable'. The NUS leaflet quotes a report on 'college discipline' produced by the Oxford University Student Council:

> In no university contacted were the hours when visitors were permitted in men's rooms more extensive than those prevailing at Oxford, and quite often they were more restricted. In other universities, as at Oxford, visiting hours in women's rooms are generally more limited than those in men's rooms. In this respect, Oxford Colleges are again the more liberal. The situation in other universities differs in one respect from that at Oxford, however. Most other universities are primarily non-residential . . . There is little attempt to make comparable regulations for students in lodgings.

The NUS survey found that the pattern in colleges of education was more restrictive than in university halls, only a quarter of them reaching the 'average' category. More than half of the colleges allowed visiting only at weekends. The NUS commented:

> Mixed visiting is not a concession: it is a reflection of the whole spirit of the day. As will be seen from the evidence cited above, resistance to mixed visiting is decreasing, but there are still Principals who contend that they are 'in loco parentis' in this and other matters of discipline. The concept of 'in loco parentis' cannot be legally defined. It is simply a moral obligation which a Principal feels that he should undertake on behalf of a reasonable parent. Obviously it would not be possible to define what is a reasonable parent, but a Principal can save himself from being 'in loco parentis' if regulations in colleges are framed only after consulting student opinion, which in turn should represent the attitude of the reasonable parent.

Where mixed visiting was still not permitted, NUS advised students' unions 'immediately to commence negotiations with their Principals' (NUS 1967: 1–3).

What was considered reasonable and unreasonable rapidly changed. Local pressure, already considerable in many places, continued into the 1970s. The Liverpool Guild of Students began discussion in 1971 of a residence policy to be urged on the University, including '24 hour mixed visiting', 'No artificial segregation of students on the basis of sex', and 'Every student should have a key to his or her room and the privacy that this entails' [Guild 6 December 1971]. The pressure at Queen Margaret College, Edinburgh, related initially to provision for the small number of male students. In 1977, if they wished residence with board, it was decided that they could be accommodated in 17 rooms 'which could be isolated from the rest of the Hall'. Four years later the students wrote to the CNAA, which had included in its review of the College a reference to 'the effect that restrictive regulations such as those governing . . . the Halls of Residence [were] having on the quality of the academic environment'. Visiting hours – until 11 p.m. for all students, not just those of the opposite sex – were one of the students' main concerns. The issue was referred to a liaison group of governors and staff (not students). In 1983 the Students' Association proposed to the Governing Body that students be allowed overnight guests, and with some hesitation it was agreed to allow one overnight guest on Friday and Saturday nights, 'with the stipulation that they are formally registered with the college authorities', thus giving the College authorities the ability to police the arrangements [GBdy 10 April 1977, 17 March 1981, 28 June 1983].

Changes in the regulation of university and college accommodation entailed other factors – including safety and security, and the protection of standards of decorum for the community in general. The means of overseeing arrangements and behaviour in halls of residence changed, though at different rates in different institutions, from the 1970s. The roles of 'wardens' and 'resident tutors' were redefined, and the transfer of a measure of authority to resident senior students (most commonly postgraduate students), and an increase in the powers of elected representatives of hall residents, meant considerable change. Institutions used the student charters of the 1990s, residence policies, general regulations and codes of conduct to set out the rights and responsibilities of students with regard to accommodation, and students' unions and/or other student mechanisms were used in the consultative process. The guidance could be in broad terms, requiring students to obey the relevant regulations, and to respect the rights and sensitivities of other students, staff and local residents. A Code of Behaviour adopted by the University of Glasgow in consultation with the Students' Representative Council lays down that:

> Students will not do or permit to be done in their accommodation anything which may be a nuisance or cause of annoyance to the University of Glasgow or the occupiers of adjoining or neighbouring accommodation whether other students or not and, without prejudice to the foregoing generality, each student will ensure that nothing is done or omitted to be done in the accommodation by that student or his or her guests or invitees which may prejudice the good order and safety of the accommodation (i.e. students are responsible for the good behaviour of their guests).
>
> [Glasgow Accommodation Office, n.d.]

Fixed visiting had been ended at Glasgow by 1975, and there was 'really only one rule: do as you like as long as it does not interfere with others and affect security, and as long as you abide by the law'. This rule was backed up by 24-hour coverage of the halls by residence assistants. Any serious behavioural problem could be reported to the hall warden next day, who might in appropriate circumstances contact the parents to say 'I cannot look after your child' (Johnson int.).

The issue of mixed halls of residence had a number of different aspects. There were pressures to open the men's colleges in Oxford, Cambridge and Durham, in order to increase the number of women students in the universities, and eliminating single-sex institutions altogether, also opening the women's colleges to male students, was a corollary. Of wider interest, however, was the issue of the halls of residence of other universities and colleges, and pressures mounted in the 1960s for these to be 'mixed', on a number of possible patterns – for example, men's and women's rooms on different floors or in different wings of the building. There was a constant search by students' unions in the 1960s and early 1970s for information and models from other places. The NUS pointed out in 1967 that there were already mixed residences at the universities of Essex, Aberdeen, Kent at Canterbury and City, as well as at the City of Leicester College of Education (NUS 1967: 3). Universities and colleges had admitted women to classes at previously male-dominated institutions from the late nineteenth century, though with various degrees of caution. Pioneering steps were taken by University College London, from the 1860s, initially with separate classes in some subjects only for women students. The early classes for women 'met and separated at the half-hours, that the men might be safely occupied at their coming and going, and the women were admitted by a side door'. When women were admitted to some mixed classes in 1872 'nothing very disastrous happened', and over the next decade mixed classes became the rule (Bellot 1929: 369–72). It was only partly the fear of 'something disastrous' happening that provoked resistance to mixed halls of residence a century later, from senior academics and lay members of many governing bodies and councils.

There were, of course, anxieties that mixed halls would mean sexual promiscuity and worse, but there were other concerns. Costs would be incurred, the expansion and possibly the viability of women's colleges would be undermined, 'romantic relationships' would develop at the expense of academic study, traditions would be lost. In some cases there was resistance from students, particularly strong in the old collegiate universities. At Durham in the mid-1960s St Cuthbert's Society, founded to bring together 'unattached' students, not based in the colleges, was divided on the issue of admitting women as members, and it took the Principal two years, until 1968, to persuade the members to accept them (Tudor 1988: 152–65). St Cuthbert's, however, was seen as exceptional in the University, and it was not until the 1970s and 1980s that the issue was faced in the residential colleges. Collingwood College was mixed from its foundation in 1972, and other men's colleges, or newly planned colleges, were either admitting women or considering doing so. After much debate in the University about the issue of 'going mixed', with divided views among the students, Grey College, a men's college, discovered that for the session beginning in 1985 it had 18 spare rooms, whereas some of the women's colleges had too many students. The Vice-Chancellor gave the go-ahead to admit women immediately. The College students had on several occasions from the late 1960s voted indecisively or against the idea, with the Sports Club particularly opposed to the admission of women. A plan for Grey College to collaborate with a women's college, with students free to live in either college, was opposed by the students in both colleges. There was, however, a danger that the College would not be able to compete with other colleges in attracting good applicants. The College went ahead, therefore, and admitted 18 'trail blazer' female students into residence in 1985 before the men arrived, and these found to their surprise a banner proclaiming 'Grey girls welcome other students'. The girls 'stormed the male bastion', and despite a backlash and unpleasantness from some male students, the female students established themselves. The staff thought the girls were noisier than the men, but that the men became more civilized (Halladay, Holgate, Watts ints).

Oxford, in the meantime, had taken cautious steps towards going mixed. The first of these was in 1972, when certain colleges were permitted to amend their statutes to enable them to admit women as undergraduates (or in one case as postgraduates). This approval to eight colleges was to be 'regarded as a closed experiment; that is to say, it should last for an agreed period of time during which no further colleges should participate'. At the end of the period 'the results should be the subject of a general review'. One concern here, as to some extent at Durham, was to protect the existing six women's colleges, which had been steadily expanding in the previous seven years. They were afraid that the new arrangements might undermine their recruitment of suitable candidates, and the investment they had made on the assumption that they would continue to expand (University of Oxford 1972: 3–7). The experiment was continued and extended. By 1980 only one single-sex men's college remained, and three women's colleges. The proportion of women undergraduates at the University had reached the national average of 37 per cent, and the social and academic problems that many people had forecast had failed to materialize (Flather 1980: 9). Cambridge was following the same path, though somewhat more slowly. One problem that was to be signalled at Durham and to some extent at Oxford was the effect of going mixed on the social life of the colleges. Students no longer needed to visit other colleges in search of companionship from the opposite sex to the same extent, and given the bar, entertainment and amenities of the college, there was a tendency for them to become more self-contained.

The position was different for the halls of residence of other universities. Opposition to going mixed came largely from the governing bodies or sections of the academic staff, and student campaigns were directed as much against the segregation of male and female students as against other aspects of institutional control. In many cases, as the NUS noted, universities were either persuaded or pressured to acquiesce, and began to see the virtues of mixed halls of residence as at least one option among those available and attractive to potential students. As the total stock of residential accommodation increased, to earmark at least some of it for unrestricted admission became more possible. Institutions had, however, to attend to some of the implications, notably those of safety for women students, and this meant in some cases allocating ground floor accommodation to male students, and more rigorous security measures. By the 1980s students could take it for granted that a mixed hall was at least one of the possibilities open to them. At Swansea, resistance at University College to mixed halls came from lay members of Council and from former students anxious to protect traditions. Three types of hall developed, reflecting the trend towards reduced supervision – traditional halls with a warden, bed and breakfast halls with minimal tutorial supervision, and self-catering halls with no residential oversight. Here, as elsewhere, strict, imposed regulations had been withdrawn (Barnes int.).

Student attitudes towards or involvement in disciplinary procedures relate not only to residence but also to the life of the institution more broadly. Wardens, assistants, tutors and resident students' committees have played an important part within halls of residence where activities variously described as 'high spirits' and 'occasional idiocy' or more serious infractions of acceptable behaviour could occur, and require some measure of regulation and discipline. Ultimately, it was an issue of who decided on the standards and sanctions. It was common until the 1960s for disciplinary matters of all kinds to be the responsibility solely of senior members of the institution. The notion of discipline inevitably changed, often dramatically, as circumstances changed, including the attitudes of students. At the Edinburgh College of Domestic Science (which became Queen Margaret College in 1972) the Students' Association Executive Committee in 1969 received a message from the Principal that

> boots, thick stockings and socks can be worn to nonpractical lectures . . . Mrs King is also considering allowing trouser suits being worn but she wants to make sure that the rules will be enforced. It was decided that if anyone turned up to a practical class with boots they would be turned away and marked absent unless they returned within the hour properly dressed.
>
> [SAC [November] 1969]

Whether trouser suits or slacks or mini-skirts might be worn by women students in a college cafeteria or class was an issue in the 1960s in colleges of education also, as it was for women in many kinds of employment, including school teachers.

As times changed the disciplinary procedures and sanctions also had to change. At the University of Glasgow, for instance, disciplinary cases were traditionally dealt with by the Principal and Deans Committee [157/40 28 April 1954]. Changes in students' attitudes were clear to academic staff from the 1960s. The deference to authority accepted without protest after the war had gone: 'one now has to earn one's authority and govern by consent' (Halladay int.). Students had become less willing to accept decisions (Reynolds int.). There was an enormous 'change in attitudes to authority', the most difficult being to persuade students to respect assignment deadlines – that 'not everything is negotiable' (Harvey int.). Students were concerned about the procedures for appealing against disciplinary decisions. At Constantine College of Technology, soon to be Teesside Polytechnic, the Staff/Student Liaison Committee in 1968 recommended the establishment of a disciplinary committee, containing members drawn from governors, staff and students [SSLC17 October 1968, 30 January 1969]. Plymouth Polytechnic in 1971–2 considered proposals for a disciplinary committee and proposals generated by the student members of the Welfare and Consultative Committee. The rules adopted by the Governing Body were made after consultation with the Academic Board and representatives of the Students' Union. The new committee was to contain three members appointed by the Students' Union, three members of academic staff, and the possibility of three members of the governing body, a quorum for the committee to consist of the three students and three staff [Academic Board 12 June 1972]. At Queen Margaret College a code of discipline adopted in the 1980s required that the Disciplinary Committee should contain two College students (alongside three governors and two full-time members of staff) [*Handbook* 1983/84: 14]. Not all students were happy with the presence of students on such committees, preferring to be judged by those in authority rather than by their peers, and in some cases students appearing before disciplinary committees asked for student members to withdraw (Reynolds int.).

Disciplinary structures and principles had become part of the student scrutiny of the nature and effectiveness of their collective and individual roles. This also included the functioning of the students' unions' own disciplinary machinery, generally in place to deal with misbehaviour in the bar, destruction of union property or other problems relating to the union and its clubs and societies. Barring a student from union premises was a not uncommon outcome of the procedures of such union committees. In the absence of student involvement in disciplinary procedures at Oxford colleges, the chair of the Oxford University Student Union's Discipline and Representation Committee commented in 1982 that college decisions were felt by students to be 'arbitrary, inflexible and made without due consideration of circumstances'. Students could not penetrate 'the blind depths of reserved business':

> The basis of student representation in Oxford University . . . has always been consultation on relevant matters rather than full participation. But students no longer accept that their teachers have a monopoly on the guardianship of long term interests any more than they believe themselves motivated solely by the short term.
>
> (Pomery 1982: 11)

All of this was of particular importance when, from the late 1970s, freedom of speech on campuses became a serious issue, with militant students seeking to prevent Conservative ministers and right-wing politicians from speaking – what became known as the 'no platform' movement (for racist, pro-apartheid and similar views). Outbreaks of violent behaviour and disorder gave rise to attempts by the CVCP and individual university and college authorities to define codes of acceptable behaviour, appropriate approaches to 'high-risk' meetings and disciplinary sanctions – an important feature of life on some campuses in Britain and the United States in the 1980s.

Many of the aspects of residence that we have discussed were paralleled in the United States, though there were also important differences. The American campus developed similar, though magnified, features of size and variety, high-rise living and student demands for mixed residential halls. In two years, 1970–2, housing capacity on the University of Pennsylvania campus more than doubled, from 3,900 to 8,400 students in residence [UPA 8/272 29 November 1979]. The abandonment of the most significant features of *in loco parentis* meant that with regard to regulation of accommodation the student voice was heard more clearly and acted upon more often. The openness of student accommodation of various kinds to police intervention, particularly when state licensing laws reduced the legal drinking age, was an important outcome. Mixed halls of residence, and in many cases the admission of women to all-male universities, became important issues from the 1960s. Geiger describes how the idea of coeducation gained ground at the two competing universities of Princeton and Yale in the late 1960s. Although each was primarily concerned with the recruitment of male students, 'each feared that it was increasingly losing good students to coeducational schools, and was even more fearful that additional students would be lost if the other became coeducational and it did not'. By 1968 they had both independently decided to admit women the following year (Geiger 1993: 249). As with their British counterparts, American students gathered information nation-wide in order to press their own case for 'co-residence'. The Association of Hall Residents at Penn State set up a committee to investigate 'co-residential living' in 1975. According to its report, 25 universities, including many of the largest and best known, five of Pennsylvania's state colleges, and even seven of Penn State's own branch campuses, offered this option. Such institutions were reported as emphasizing the contribution co-residential living made to the educational and social atmosphere of residence halls. One of the greatest advantages was:

> the opportunity of learning to live with members of the opposite sex. By producing a more natural atmosphere, Co-Residential living decreases tension and abolishes many of the stereotyped images that accompany students where sexes are more strictly separated . . . Schools with Co-Residential living systems also reported more extensive and more successful educational programing.

Co-operation between men and women resulted in more discussion groups and speakers, increased male competence at the ironing board and female competence with repair work. The report suggested that there was more mutual respect, an improvement in the students' dress code, manners and room cleanliness. The conclusion was that co-residence was 'a rapidly growing institution . . . now the rule rather than the exception' [USG 1976–77, Association of Residence Hall Students 30 January 1976]. Not all of these perceived advantages were to persist! The reference to the 'educational' benefits, however, points to an interesting American campus phenomenon.

American campus authorities have often in the recent past seen residence as integrated with academic studies to form a somewhat different context for student hall culture than in the United Kingdom. American approaches to the provision or co-ordination of certain kinds of services have often been different from those of British institutions. The roles of 'students' unions' have not been the same in the two countries, the term being used in the United States normally for the buildings in which student entertainment and other activities take place, while other functions belong to separate 'student government'. This is a difference to which we shall return, but it is important here to note the emergence of a substantial cadre of American student affairs professionals out of their roles in student residences. The University of Pennsylvania is not unusual in this respect, with the University developing an educational role for residence, and with students sharing in the development. In 1973 the University was promoting what became a feature of its philosophy – 'residential living in the implementation of an Integrative Educational Life' – an approach based to a great extent on the role of the residential life staff: 'it seems clearly desirable to stress the development of a staff that meaningfully contributes to the richness, intensity and seriousness of the intellectual life of the residence' [Report on University Life 1973: 11]. Seventeen years later the University's committees were, in an expanded university, using the same emphasis, as was the Student Committee on Undergraduate Education:

> The establishment of a collegial living environment is essential in creating and enhancing a vibrant intellectual community at Penn. Although residences are not primarily academic centers, they cannot be void of intellectual vitality. Intellectual activity outside of the classroom complements and amplifies students' quest for knowledge; the residences provide a unique setting in which to combine academic and extracurricular exploration.
>
> [SCUE White Paper 1990: 32]

The ideal and the reality, however, did not always match. In 1987 a survey of students living in the University's 'highrises' by the University Assembly (the student government organization) recorded that 79.9 per cent of those who responded had attended either 'few or very few programs', though those who did attend were satisfied with them [UA High Rise Experience 1987: 2]. University and student committees in the 1990s were concerned about the impact of the high rises on university life and community. Residential students indicated in a 1990 survey that they had chosen to live on campus mainly for reasons of 'proximity, security, private bedroom space (when available), room conditions and furniture provided'. Preserving a sense of community for these students produced plans from the 1970s to establish smaller units or 'colleges'. A new generation of 'virtual colleges', as they were described in 1992, were for 300–350 students, each student being affiliated for 'meals, academic and programmatic support'. The aim was to identify each such college with a particular theme or collegiate experience that would bring students from different schools of study into a unifying 'connectedness' [Penn *Almanac* 1 December 1992: vii–ix].

At Penn, as at other universities internationally, the building expansion, and the types of building, had produced a new experience of the campus. One student reflected on her time at the University:

> Although the housing projects . . . are a great success, and there is a genuine community feeling there, the high-rises can only be called a failure. They isolate students, and this isolation is heightened by the fact that most students eat in their apartments and therefore do not have the opportunity to socialize with each other over meals.
>
> [UPA 4/348 9 8 January 1976]

A 1991 student survey also summarized the feelings of students who had chosen to live off-campus. Their reasons for doing so, in descending order of importance, were:

> greater autonomy and independence, larger rooms, lower rent, more space, condition of rooms and other general reasons such as desire for pets, for year-round leases, for cable TV, better kitchen facilities and parking. At the same time, students who have made this choice have described their ambivalent feelings, missing the community, the collegiality, and the opportunities for more spontaneous engagement with the University on a daily basis. This choice to move off-campus is clearly made at some cost, sometimes not fully realized until the student reflects back on the experience.
>
> [*Almanac* 1 December 1992: vii]

There is no need here to pursue in any detail the vicissitudes of the particular American tradition of fraternities and sororities. In recent decades these forms of self-perpetuating student-run housing, with their Greek symbols, have been through varying fortunes nationally and across the campuses. Their numbers as a proportion of the student population have fluctuated. At Penn, the percentage of first year students who 'pledged fraternities' declined from more than 70 per cent in the early 1950s to 21 per cent in 1970–1. By the same date, women members of sororities had declined in ten years from 526 to 15 (Goddard and Koons 1973: 232). Sorority membership at Penn State declined by 8 per cent in 1969–70, when it averaged 1,350 women, 20 per cent of the total. In the 1980s and 1990s there was a resurgence in the number of recognized fraternity and sorority chapters and members. At Penn State in 1995 there were some 5,000 students in fraternity and sorority houses (as against some 12,500 in the University's residence halls) (Latta int.). The fraternities have traditionally had an image of macho attitudes, drunkenness and intolerance, and at various times the image has matched the reality. The fraternity system embodied degrees of 'institutionalized intolerance' and discrimination against black, Jewish and other groups of students (Goddard and Koons 1973: 233). There were much publicized occurrences of what the Trustee Committee on Student Life at Penn in 1980 described as misconduct in some houses which had 'taken the form of violence and gross insensitivity' [UPA8/274 17 January 1980]. The view on both of these campuses, however, is that there has been a substantial change, particularly a decline of intolerance towards women and minorities, and a greater willingness to share in university and off-campus service activities. The fraternities were described as being neither more nor less liberal or intolerant, and drinking neither more nor less, than among other students, though since the lowering of the legal drinking age to 18 in an increasing number of states in the late 1980s access to alcohol in fraternity houses has been to some extent easier than in other campus accommodation. These fluctuations in the numbers, influence and conduct of the fraternities in particular have also meant fluctuating relations with their parent universities, and at different times varying degrees of intervention, hostility and support by their authorities. Students not belonging to fraternities have also held widely different and strongly held views of the fraternities and 'Greek life', and particularly of their exclusiveness. The former Penn student who in 1976 sent her reflections to the University commented also on the fraternities:

> The fraternities are too numerous and, I think, should be abolished as they are in principle dedicated to what college should not be; that is, members are all too often of the same background (i.e. each fraternity attracts a certain type of person. There are jock fraternities, Wasp fraternities, Jewish fraternities etc.) These students are not participating in the social melting pot college should be.
>
> [UPA 4/348 9 8 January 1976]

By the 1990s the principles of fraternity and sorority organization had not changed, though their public attitudes and activities to a considerable degree had.

In many respects British and American experiences of residence have been and remain different, but the common elements are important. Perceptions of student 'adolescence' and 'adulthood' are made within structures which are imposed upon them, but which they themselves adapt and develop. The American student in Oxford in the 1990s thought that such features of the University as the lower permitted drinking age and the tutorial system emphasis on independent study 'reinforces an attitude that students here are responsible, mature, intelligent young people. I think most American college students would say that they feel they are far from receiving the same treatment' (Rooney 1993: 25). This student's impressions may be no more 'typical' than Oxford is 'typical' of British universities, but there is an important emphasis on the relation between the expectations engendered by structures and perceptions of the characteristics of students. Such suggested comparisons help to clarify issues surrounding the partners in the campus experience – the students, their relations with academic and administrative staff, the nature of the academic processes, the institution's understanding of its responsibilities. The last of these embraces the aspects of residence and discipline we have discussed, but it goes further, and before looking at some of the experience of extra-curricular activities on campus it is to understandings of the nature of shared responsibilities that we turn.

4

Student Life, Students' Lives

In 1983 the President of the University of Pennsylvania, Sheldon Hackney, wrote to the Provost, who had drafted a paper on *in loco parentis*. 'One point that I sometimes make during discussions of the collapse of *in loco parentis*', Hackney wrote,

> is that colleges and universities now do not serve as arbitrary rule enforcers, as they did in the 1950s, but as a consequence we offer many more services and support systems than we did in the 1950s. In short, it was cheaper to have codes of conduct and strict regulations. I don't believe it was healthier, however.
>
> [Hackney 184 14 November 1983]

How American and British campuses reacted to the ending of *in loco parentis* is of interest not just as a comparative exercise, but because it may suggest ways of interpreting students in changing situations. In the American situation 'more services and support systems' was represented by the range of descriptions of services and personnel, which included 'student affairs', 'student activities' and 'student life'. At Penn State we met administrators whose titles indicated their responsibilities for 'student programs', 'student affairs', 'counseling services and program assessment', 'campus life' and 'student activities'.

The extent of these services at this and other institutions is indicative not only of their increased size but also of the way in which American universities and colleges have interpreted their responsibilities towards students and their vision of the campus. One of the emergent leaders of American student radicalism, Tom Hayden, speaking in 1962, drew attention to the fact that 'student extracurricular activity is articulated by the administration in terms of either the "preparation" theory or the "privilege" theory'. Students were either involved in a make-believe world, practising being a citizen, presented with an empty gesture, making only decisions that have no consequences, or defined as outsiders, presented with the privilege, not the right, of attendance (Hayden 1967: 275–7). Hackney and Hayden in their different ways point towards the professionalization of 'student life', a form of 'articulation' which substituted for *in loco parentis*. The development of 'student services' on British campuses was more limited until the late 1980s and 1990s. In the British circumstances some of the roles were adopted by students' unions, with their more comprehensive functions and powers than was generally the case on American campuses. The lives of students in both countries have been strongly influenced by the ways in which American 'student life' services or their British equivalents, and the diverse roles of student organizations, have been interpreted. The realities, the relationships, the traditions and the outcomes have been different, though in the 1990s British students' unions became more similar to their American counterparts.

From various points in the nineteenth century British students developed campus students' unions and eventually a National Union of Students to represent them in campaigns not only against their parent institutions, but also against the state, on aspects of autonomy, influence and change. This was particularly true from the last decade of the nineteenth century, when universities received their first injections of government finance, and after 1919 when government formalized its financial support through the University Grants Committee. Ashby and Anderson (1970) described the history of student organization as the *Rise of the Student Estate*. The outcomes, particularly in the second half of the twentieth century, were strongly established student organizations, which drew – as did the institutions themselves – on public finance. Despite a Conservative government attack on students' unions' finances and activity in the 1990s, and a legislated move to voluntary membership, British students' unions have remained a powerful symbolic, and in many respects effective, representative of student affairs. They may not have the strength of influence on academic affairs that they sometimes wish, but they are the conduit through which higher education institutions conduct their formal liaison and consultation with the student body, including as the means of ensuring student representation on the institution's committees. They have substantial budgets and run their own food services, second-hand bookshops, bars and many other services, either alone or in conjunction with the institution, not unlike the services (with the exception of bars, given the lower legal drinking age) provided in American unions. In spite of recent legal limitations on their activities, British students' unions remain the voice of the student body. Their elected sabbatical officers (students paid by the students' union for their full-time work for a year) and often extensive staffs are points of information and advice on, for example, welfare, residence and rights, and sponsors or providers of training for committee representatives, campaigns on the rights of students in general or of particular constituencies, legal and financial advice, and pointers to other sources of advice and support.

The University of Sussex Students Union has six sabbatical officers, a president and five vice-presidents (covering finance, welfare, communications, education and sport). They and the 16 non-sabbatical members of the Executive Committee are supported by a full-time staff of 25. USSU operates a small 'union shop' and a larger 'union store', a print shop and a second-hand bookshop. It also runs a café and two bars on campus.

Extensive entertainments facilities and programmes are run by a full-time entertainments manager, and the staff are headed by a full-time general manager. The Union's Welfare Centre, apart from the involvement of the sabbatical welfare and education vice-presidents, is staffed by two full-time welfare advisers, a welfare administrator, and a student community action co-ordinator. It offers advice on students' finances, housing, health and safety, employment, legal matters, equal opportunities and special needs. It runs a parents' group, a kids' club, a families' room and a play scheme, provides a list of volunteer baby-sitters, and has been developing its work with international students. It supports a Nightline, gives advice on patients' rights, and issues an extensive range of regular and occasional publications of interest, for example, to students living off campus and to mature students, and on women's, gay, lesbian and bisexual issues. USSU represents students on almost all University committees, publishes a serious 'alternative prospectus', negotiates with the administration on such matters as the timing of examinations, and is deeply enmeshed in all aspects of the University affairs of importance to students.

The range and extent of union services elsewhere varies, but the pattern is similar. The Guild of Students at the University of Liverpool has four sabbaticals and 65 permanent staff. Larger unions have this scale of sabbaticals and staff, obviously smaller in smaller institutions – Queen Margaret College has three sabbaticals. The Liverpool Guild in 1992 had 45 'departmental' clubs and societies, and 79 classified as 'pastimes, religion, political'. It houses a shop, a travel office, a print shop, an optician, a bank branch, a photographic service, a textbook and second-hand books sales service, a launderette, hairdressers, three bars, a restaurant, a coffee bar and a snack outlet, and a location for market traders. The Union at Plymouth has two bars, an insurance office, a games room, a launderette, a print shop, a union shop and a travel office, and sells produce from its smallholding on Dartmoor. At the University of Wales Swansea the Union has two bars, two shops, two launderettes, a travel shop, a nursery, a print shop and a welfare advice centre. In 1995 its turnover was £2.2 million, and it employed 23 core staff, a total of 40 full-time staff in term time, as well as 80 students part-time [*Handbook 1993–1994*] (Tregoning int.).

Students' unions provide other services, particularly in the field of welfare. The Strathclyde Union announces this support service as dealing with

> anything from grants and finance to drugs, sex and relationships. University can sometimes be an isolating experience and Welfare is here to make sure that ALL students have someone to talk to and offer practical advice. Please, please, please, if there is something bothering you pop up and see us ... Nobody gets through University without some kind of hassles.
>
> [SA student diary 1994–5: 11]

The Students' Representative Council at the University of Glasgow has two trained welfare advisers at its Welfare and Advice Centre to deal with financial, accommodation and legal problems, a job shop dealing with part-time and vacation work, and a campus-to-halls-of-residence minibus service. The Students Union Advice Unit at the University of Wolverhampton deals with accommodation problems, runs legal advice sessions twice weekly by qualified advisers, has a financial surgery fortnightly, also run by qualified financial advisers, advises overseas students, provides personal counselling and an information system on issues of concern to students. The Unit is staffed by experienced, professional counsellors/advice workers with secretarial and administrative support. The University of Sussex Union publishes a pack of materials entitled *Moving Off Campus*, containing British Gas, Health and Safety Executive, Borough Council and its own and other information leaflets. Its Welfare Centre runs a grant enquiry service every day, organizes support groups on particular health problems, and issues leaflets on a variety of other student-related topics. Students' unions and their handbooks draw attention to the services provided by public or their own institutions' student services, and in some cases publish general or specific guides jointly with the latter. In 1991 the Students' Association at Queen Margaret College drew attention to changes in 'external influences', including the removal of state benefits for students, and the introduction of loans, and as a result 'we now find ourselves in a new role which is perhaps more akin to the Citizens Rights Office than the Students' Association of old' [*Annual Report 1990/91*: 11]. In areas of welfare and counselling students may sometimes therefore have a choice of service.

The National Union of Students backs up its affiliated campus organizations with legal, campaign, information and other services. As an umbrella student organization the students' union itself plays an important role in all aspects of academic and administrative relationships, and in the policy- and decision-making processes of the institution more prominently than may be the case with an American student government organization. An American campus institution may itself provide offices, often in the same building and in close collaboration with the student organizations, for the vice-presidents, provosts, deans, directors and others, including the great range of student service personnel, who deal in some way with matters relating to students, underpin, help to co-ordinate or keep a watching brief over their activities. The reality and the philosophy of the ways in which the college or university, and the students within it, are organized, have therefore often seriously differed from the traditions of the British campus. Institutions' student service units in the United Kingdom do indeed cover a range that has widened in recent years, invariably including health and medical, careers, counselling and accommodation services, as well as support services for students with disabilities and international students, and in some cases childcare, financial advice and a chaplaincy. In 1982 at Plymouth Polytechnic the Student Services Centre recorded 2,000 student visits to the nursing sister for advice, counselling and/or treatment; 2,381 visits to the five doctors who provided eight surgeries a week; an 'almost alarming increase' in the number of visits to the Careers Information Room to 9,120, from 3,651 in 1980–1 and 2,132 the previous year; 1,297 individual interviews with the Student Counsellor, and visits by nearly 200 students to obtain advice from law surgeries run by lecturers from the Law Department [Student Services Committee 15 October 1982]. Student services at the University of Wales Swansea have 'increased beyond recognition', with four student counsellors, ten careers advisers, an accommodation service, a medical practice on site, and occupational therapy staff (in the 1960s one person covered careers and accommodation) (Barnes int.).

Although such services are often in parallel with those provided by students' unions, they are also different in scope and the range of available expertise. A careers service, for example, has a more comprehensive and more sustained role than it would be possible for a students' union to provide, as is true of medical and many counselling services. By whom some of these services are provided and to whom they are responsible are often matters of the local history, for example when a students' union began a service because the institution did not, or because of dissatisfaction with an existing service. To enter a university and ask for the welfare service may result in being directed to a university centre or to the students' union. The concept of service or support applies in both the British and American cases; given the scale and purpose of American administration and provision the differences have been clear, but are becoming less so.

The American campus life offices have traditionally been much more concerned than their British counterparts with programmes, training – including for 'leadership' – and a much more active interpretation of student service, one which is more dynamically integrated with the notion of providing education, fostering community. American student services reach out into wide areas of student experience. One 1960s account of the 'new offices' which came into existence in colleges between the wars lists

> deans of all kinds and functions; chaplains and career consultants; elaborate departments of health, containing a corps of psychiatrists in the wealthier institutions . . . offices that dispense financial aid to students . . . offices of research to advise the colleges in the problems of admissions, scholarships, examinations, and standards.
>
> (DeVane 1965: 59)

The story of the 'new offices' in fact stretches further back to the late nineteenth and early twentieth centuries, to the forms of control subsumed under *in loco parentis*, to ways in which students were more closely incorporated into the ethos and cultural, religious, residential and other continuities of the great range of American institutions.

The development has also related to the longer American tradition of interpreting students as 'consumers' and therefore of providing a range of 'consumer services'. American administrators were given increasing responsibility not only for attracting but also for retaining students, at a time when a far smaller percentage of British school students went on to college, and when British institutions were almost entirely dependent on public financial support. American student services personnel, as we have seen, grew rapidly between the wars, particularly in relation to residence halls, in order to provide programmes or oversee behaviour. American 'student government', it has been argued, grew in earnest at the same time as the student personnel movement in the 1920s,

> and the dean of students often served as coordinator and watchdog of the student government activities. With few exceptions, students shied away from the major business of governance and seemed happy to select homecoming queens, school songs, mottos, and the senior class play.
>
> (Hodgkinson 1971: 42)

Hackney's pointer to the later growth of services, and the reasons, was echoed elsewhere. The President of Chatham College, a small liberal arts college for women in Pittsburgh, considered in the mid-1970s that campus values were 'fragmented and all but impotent; student services have been multiplied many times over . . . Most colleges are like parents experiencing a change in roles' (Eddy 1977: 8). He was also provost-elect of Penn State University.

Every aspect of American 'student life' (not unlike trends in society generally) came to be seen by institutions and their 'watchdogs' as needing its expert, and the aggregation of this official expertise came to be not only a significant feature of the administration, but also an essential element of what was understood as a campus community. Indeed, the community has been held by the professionals not to exist without student services personnel to promote and uphold it. The professionals have served two main functions. First, they have pointed directions for the whole institution. One of the founders of the student personnel movement helped in 1937 to define the role of student personnel,

> which many college educators in the late nineteenth and early twentieth centuries were beginning to find essential. That role would require paying special attention to students and considering them as they lived in community with one another. It has been gratifying to find that the orginal concepts we sought to define have survived so potently. It should well be so, because the role of the dean of students emerged from and enhanced the total concerns and purposes of the faculty . . . while the teaching faculty of a college or university are important, the student personnel can do much to make or break an institution.

These student personnel are seen as the experts in 'the quality of human relations' and without their programmes 'the students' college experiences will not be as good as they might be, and the college will not affect students' lives as richly and beneficially as it should'. This vision goes beyond the simple provision of services: 'The most successful educational and developmental environments will be those that infuse all campus staff with the goals and purposes of student personnel experts' (Lloyd-Jones 1989: 2).

The second function arises from the fact that this expertise requires a basis in sustained data. This includes not only institutional, regional and national statistics, but also operational, experiential and attitudinal information. The student personnel professional journals disseminate findings which have a use in detailed decision-making. The 'level of rapport and compatibility of residence hall roommates' is 'an important focus' for college student personnel research: 'if factors associated with healthy relationships are discovered, it will be possible to design optimal growth-promoting relationships through interventions such as roommate assignment' (Carey *et al.* 1988: 239). Participation in student activities and organizations is seen as 'of particular interest to student services professionals who consider this type of involvement as an integral part of development' (Abrahamowicz 1988: 233). A conference on undergraduate education at Penn in 1971 was told that Student Affairs felt strongly 'that non-classroom activities which contribute to the intellectual and cultural life of the campus are critical elements of the University's educational mission and, therefore, should be given some priority in the distribution of finances' [21st Century Project, Robinson, October 1971: 1].

The purposes of the American system of student support are extensive and explicit. At Penn the mission statement of the Division of University Life in 1994 began with its intention to provide 'leadership, supportive services, and programs', which:

– partner undergraduate, graduate and professional students . . . as they undertake their academic programs, fulfill their educational objectives, and engage in learning, service and leadership activities;
– improve the quality of campus life for students and other members of the University community; and
– promote a caring, supportive and humane campus community in which the dignity and value of each individual is respected and the diversity of the community is nourished and sustained.

Its priorities included to

> create formal and informal opportunities for learning . . . improve computer clusters to support academic and other activities . . . improve physical space for learning and teaching . . . promote greater adherence to community norms supported by University policy . . . increase opportunities to learn and practice leadership and teamwork skills . . . stimulate inter-disciplinary academic support programming . . . stabilize occupancy (of residential facilities) and increase student satisfaction . . . coordinate with schools and departments to design retention strategies.
>
> [Division of Student Life 26 August 1994: 1–5]

At Penn State the Student Life annual report for 1993–4 suggested that its vision was 'to be recognized for shaping and enhancing the learning environment by providing support, assistance and information, encouragement, and opportunities outside of the classroom for students, organizations and other members of the University community'. It also wished to

> train students in the development of career and lifelong educational skills ... enhance the quality of the student experience by providing accessible, individualized and coordinated assistance with the issues affecting their personal and academic progress ... serve as role models, advisors, and advocates for students, student organizations, and student government groups ...

Its mission statement reads:

> Student Life assists with the transition to and through college and offers diverse opportunities which support and challenge students to achieve their educational, personal and career goals. We accomplish this by providing quality services and programs which increase the involvement of students in leadership and community activities and by creating an accepting campus environment which reflects the changing social and cultural background of our students. In addition, Student Life provides experiential learning opportunities in the University community which have a positive impact upon the academic and personal development of students.
>
> [Student Life 1993–94: 2–4]

American 'student government' has been concerned more exclusively than in the British case with what a former US Commissioner of Education described in 1970 as 'the social, or non-academic, aspects of the college experience':

> 'Student government,' as it developed almost universally on campuses across the nation, remained entirely extracurricular. The officers of student organizations enjoyed neither the right to nor the responsibility for collaboration with the faculty in determining academic purposes, policies, or practices.

Even those activities with which they were allowed to concern themselves were 'more often than not ... subject to review by faculty advisers and administrative officers' (McGrath 1970: 19).

The roles of student government often widened, however, to include varying degrees of representation, though rarely at the level of boards of trustees or other senior policy-making bodies. Some of this restricted view of the student government role was true, though less true, of British students' unions in their developmental stages, but these had much more independence to campaign and act, and were (and are) less 'subject to review by faculty advisers and administrative officers'. In 1969 the rapporteur on an Anglo-US conference on 'Students and Universities' concluded that the British student 'has greater autonomy in his extra-curricular life' (Herrman 1969: 16–17). Twenty years later a Scottish student observer of five American students' unions found similar problems, activities and services, 'the major organisational difference in our respective Student Union systems [being] that we are run on the basis of "student control"' [Council, Johnson ACUI report 11 March 1991]. The Assistant Vice-President for Student Programs at Penn State meets fortnightly with student leaders, and he concludes from international meetings that the University's approach is 'more structured than in the British system' (Eakin int.). Penn's elected Undergraduate Assembly (the 'lobbying body') has five branches, covering Social Planning and Events, Student Activities (funding clubs and programmes), the Student Council on Undergraduate Education, Nominations and Elections, and 'class boards'. The University's Director of Student Life Activities and Facilities explained:

> My colleagues and I act as advisors to three of these bodies, that, is as resource persons and a historical memory. I attend UA Steering Committee meetings. Students ask for advice on whether something is a good idea, whom to talk to. Our role is one of personal interaction. The Office supervises 23 people who operate the building.
>
> (Walker int.)

Despite important differences between the two countries, the *in loco parentis* regulation of student codes of dress and behaviour, residential curfews, the policing of relations between the sexes, and other aspects of the college operating as proxy for parents and public morality, declined roughly in parallel. The effect was in various ways to reduce student dependency on the institution, but the development occurred in neither country in a vacuum. The demand for greater control of students' own lives was accompanied by other prominent demands for greater participation in academic and administrative decision-making. All of these had different levels of support, and were given different priorities by students and student organizations. The different traditions of student and institutional organization affected the outcomes. The British students' unions emerged into the new conditions of the 1970s with stronger antennae and links in the committee and decision-making processes of their institutions. There were, and are, difficulties in sustaining some of their activities, and student representation varies in its effectiveness. With the rapid growth in the size of many universities, their greater competitive position in the market-place, and the funding limits now in place on students' unions, some convergence with American practice is visible. In order to sustain their educational, advisory and representative roles British students' unions are having to boost their shrunken public funding by trading and entrepreneurial activities, and students' union executive and staff energies for some of their traditional roles may have to be diverted by new financial imperatives.

We have focused on these transatlantic similarities and differences because they illustrate clearly the various ways in which the student role can be 'idealized'. There are differences in emphasis between university services which 'partner' students in pursuit of their academic objectives, and those, for example, of the department at the University of Glasgow which deals with accommodation, catering, visitors' centre, and conference and vacation service, and is described by its director as 'part of the University welfare state' (Johnson 1994). The extent and nature of the student-as-consumer, for example, is involved in these descriptions. It is arguable that in the United States there was an escape from *in loco parentis*, and then a recapture of the terrain. This is not just in connection with those institutions which have in the recent past sought to reintroduce regulations covering, for example, dorm visiting, or to strengthen the policing of regulations on under-age drinking. One American commentator has argued that 'some aspects of *in loco parentis* never disappeared completely during the turbulent years of the late '60s', particularly as students continued to press for protection from outside law enforcement (Fass 1986: 33). A summary of 'The new *in loco parentis*' in 1991 underlined an ambiguous legal position in the United States:

> Courts continue to expressly reject the arguments that colleges and universities stand *in loco parentis* and act as guardians of student morals and safety. Institutions may nonetheless be held accountable for and to students . . . The Massachusetts Supreme Court refused to reinstate the *in loco parentis* doctrine, but found the college liable nonetheless . . . To some extent, these federal laws impose upon institutions obligations to regulate student behavior – a role many institutions might otherwise decline.

In some respects, comments the doctoral law student writing this, 'the days of *in loco parentis* were preferable. At least institutions and students had an identifiable set of expectations to meet' (Thomas 1991: 38–9).

Together with the institutions' motives of providing caring services and frameworks for student development there have been those of improving retention rates and responding to criticism that the absence of firm *in loco parentis* structures has reduced institutions' capacity to regulate significant aspects of student behaviour, including drug abuse, sexual promiscuity and under-age drinking. Students themselves sometimes want 'more administrative involvement' (Koons int.). An important feature of consumers, of course, is that although they have rights they are also dependent on providers to fulfil certain defined obligations. Over a longer period in the United States, but increasingly in the United Kingdom, an element of post-*in loco parentis* dependency is part of the discussion of what it has meant and means to be a student.

The expansion of student services has had to do with all of these issues about responsibility, professionalism and care. It has also had to do not only with the size of student populations, but also with the greater diversity of student constituencies which we have discussed. The 'new students' were from racial and ethnic minorities, disadvantaged social groups, women, the employed in need of first or further qualifications, access, franchised and other students in programmes sub-contracted to further education colleges. An additional word needs to be said about some of these and their relationship to the services that have grown in recent decades. An important example is that of students with disabilities, variously described across this period also as handicapped or disabled students, and later as students with special needs or learning difficulties.

The model for developments in this field was the United States. Many states and higher education institutions were rapidly expanding their provision in the 1960s for what were then described as handicapped students. Additional impetus was given by the effect, particularly on the schools, but with knock-on effects in higher education, of Public Law 94–142, the 1975 Education for All Handicapped Children Act. More directly applicable was the Rehabilitation Act of 1973 which required institutions to maintain an affirmative action programme to employ the handicapped, and to correct architectural barriers to employment and/or attendance by students. Penn had been developing programmes for the handicapped since the late 1960s, but began to invest particularly from 1977; in the three years between then and 1980

> [a]bout $1.25 million has been spent to add wheelchair ramps to buildings, widen doors, install elevators and modify toilet facilities. The City of Philadelphia cooperated by installing small wheelchair ramps at street corners through the campus. There is campus transportation in which a radio-dispatched station wagon and a van with a wheelchair lift are used to transport about 25 students, faculty members and employees each day. Many improvements have been made to Penn's gym and athletic fields, its swimming pool and ice rink to provide easy access to the handicapped to be both spectators and participants . . . The disabled can arrange for recorded textbooks, readers, tutors, typists, editors, proofreaders and research assistance . . .
> [UPA 4/284 265, news release 1980]

This was part of a pattern of increased or changed provision across large numbers of universities and colleges in the 1960s and 1970s, developing services, improving access, and involving student organizations and able-bodied studies in providing support.

There was British interest in the experience – particularly after the emphasis on university provision in the Warnock Report on *Special Educational Needs* in 1978 (DES 1978). Before that, however, institutions were looking at opportunities to improve their facilities and services, and working parties sometimes looked closely at what was happening in the United States. A working party of the Academic Board at North East London Polytechnic in 1973 reported on the 'great deal of interesting work being done for disabled students' in UK institutions of higher education and in the United States:

> We have also studied the appreciable documentation from the United States where a number of institutions such as the University of Illinois have made extensive provision for disabled students. The work of such

institutions has been a source of inspiration to us and a constant reminder that educational establishments in the United Kingdom have a long way to go before they can match our American colleagues in providing help and hope for the physically disabled.

The aim at the Polytechnic was defined as enabling the student 'to become an independent member of the student community who is not continually dependent on others during his or her stay at the Polytechnic', and this definition drew 'on the experience of American universities' (NELP 1973: 3, 7). In British universities pockets of specialized development were appearing, including the education of the deaf and hearing impaired at Durham and a specialized residential unit at the University of Sussex.

The NUS took a particular interest in reporting and encouraging such developments, notably from 1978, when it surveyed provision for students with locomotive disorders in halls of residence (NUS 1978). There were more universities and colleges making some provision, however limited, than those reporting none at all. The third edition of the survey report in 1981 reported some slight improvements (NUS 1978, 1981). The same year (which was coincidentally the International Year of Disabled People), the NUS, together with the National Bureau for Handicapped Students, issued a set of Guidance Notes for Student Unions, underlining that the number of handicapped students was only a quarter of the number it should have been if 'handicapped young people were fully represented in the student population', and that students' unions needed to make a major effort to ensure access to further and higher education for handicapped young people (NUS and NBHS 1981). In the late 1970s and early 1980s there were working parties at universities all over Britain, appointed by senates and academic boards, welfare committees, students' unions, or some combination of these and others. They acknowledged the poor facilities and their deterrent effect on potential applicants, surveying in detail the campus and the needs of students in specific categories of disability, recommending the appointment of responsible or co-ordinating staff, exploring the local and national support services, and drafting policy statements. Support services ranged from competent to negligible, but many institutions were deciding which categories of disability they could realistically attempt to support with appropriate facilities, by adapting rooms, installing loop amplification systems, running signing courses for staff and students, purchasing equipment. Institutions reviewed their prospectuses, application procedures and departmental and faculty support systems. Students might initially find services inadequate because institutions made the investment or arrangements only when students with particular disabilities had been admitted. These and other students and students' unions campaigned to be consulted or to be represented on working parties and committees. Some institutions made access for students with disabilities in general part of their mission, some focused on particular disabilities. There were major differences in the ability of campuses to cope with certain kinds of disability, and reluctance by teaching staff in some places to enter into unfamiliar teaching situations. Services for students with disabilities increased.

In 1990 the present authors conducted a study of 'Students with disabilities in higher education', considering the admissions procedures, relevant institutional structures and policies, personnel and provision. It did not deal with the special case of the Open University, which at the time had 2,800 students with disabilities among its 84,000 students (3.3 per cent), and which had an outstanding record of encouraging and helping such students. The report included a portrait of the roles and relationships of students with disabilities on a range of campuses, and the directions in which developments had gone since the 1970s. Given the relative neglect of these students in discussions of higher education, it is worth recalling the picture in some detail:

The degree to which students with disabilities, other students, students' unions, are involved formally or informally in these various procedures is to some extent influenced by the numbers of students with disabilities in the institution. The same is true of the types of disability represented on the campus. The presence of deaf students may encourage individual students to take up signing, as was the case in the early 1980s when Bulmershe College of Higher Education began to make particular provision for such students. A students' union may become involved in obtaining volunteers for a particular category of help, or in pressing the institution to provide a facility or remedy a defect. Individual students, as at the University of Nottingham, may become involved in an open day to help a disabled student at meal time, or in a variety of other ways. Middlesex Polytechnic arranges where possible for current students with disabilities similar to those of applicants to take part in the discussion with them following consideration of a place on academic grounds. Students with disabilities have collectively exercised pressure for specific changes or developments. At the University of Birmingham, for example, a group of blind students pressed successfully in 1990 for a resource centre, and at Lancashire Polytechnic it was the students with disabilities who persuaded the Director to take the first steps in setting up the advisory and resource arrangements now in existence. Dyslexic students at Bradford and Ilkley College successfully pressed for a specialist tutor. On their own and through their students' unions such students have secured changes in a prospectus or – as at the University of Leeds – the establishment and maintenance of the Recording Centre for the Blind. Some institutions, like South Bank Polytechnic, have an established procedure: 'comments, enquiries or suggestions from students with disabilities concerning improvements in facilities should be passed to the Dean of Student Services, who will consult the Registrar and liaise with members of the (disabilities) steering group as necessary'.

Students with disabilities and other members of students' unions regularly represent the union on committees concerned with welfare, student services or the specific needs of students with disabilities. The Disabled Students' Advisory Panel at the University of Liverpool, for example, contains the President and Welfare Officer of the Guild of Students, and 'disabled students are regularly co-opted onto the panel'. The University of Lancaster has a Committee for Handicapped Students which, as part of its membership, includes 'three persons, of whom two at least should (if possible) be students who are handicapped persons (appointed by the Student Representative Council/ Students Union)'. Working parties of various kinds, particularly where student welfare and disabilities are concerned, often include students with disabilities as members. West Glamorgan Institute of Higher Education had by 1990 accepted students with a wide range of disabilities (including wheelchair bound, non-sighted, epileptic, thalidomide victims and others) and was in the process of devising – at the request of the Institute's disabled students – a questionnaire for all new entrants to be completed on a voluntary basis, 'so that hidden disabilities are known about by someone on campus'.

Students' unions are in a position to make many kinds of contribution to the welfare and support of students with disabilities, sometimes in the absence of initiative elsewhere or of other relevant machinery. [The union] may, as in the University of Cambridge, produce an access survey. It may supplement the institution's welfare arrangements with its own, and there are students' unions with their own sabbatical welfare officers and welfare services, which may contribute substantially in the disability field. Some, as at the University of Lancaster, have their own Disabled Student Committee, or as at the University of Leicester share a Sub-Committee for Disabled Students with staff as a sub-committee of the Student Welfare Committee.

Students and their unions have in some institutions strong, active records in these connections. The Students Union at the University of Durham, for instance, keeps a small disabled students' fund, making grants of, for example, up to £100 for dyslexic students. Brighton Polytechnic students raised £6,000 to fund a private operation not available on the National Health Service to enable a cerebral palsy sufferer who had become wheelchair bound during his studies to walk again. In 1990 the Students' Union at the University of Leicester was planning a 'twinning' exercise, in which able-bodied students would guide disabled students from their Faculty around the campus for the first few days of the autumn term. The students had already established a Visually Impaired Student Friendship Network 'to improve student awareness of the problems faced by visually impaired students and to provide a meeting place for them'. Brighton Polytechnic students have operated a scheme not only to provide volunteer help for students with disabilities, but also to ensure a continuity of service (placing a disk in a student's window when a regularly needed piece of help has been given). The Students Union at Bulmershe College of Higher Education (before it amalgamated with the University of Reading) had [Britain's] first deaf Students Union president, following the involvement of the Students Union in the College's development of its work with the deaf.

There are also students' unions with little or no involvement with the disabled, even in institutions with active policies and procedures and substantial numbers of students with disabilities.

The conclusions reached in this report included specifically the roles students' unions could play in association with students with disabilities, and the need for the institution, its committees and services to recognize and encourage the union's role (Silver and Silver 1990: 3, 15–16).

Related to these snapshots of developments were the structures and increasingly systematic support processes of many of the institutions. By the 1990s many of them had a service for students with disabilities built into their Student Services. Student Services at Oxford Brookes University, for example, described its advisory service in the context of the University's policy to improve access and make a central fund available to assist with the purchase of specialist equipment. The Disability Action Group keeps the needs of students with disabilities under review. A part-time adviser arranges informal visits to assess the services required by prospective students, briefs staff, plans special examination arrangements and monitors progress. Plymouth at the same time was providing assessment, guidance and support for students with dyslexia in particular, including help in claiming special grants, technology advice, a student support group, and special examination provision.

For reasons which have partly to do with the attitudes and changes in the institutions themselves, including the provision of such services, and partly to do with developments in the schools, pressures from national advocacy bodies, and equal opportunities demands in general, the numbers of students with declared disabilities applying to and being admitted by universities and colleges increased sharply in the 1980s and 1990s. The numbers and proportions of applicants indicating a disability, being offered and accepting a place varied for many reasons. In 1993, for example, at the University of Liverpool 1,757 indicated a disability, 663 places were offered, and 262 were accepted; at Bristol the numbers were 1,432, 712 and 352, respectively; at Manchester 2,054, 818 and 347; at Plymouth 1,222, 687 and 321; at Wolverhampton 1,170, 657 and 286; at Nene College 508, 328 and 154. Seventy-seven institutions had received acceptances of their offers from 9,529 students (PCAS 1993). In 1995 there were 11,500 students with declared disabilities in the first year of full-time higher education, and 3,400 in part-time, accounting for 3.8 per cent of the total (*THES* 29 September 1995: iv–v). These figures are no more than an indication of the spread of students with all kinds of disabilities considering and entering higher education, as well as the situation to which institutions' services were responding.

The existence of such services was important in encouraging potential students and enabling them to enter higher education. Large universities in Britain and the United States provide increasingly comprehensive and technologically sophisticated services. At Penn State these cover students with visual and hearing impairments, students with learning disabilities, and those with mobility impairments. Whatever the disability, the University announces that it is 'interested in all academically qualified students' [Office for Disability Services, leaflets]. The position is not static. Students, in Britain as in the United States, are entering with greater expectations, aware of established rights, having had their needs identified at earlier stages of schooling and expecting more of the same kind of support, and critical of institutions which do not sufficiently recognize their disabilities (Hameister int.).

Not all categories of students have, or need, special services, and some needs are met with difficulty or not at all. Part-time students, for example, are an extremely diverse category, with particular academic needs that it is important but difficult to meet, but also without a common pattern of social or other support needs. Providing personal tutor support, for example, involves problems relating to the diversity, timing and frequency of their attendance on campus. It is difficult for them to be involved in the life of the students' union and the campus in general. Commuter students are a similarly diverse category, full- or part-time, local or travelling considerable distances, traditional or non-traditional, dependent or independent. This classification of students is of particular significance in the United States, but also important to large, British urban institutions and those in rural areas such as South West England. A study of American commuter students in 1989 indicated that they accounted for over 80 per cent of college students, but 'the residential tradition of American higher education has impeded effective, comprehensive institutional response to their presence . . . some institutions still barely acknowledge the presence of their commuter students'. In spite of the difficulties of these students and their 'greater risk of attrition', there was a strong tendency to perpetuate the values of residential institutions from which administrators and faculty had themselves graduated (Jacoby 1989: iii–iv).

Although discrete services are not targeted on part-time and commuter students as such, there are often services for mature students who have in recent decades accounted for rapidly increasing full-time and part-time numbers, and certain categories of whom are by definition home-based or commuter students. As we have seen, the expansion of British mature student numbers was associated initially with the development of the CNAA and the polytechnics, and since the 1970s more and more attention has been given to the recruitment of older students. At Queen Margaret College in 1975 the Academic Council discussed a paper on provision for adult students and proposed the establishment of a working party. A report in 1978 was the subject of a special meeting of the Academic Council, which considered the two types of older student in the College: 'the "postponed-entry" students following courses normally taken by school-leavers, and the "mid-career" students who entered College to build upon qualifications or experience already achieved in a particular professional field'. Population trends might lead to developing more courses to attract older students. Initiatives for new courses, a review of course materials and teaching strategies, staff development and the allocation of resources, were all recommended [AC 4 November 1975, 5 July 1978, 21 February 1979]. In the 1980s the College was specializing in preparing students for careers in the health and consumer services, and its publication for mature students in 1987 emphasized that would-be students over the age of 21 were 'eligible for special consideration for entry', and that mature students

> bring a distinctive contribution to the classes they join . . . Many people who did not have the opportunity or inclination to enter higher education after school, decide, sometimes after a long period away from education, that they want to begin to study again. Many of these are women whose family commitments have prevented them from fulfilling long-cherished goals of pursuing professional careers . . . There is no pretending that being a mature student on a full-time course is easy . . . [but] mature students have a high success rate.
>
> [*A Second Chance to Learn: Opportunities for Mature Students* 1987: 1]

Other institutions in the 1970s, for similar demographic and other reasons, were planning such increased recruitment, while in many cases reluctant to develop part-time courses or accept part-time students, or anxious about the difficulty of assessing the abilities of candidates with 'non-standard' entry qualifications – for example, Higher National Diplomas and Certificates, National or Scottish Vocational Qualifications. The pressures to admit and support older students were not new. The NUS told the Robbins Committee in 1961:

> we would expect . . . that for many years to come there will be an increasing demand for higher education from older people who missed the opportunity for full-time higher education at the usual age, and who are prepared to make considerable sacrifices in order to return to full-time education.
>
> (NUS 1963: 218)

It was not alone in believing this.

The special difficulties of many mature students are recognized, but institutions often have their own difficulties in offering support. Just as mature students may have strong family ties and social networks outside the institution, so they may also prefer to look elsewhere for formal or informal sources of support. The more than a quarter of a million students over the age of 21 who began higher education courses annually from 1990 are an extraordinarily disparate constituency for the institution or the students' union easily to encompass. Students' unions are as prone as their parent institutions to assume that full-time, residential provision remains the planning norm. A solution that mature students themselves or the students' union have often sought is the organization of mature students' organizations. At Teesside the Students Union supported the creation of a mature students' association from 1978 and it established one in 1981 [EC 6 March 1978, 16 March 1978, 25 May 1978, 17 February 1981]. At Durham, with only a small population of older undergraduates, the Union nevertheless took the initiative to establish a Mature Students' Association, which 'really got off the ground' in 1979–80. The Union Council recorded in 1980 that

> mature students have an important part to play in higher education, especially in Durham, where you can go from one year's end to the next without seeing anyone outside the 18–22 year old age group . . . Mature students have many problems, which the 'normal' undergraduate never has to face.
>
> [Council 5 March 1980]

In 1990 the Mature Students' Association at Strathclyde described itself as 'the most active and dynamic society in College' [*Strathclyde Telegraph* 24 September 1990: 13]. A journalist who had been a mature student in the 1960s, reflected in 1992 that mature students used to be

> a potent force within the universities and colleges. Most of them hailed from backgrounds in which educational opportunities had not been sufficiently available to reach higher or further education, and many of them had cut their teeth in the trade union movement . . . Yet there was always a problem with mature students. For a start British academic life was not prepared for the phenomenon.

Some of these students felt this was their last chance, 'studied assiduously, and had wives and children and jobs they desired . . . [They] had aspirations less well formed . . . had a great time'. For mature students now the burden, financial and emotional was 'excessive to the point at which only the most dedicated or even obsessive, will consider the option' (McLean 1992: 5).

It was clear from research from the 1970s that the success rates of these students 'show up very favourably against straight-through students' (Jones and Williams 1979: 19; Molloy and Carroll 1991: *passim*), and in spite of the difficulties they face, for a variety of reasons 'in the perception of those who teach them, adult students in higher education appear to be more confident than younger students' (Percy 1985: 46). In its programme for 1995–6 the Mature Students' Association at Strathclyde told students over 21 to 'take your head out of the books for a while. The biggest problem faced by mature students is working too hard, on their own' [MSA, leaflet].

Other groups of students, including racial and ethnic minorities, franchised students and distance learning students, may overlap with some we have discussed, but they may not relate to the services and organizations of their institutions in the ways we have outlined. Two other categories, however, relate more directly to this discussion, women and overseas students.

First, women students, whether older or school leavers, face particular problems which Student Services and students' unions often do directly address – issues concerning harassment or rape, child minding or nursery, or stresses from their presence on traditionally male-dominated campuses. In the 1960s an American review of research drew attention to work which indicated that it was easier for women to stay in some institutions than in others, and 'the masculinity of the college' was related positively to women's dropping out' (Yonge 1965: 256–7). Female minorities in former all-male Oxford and Cambridge colleges continued to have difficulties with the 'masculinity' of the college culture. In 1994 the Dean of Churchill College, Cambridge, resigned in protest at the lenient punishment imposed on a male student who stripped at a mixed soccer club dinner, reflecting what the *Guardian* reported as the 'rugger bugger' culture of Oxford and Cambridge. An Oxford study suggested that the move to mixed colleges had had a disastrous effect on women's examination results, in part as a result of the intimidating male-dominated culture of the colleges (*Guardian* 30 April 1994: 4). The issue of women students' security on campus has loomed large in many places, and campus security measures have been increased. 'Date rape' has reached the courts and the media in Britain as in the United States. Interviews did not suggest widespread anxiety about security on the campus itself, and a 1991 survey of second and third year women students conducted at the University of Manchester points in some important directions. Students were asked to rate answers to questions on a five-point scale – very troubled, troubled, OK, contented and very contented. On personal security at the University no second year student was very troubled, and 16.2 per cent were troubled; 79.6 per cent answered contented or OK. Third year students were marginally more troubled. Thirty-three per cent of second years and 46 per cent of third years were troubled or very troubled about security in their housing, and 51 per cent and 62 per cent respectively were troubled or very troubled about security while travelling to and fro. The overwhelming majority of the respondents considered their social life to be OK (11 per cent of second, 24 per cent of third years), were contented with it (37 per cent of second, 31 per cent of third years) or very contended (47 per cent of second, 41 per cent of third years) (Berry 1995: 212).

Women students share some of the campus roles and relationships we have discussed, but have become increasingly involved in mutual support groups, or have been the object of increasing support and security measures. Students' unions or independent groups run women's advice centres, half-term play groups or baby-sitting networks. Some Student Services are responsible for nursery or childcare facilities, and in other cases students' unions have in recent decades taken the initiatives for these and provide them. Campaigns for nurseries or crèches have been among the most prominent campaigns of students' unions since the 1960s, reflecting either the presence of student parents in the institution or pressures to widen recruitment to mature women students. Such campaigns in the 1970s and 1980s were most prominently a feature of polytechnics and colleges of higher education, many of whose mature students accounted for a quarter or a third of the total, although other urban institutions such as those of the University of London were also involved. A Students Union campaign for nursery provision was launched at Teesside in the mid-1970s [Council 3 December 1974, 25 March 1976]. In 1988 the Strathclyde Students' Association's nursery was ten years old, but was at risk financially and needed, and received, additional University finance [Council 17 October 1988, 27 October 1988, 12 December 1988]. In 1977 Durham Students Union was negotiating with the University for a full-day crèche, and submitted a paper to a joint committee of University Council and the Union:

> Students who study at Durham University do not, under normal circumstances, have children. However, with a number of married postgraduates, a growing number of mature students, the trend towards earlier marriages amongst students and the needs of members of university staff, there is undoubtedly a need for a creche to be provided.

Some steps towards provision were taken by the University, but full-day care had been postponed, and a morning crèche had been opened. The Union emphasized how helpful the University had been and hoped that full-day provision would become a reality when finances permitted [Joint Committee 26 January 1978]. Costs, inappropriate buildings and safety regulations, and in some cases hesitations by university authorities about the need and responsibility for making provision, led to prolonged campaigns on many campuses through the 1980s and into the 1990s. In 1995 the NUS joined with the Association of University Teachers, the National Association of Teachers in Further and Higher Education and Working for Childcare, to launch a campaign around a document entitled *Childcare on Campus*, pressing for suitable provision: 'the desperate lack of childcare provision in colleges and universities is a major obstacle to equal participation at work or in learning for people with children' (McHardy 1995: 6). Provision for children had not kept pace with the implications of increased numbers of older students.

Some 10 per cent of the million and a half students in UK higher education come from overseas, the majority from EU countries and Asia (*Higher Education Digest* 1995b). This number has grown from some 28,000 in 1955–6 and 64,000 in 1962–3 [CHE 2A 1993: 252]. They have been seen as a contribution to international relations, an enrichment of campus life, a source of students for vacant places, and a source of revenue. A decision in 1979 to charge students from non-European Community countries full-cost fees 'sent shock-waves through a number of Britain's international relationships' (Overseas Students Trust 1987: 1), severely affected the flow of students from Commonwealth countries and led to prolonged re-evaluation of policy towards overseas students. The nearly 50,000 new entrants annually are spread unevenly across the sector, and the extent and nature of the formal institutional support varies, but support of some kind has become inevitable as major difficulties have surfaced over, for example, immigration controls, payment of fees by foreign governments and the funding of students. Oxford Brookes was one of the first institutions to establish an Advisory Service for International Students. A full-time adviser and a part-time assistant have responsibility for providing 'pre-arrival information', orientation programmes and advice and support for international students throughout their course, as well as working with the International Office on matters relating to student recruitment, and a network of specialist tutors [Student Services, September 1994]. The University of Liverpool has an international students' adviser who offers advice and help, can direct students to appropriate services, and can give assistance with immigration, financial, legal and other problems [*Guild Handbook* 1994: 32]. Students' unions also often make special provision, and the students themselves establish international students' societies. The union at the University of Plymouth tells students:

> As an international student you can face additional problems that home students often don't. These could be difficulties with tuition fees, visas/ entry certificates, council tax, working, racial prejudice and isolation from other students. All is not bad news though, the Students' Union has an International Students' Officer who is there to help and support you through your time at Plymouth.
>
> [*UPSU Handbook* 1993: 14]

The reception and treatment of overseas students, by the universities and colleges and by the community more widely, has often been judged negatively, from their description as *Disappointed Guests* in 1965 (Tajfel and Dawson 1965). A study in 1970 considered their adaptation difficulties, and the difficulties they faced in establishing close contact with British students, families and the community in general. They encountered discrimination in various ways, had particular difficulties over accommodation, but did find support from within their institutions, from the British Council and other organizations, and in many cases from their own embassies or high commissions. The wastage rate was high, at 25.9 per cent – highest in colleges of technology and further education, and lowest in colleges of education (Sen 1970: 30–7, 78–87, 141). American research produced similar results. In the late 1970s, for example, only 52 per cent of foreign students were found to have contact with American people as frequently as they wished. Forty per cent spent time mainly in the company of American students, 33 per cent mainly with their fellow nationals, 21 per cent with other foreign students. Loneliness was a significant feature of the students' experience (Hull IV 1978: 106–11). In some British institutions, in the 1970s particularly, international students set up their own organizations as much because of their dissatisfaction with students' unions as for other reasons. At Strathclyde, for example, in 1978 an Overseas Students' Committee was formed, explaining that this was because of 'growing discontent among overseas student groups over the irresponsible attitude the Students Union has shown towards overseas student problems' [*Strathclyde Telegraph* 30 November 1978: 6].

Much of this discussion of services and support relates to the changed circumstances of higher education following the upheavals of the late 1960s and the abandonment of formal *in loco parentis* roles by the institutions. It has been concerned both with the changing constituencies in higher education, and interpretation of the rights and responsibilities of students. In Britain more than in the United States, this has also concerned the enhanced role of students' unions and the government review of their roles, practices and finance in the 1990s. From the 1960s, however, interpreting the roles of students and their organizations has meant considering them not just as recipients of services but as judges of and participants in the governing, administrative and educational processes of the institutions. On questions of representation, at levels closest to and most remote from the daily lives of students, there is no escaping the 1960s, not only *in loco parentis* issues, but also the student movements which, among other things, generated concern about what roles it was legitimate, fitting and possible for students to play in these various processes.

5

Action and Representation

Students in the 1990s, despite all the changes in their conditions and attitudes from the 1970s, remain heirs to much that was fashioned by the student movement of the 1960s. It is important to signal some of the directions in which their militancy and action pointed. The postwar world had changed in fundamental ways, and the implications were described with some drama by anthropologist Margaret Mead in 1970. The younger generation at the time, 'the articulate young rebels all around the world who are lashing out against the controls to which they are subjected, are like the first generation born into a new country. They are at home in this time'. They neither understood nor were understood by their parents: 'The young do not know what must be done, but they feel that there must be a better way . . . Today, nowhere in the world are there elders who know what the children know'. Mead conveys a sense of global drama:

> The elders are separated from them by the fact that they, too, are a
> strangely isolated generation. No generation has ever known, experi-
> enced, and incorporated such rapid changes, watched the sources of
> power, the means of communication, the definition of humanity, the
> limits of the explorable universe, the certainties of a known and lim-
> ited world, the fundamental imperatives of life and death – all change
> before their eyes . . . At this breaking point between two radically dif-
> ferent and closely related groups, both are inevitably very lonely, as
> we face each other knowing that they will never experience what we
> have experienced, and that we can never experience what they have
> experienced.
>
> (Mead 1972: 99–102)

Much of the commentary on the student events of the 1960s was in terms of their irrationality and inexplicable revolutionary politics, the unacceptable behaviour of at least the most visible activists. Mead, however, recalls us to the rational explanations of the larger stage, and she was not alone in doing so. In Britain in 1960, the Albermarle Committee on the Youth Service had already emphasized, as we have seen, that teenagers were 'living in a world more than usually different from that of their parents'. Most of the generalizations about youth and their reactions to their world were 'untrue and distorting. But they have hardened into some of the most striking clichés of the last decade'. Young people were described as 'teenage delinquents', rejecting family life, increasingly materialistic, without moral values (Ministry of Education 1960a: 31). The difference between these 1950s 'clichés' and those of the 1960s reflects the move from rejection to confrontation. Students, wrote Schwab, 'are men and women without a country'. They are tolerated aliens in the collegiate community' (Schwab 1969: 41). They were alienated in their increasingly large institutions, no longer engaged to the same extent, or at all, with their academic elders, aware of the military, financial and other evils of the world that had been created but of which they did not feel a part.

There were commentators who accepted the analysis of the big stage, but were less convinced that the scene was new. Lord Robbins, speaking in the United States in 1967, thought it would be 'a great mistake to treat much of what is happening today as if it were an entirely novel appearance in history'. He had been reading Turgenev's *Fathers and Sons*, which dealt with 'just this problem of alienation and revolt among the younger generation. Indeed, I am inclined to argue that there are profound psychological reasons why this should be a more or less permanent feature of the human situation' (Robbins 1969: 182). The history of students in particular does contain if not a constant thread at least a recurrence of types of protest and conflict. Medieval university students rioted and worse, and the histories describe internal conflict and bloody warfare with townspeople. Students have over the centuries assessed the quality of their colleges and universities in 'colorful ways', in the words of one American description: 'They have thrown rocks. They have boycotted their classes. They have rioted. They have harassed their professors. They have thrown their food upon the floor' (Williams 1971: 13). Reflecting on the activism of the 1960s, various American analysts went out of their way to underline how adversarial students were in the 1930s (Swirsky 1971; Lee 1970).

It is important, however, in spite of the history of student dissent and generational conflict, to see the events of the 1960s in two searchlights – one which illuminates the recurring need of students to make their presence felt, to take the opportunity of influencing situations and events, and the other which shows up the particular urgencies of the youth movements of the 1950s and the transition to the dramatic confrontations of the mid- and late 1960s. There are various ways of representing this transition. Another American view, while the momentum of events was still evident, was that the generation gap was not new, but that the power relationship had changed. There had been a 'steady loss of power and authority over social decisions by the older generation', and the ideas and occasional militancy of students were 'spreading among campuses with the speed and power of a flood – unstoppable on a national scale'. What was new was that 'recently the young generation has begun to win' (Johnston 1971: 85–6). With hindsight this is an exaggerated view, but it was not an uncommon feeling at the time, and the response of the universities and colleges internationally was to concede as much as was necessary to stop the 'unstoppable' and to try to remodel a sense of institutional community in new circumstances.

This discussion carries forward into all aspects of students' lives and roles in recent decades and the present, as well as our earlier concern with perceptions of adolescence, youth and adulthood. Judgements about developments in the 1960s were not just about the legitimacy of political attitudes or action, they were also about the profile of 'the student' amidst these new phenomena. They were about technology, war and poverty, but they were also about dress and behaviour. It was not always clear to the world outside why and to what extent students were exercising a version of what one vice-chancellor called 'the new independence of young people, and the implications this has for institutions which have in the past stood *in loco parentis*' (Sloman 1970: 39–40). Since more students were living off campus, and shared in aspects of the highly visible and audible youth culture, the question was whether one of the roots of 'displays of generalized dissidence' lay in mass youth entertainment and the 'dissident youth' made possible or promoted by the entertainment industry's attack on a 'received cultural tradition' (Wilson [1970]: 80, 218–22). Much was made of the student adoption, in Britain as in very many countries, of the features of generational conflict represented by psychedelic drugs, rock music and the 'angry' content of theatre and film. Puzzling for many was the changed appearance of students. The Warden of All Souls College, Oxford, produced one of the most vivid responses in an article entitled 'Why do the young look like this?' On both sides of the Atlantic the young 'have in the last few years undergone a metamorphosis in their speech, their dress, their bearing – in the whole style and conduct of their physical life'. The classic image of youth

> no longer decorates our college quadrangles and our city streets; its place has been taken by a strange, unprepossessing crowd. Shock-headed and dishevelled, ill-clad and ill-conditioned, a new breed of adolescents presents itself to view, padding hand in hand along our pavements, soft-shod or bare of foot. Common to either sex are the patched jeans and dirty sweaters; hair seems to have run to seed, hiding ears and neck and fringing young men's faces with a fuzz of beard or whiskery overgrowth. Many of these male and female sluts are evidently, like Dr Johnson, 'no friends to clean linen'.

The ones who still had clean necks and clear complexions 'are jostled by a sloppy, shaggy, crowd of miscellaneous anthropological types – the human golliwog, the hairy Ainu, the fuzzy-wuzzy, the Struwwelpeter, the Barbary pirate, the Robinson Crusoe, the Jesus Christ'. It was obvious that students were not just protesting against a set of middle-class sartorial conventions, but 'all conventions alike' (Sparrow 1970: 25–6).

The American version of that kind of response, as viewed from Berkeley, was summarized by Tussman:

Students en masse are apparently a disturbing spectacle. Beards and miniskirts, mysterious potions and simple musical instruments, evoke ancestral memories of nymphs and satyrs. In our puritan nightmare they have emerged from the wooded fringes and swarm unheeding and shameless in the public streets, the parks, and the campus . . . Or, in the other nightmare, the sullen cast of *Lear* – Gonerils, Edmunds, Regans – monsters of ingratitude, are turning heedless and destructive energy against the aging nurturer. The college, when it is not blamed for causing all this, is at least expected to cure it.

(Tussman 1969: 23–4)

By the end of the 1960s, however, confrontation had begun to alter the image. Maxine Greene pointed to the change this caused. Before the campus disturbances young people could be treated as a kind of spectacle. They were the 'now', the 'mod', the 'protest' generation, the hippies and the flower children, the draft resisters and some New Left revolutionaries: 'one could, if one chose, talk entertainingly about beards, long hair, sandals, head-bands, beads. One could refer pleasantly to the sound of folk-rock music'. But that was before the confrontation and the violence, with the symbolism of Che Guevara boots and black jackets. Like Margaret Mead, and quoting her, Greene set all of this in the wider context: 'we too often forget how radically the world has changed from the days of our youth' (Greene 1970: 13–15). The consensus seemed to be that the student 'troubles' were related to but a specialized version of the youth culture, aimed at new targets, and finding new energies. Observers commented, as we have previously noted, on the particular position of students, most of whom were isolated from the labour market, which had become so important to youth generally and which had given them the basis of their independence. An American study of 'The student revolt: a special case of a youth culture' found it appropriate to apply the term 'youth' to students, and reasserted the view that students were placed in an ambivalent position:

An ever growing percentage of the young-adult population is pouring into the universities and is consequently being withheld from participation in the adult-role system, although these students are intellectually, physically, and emotionally capable of such participation. At the same time, there seems to be little doubt that the university is a most conducive environment for the development of a rather independent sub-culture, in terms of students' forms of behavior and modes of expression.

(Adler 1974: 124)

They were young adults, youth, adolescents, children, and some kaleidoscopic mix of these, and they called themselves 'kids', 'out to remake the world they had not joined' (Farber, quoted in Davis 1988: 52).

Prime targets in this remaking of the world were of course the Vietnam War, the dominance and ethics of corporate capitalism, white racism, and a variety of related economic and social ills. The extent of the 'educational' content of the various protest movements is less clear. Students were often translating their adolescent/adult destinies and their disaffection with their higher education institutions and experience into broader forms of confrontation. They did so, however, in different forms and with different emphases. The idealism inherent in much of their protest often simply included the university in the global interpretation. As Crouch put it, student militants saw authority as 'a vast international monolith; to distinguish, say, the Vice-Chancellor of the University of Warwick from the commander of U.S. forces in Vietnam is to make a false and probably deliberately deceptive distinction' (Crouch 1972: 203). It is probably more true of the United States than of Britain that the educational or academic issues did not surface unambiguously as targets of protest. A University of California sociologist made the point with some force that 'none of the student insurrections, at least in such major centers as Berkeley, Harvard, Columbia, Michigan, and Wisconsin, were motivated by concern with *academic* matters'. Student revolutionaries, at the beginning, were not interested in the structure of the university, and even later, when they claimed an interest in the curriculum and academic policy, it 'had a rather hollow ring alongside their manifestly transcending, ostentatiously millennial interest in, first national, then world revolution'. The condition of the university mattered to the major student revolutionaries only as 'one more illustration of a social order that was in their view irredeemably corrupt and obsolete' (Nisbet 1971: 157, 165–6). This, as a broad view, is overstated. Student demands for representation and a voice in university affairs, as well as immediate campus changes, were not uniform, but they were widespread. Such demands, as we have seen, might include concern about mixed residence and curfews, but they also included issues relating to the curriculum, assessment, class size, faculty–student relations, and student representation as a symbol of student maturity and status. A study of reform movements at five US west coast colleges and universities pointed to the difficulty of separating campus and broader issues. Many student demands concerned innovative approaches to their problems, including:

> experimental curricula; student participation in university decision making; special attention to the curriculum and related needs of black and other minority students; a general reduction in the size of classes; insured consideration of quality of instruction in the promotion and tenure of faculty; a general humanization of the university's bureaucratic directive machinery, and withdrawal from collaboration with military operations.
>
> (Fashing and Deutsch 1971: 10)

That all such demands challenged the legitimacy of authority, power and policy does not mean that the 'domestic' issues were universally unimportant, or that the view of the 'major centers' is more widely applicable. It also does not mean that the targets set by the 'major student revolutionaries' were also the targets of all those who participated in the 'insurrections'.

At Penn's relatively 'quiet revolution' a six-day sit-in in 1969 resulted in the Trustees agreeing to raise $10 million for community renewal programmes, and the establishment of a joint faculty–trustee–student commission to oversee future University development plans, including the use of land for low-income housing. The Community Involvement Council, a student-led organization, had been active in opposing the University's expansion into a disadvantaged area, and in organizing student community service. Following the sit-in, the head of the students' negotiating team considered that 'we have won more than any other college movement in history' [*Daily Pennsylvanian* 24 February 1969: 1]. The Politics and Education Collective at the University demanded the right of students and teachers together to 'determine the direction of the course, its approach and structure, its work or exam format, the grading system, when and where it meets, etc.' It also wanted the right to initiate new courses, and to have a say in the hiring, firing and promotion of faculty and administration [UA 'The Case for Student Rights' 1972]. Angry confrontations at Penn State were concerned with demands for the recruitment of more black students, a University bookstore, the removal of restrictions on mixed visiting, increased accommodation, and representation on Senate (Bezilla 1985: 294–9). There were other demands, including those relating to Vietnam, and the University administration was regularly 'under siege', with the two sides frequently unwilling to hear each other. In these two institutions, however, it would be misleading to exclude academic considerations from the agenda of confrontation.

It would also be misleading, in the United States as in the United Kingdom, to leave out of the picture student disappointment with the university or college experience, the scale, the resources, the processes, the roles of academic staff, the absence or weakness of the student input. There is a helpful description of the American student response to the higher education environment, by Paul Potter, immediate Past President of the radical national body, Students for a Democratic Society:

> The reality of universities was, to a great extent, the opposite of what we had hoped for. In the place of intellectual and personal seriousness was substituted the academic grind of large classes, intense competition for grades, exams that were irrelevant and intellectually damaging, and an environment in which the chief academic occupation seemed at times to consist of learning to beat the system . . . In place of personal independence in shaping life and education were substituted numerous requirements characterized mostly by dullness and massiveness, the confining and degrading existence of dormitories and their regulations . . . Independence, university-style, meant isolation in an environment that was essentially callous to personal needs. For most, it was the first encounter with the full inflexibility of mass bureaucratic

organization . . . and a system of external pressures and deadlines that substitute for internal initiatives and concerns . . . If, on occasion, students found good teachers or exciting classes, it did little more than underscore their sense that the rest were bad or useless. Perhaps the most difficult thing to assimilate, however, was the phoniness of the presentation of the university experience . . . On the whole, colleges seem to try to present themselves as permissive and mildly parental when in fact they are neither.

All of this helped to explain, Potter added, the origins of student discontent, not necessarily its explicit focus: 'in general, the university experience outside of the classroom is the catalyst that begins to give students new insights into the way the society operates, the way people are treated, and the way cultural values are misrepresented' (Potter 1965: 72–3). There is no reason to doubt that these springs of discontent continued to operate for very many students.

In Britain it is equally true that the most militant students were targeting war, militarism and corporate capitalism, and education was equally subsumed in the society that was shaped by them. A similar ambiguity exists in the analysis, since 'the first issue to gather widespread support was the search for student participation in the government of universities', at the same time as this challenged the legitimacy of university authorities, and 'purely educational issues have predominated only in a few revolts . . . Where education has figured directly it has concerned either course content or examinations' (Crouch 1972: 198–201). As in the United States, students at British universities and colleges of art particularly, encountered some of the same sources of discontent, and framed their protests and demands in terms of those and other issues which matched on the larger canvas those they experienced in their institutions. The crucial point is the relation between the experience and the protest on the one hand, and the self-definition of the young adults in the face of that experience and the perceived failures of the older generation on the other. An Oxford student is reported as observing in 1968 that 'as far as the universities are concerned, we want them run on a completely democratic basis. We want them run on the assumption that every member of a university is an adult and capable of participating in its affairs' (Green 1969: 324). What students inherited most from the events of the 1960s was a sharpened attempt to redefine the nature of a university or college community, and their position as adolescents and adults.

Defining the nature of the community was symbolized for students in the 1960s and 1970s particularly by the purpose, extent and effectiveness of their representation in those areas of policy- and decision-making which governed the central features of the academic community. As the radical energies of the late 1960s and early 1970s declined, issues of representation, authority and legitimacy became more distant from the routine concerns of the great majority of students, and the relative political conservatism of students from the mid-1970s established other student priorities. The changes of the 1970s and after altered the students' experience of the students' union and the campus. The demand for representation, as a direct outcome of the 1960s student movement, first needs some consideration.

Whatever student representation became, and with whatever limitations, it was in the late 1960s and 1970s symbolic of students' entry into a new relationship with their institutions. To be consulted was one thing, to be present at the table when the major decisions were taken was another – though many students were soon to find that 'real' decisions often seemed to be taken at some other table. There were, of course, students who wished to control, even to abolish, the process, and others who merely wanted to influence it in a more open environment. It is likely that the majority of students simply welcomed a vague reassurance that they 'belonged', that their voices, however small, might be heard. They may not have expected a great deal, and into the 1990s it was not always clear what they had in fact gained. Representation at all levels, from the course or department to the council or governing body, was indeed widely attained between the 1960s and 1980s, but to the activists the negatives became increasingly apparent. Representation was for many students a hard and unattractive commitment. Experienced chairpersons, whether lay, administrative or academic, knew how to colonize, intimidate or talk down students on every kind of committee. Much was gained in the adjustment of authority's attitudes, but rarely in adapting them to any of the more far-reaching notions of student participation, partnership or influence that had been formulated particularly in the late 1960s and early 1970s. Representation in relation to perceptions of the student role can be glimpsed by briefly considering a sample of student demands and institutional developments across recent decades.

At Liverpool a joint committee of Senate and the Guild of Undergraduates was appointed in 1969 to consider where students had a part to play in University life, possibly extending their past involvement in committees to include Council, Senate, faculty and departmental levels. One of the stumbling blocks was opposition in some faculties, but agreement was reached in 1971 that the Guild president and deputy president, together with one student representative from each faculty, would take part in Senate, and that two of these would be invited to attend Council meetings [*Report to Court 1970–71*: xii; ibid. *1971–2*: xviii]. The Guild had wanted 12.5 per cent representation on faculty boards but Senate 'discovered' (the quotation marks are those of the student newspaper) that University statutes did not permit students to have voting rights there. The radical Socialist Society opposed participation altogether, but the more moderate Students for a Democratic University supported acceptance as a step towards something more comprehensive and as 'a means of challenging the university administrators' pre-conceptions about what students are and their role' [*Guild Gazette* 27 June 1972: 1; *ibid.* 7 November 1972: 1]. The 'experiment', as the University saw it, began with elections in 1972. One of the Guild's negotiators attended an NUS conference in May 1972 which (apart from abrogating the CVCP–NUS 1968 joint statement) provided warning signals not to be too optimistic. The conference did not formally discuss representation, but the Liverpool delegates

> carried out an informal survey and detected considerable disillusion. In many cases, we may conclude that too much was expected of student participation from the start. Some Universities, Edinburgh for example, suffered from too much participation and the student effort was dissipated on a string of committees. I believe that student representation at Liverpool could be similarly disadvantageous unless it can be shown to be positively useful. It should not be accepted merely because it is the 'thing' – in fact, Liverpool is so far behind the others that in 1972 representation is distinctly unfashionable . . . All this does not alter the fact that that representation could only be a marginal improvement on our present position.

Presence at Senate, Council and faculty boards might make some contribution to student interests, but 'it does not mean progress towards the democratisation of the University' [A.032/45, Graham 1972: 3–4]. Liverpool students found that departmental and faculty representation could be extremely frustrating. Not every department had a staff–student liaison committee, and at both levels students found that 'staff members are not prepared to take forward the business of the Staff/Student Committee'. Meetings were 'dominated by the Head of Department' [A.032/85 Report on Staff/ Student Committees, n.d.: 1–2].

A Guild Council meeting in 1973 elected two members to each of ten University committees and one to each of two others (including Discipline, Library, Health and Welfare, Car Parking, and the Training of University Teachers) [A.032/86 2 July 1973]. Throughout the 1970s, however, the issue of sufficient representation on the main bodies remained a preoccupation of the Guild, pressing, for example, for 20 per cent representation and voting rights on faculty boards. Although by the 1980s energies were being devoted to other acute issues, including accommodation and grants, representation was not dead as an issue. In 1991 the Guild Council minutes reported that 'it is generally recognised that in the past the quality of our representation has not matched the increasingly complex demands placed upon it'. The Vice-Chancellor was reported as having agreed that 'the present system of representation by Students on Faculty Boards and Senate is outdated and inadequate' [Guild Council 21 May 1991].

At Durham, as a collegiate university, issues of representation were addressed at three levels – that of the University and its controlling bodies; that of departments, powerful units in a highly devolved university; and that of the colleges, with their own management structures. These were issues for the Students Representative Council (which became Durham Students Union in 1970) and in the third case also for students in the colleges with their Junior Common Rooms. The purposes of representation were seen by students as different in the three cases, with discipline, regulations and day-to-day life uppermost in the colleges. Senate had debated the issues in 1968, in the light of the arguments advanced by the students, by events across higher education, and by the need to respond to the CVCP–NUS joint statement of that year, which suggested that 'the machinery of student participation can and should be extended and improved' (CVCP and NUS 1968: 3). Senate held an extraordinary meeting in October 1968 to consider student disturbances elsewhere and procedures if attempts were made in the University 'to obstruct or disrupt its work', and in December it considered the CVCP–NUS statement, proposing a committee to discuss what action, if any, should be taken regarding student participation in Senate and its committees [Senate 1 October 1968, 3 December 1968]. From 1964 the SRC had been urging more representation on University committees, and in 1967–8 was reasserting its policy that students should be represented on Senate and Council and their committees and on the governing bodies of the colleges, and should have formal staff–student meetings in all departments. Departmental meetings were seen as particularly important, and the SRC President produced a detailed account of the existing consultation arrangements, mainly informal, in each of the 33 departments [SRC memo January 1969]. Senate initially opposed representation, accepting students on some of its committees, but confining participation in Senate to inviting the SRC president to attend meetings for discussion of the minutes of the Joint Committee of Senate and the SRC [Senate 4 February 1969, 4 March 1969]. The working of student representation was to be kept under review by a committee of which one-third would be students, the others representing Council, Senate and the heads of colleges, and academic staff [*ibid.* 21 October 1969]. A critical moment occurred in 1971–2, when Senate approved participation by up to two students in Senate, except for reserved areas of business. At the next meeting seven members of Senate attempted to rescind the decision, but their motion was defeated [*ibid.* 30 November 1971, 1 February 1972].

At Durham throughout the 1970s and 1980s the Union, the Joint Committee and the Senate discussed the existence, membership and functioning of staff–student departmental committees, the constitution of faculty boards, the work of the two student representatives on Council and two on Senate, and the various kinds of resistance to effective student participation. Junior Common Rooms began to be represented by their presidents on college governing bodies, though given the nature of the colleges it was often felt that most issues could be resolved by informal means. Representation was most important to students at this level when questions of fees, bars, discipline and the formality and informality of college functions were on the agenda. A Senate Review Committee in 1983 reaffirmed the general principle that

> whilst it is in the nature of a University that the academic staff should
> play the leading role in government, the structure must readily enable

the lay members of Council, the non-academic staff and the student body to make their distinctive contributions.

It pointed out that students were already members of Council and a large number of committees, Senate (except for reserved business) and governing bodies of the colleges and many of their sub-committees. Only some changes in practice, not in membership, were suggested, and the report recommended that a staff–student consultative committee should exist alongside all boards of studies, to which students could be invited as observers. The Joint Committee welcomed these last proposals, in particular that boards of studies be asked to consider 'the greater and more positive use of students as observers' at their meetings [Senate, Holgate report 1983: 3 and *passim*; Joint Committee 23 February 1987]. The Union had submitted a paper to the Review Committee complaining that 'the particular area of neglect in the University is at a Board of Studies level, where the amount of consultation varies enormously. Some boards allow student members, while other departments appear not even to entertain the thought' [Holgate report, document 84: 4]. The attempt to make student participation at this level more effective and consistent appears not to have been wholly successful. When the CVCP's Academic Audit Unit visited the University in 1992, it noted problems relating to its 'highly devolved' nature, and reported that the effectiveness of staff–student committees

> caused the audit team some unease, since there appeared to be wide variation in the seriousness with which they were regarded by departments. In some cases which it examined, the team found that meetings were irregular and more infrequent than the expected once a term; in another case no minutes were kept of meetings, which made it as difficult for the audit team as it would have been for the students, to discover whether any of the issues raised had been followed up. In some examples seen, the agenda focused almost entirely on domestic issues such as the operation of coffee machines; in others it appeared that complaints were merely noted and that there was no record of subsequent staff or board meetings to follow up what, on the face of it, appeared to be substantive items.

Although some departments treated students' views seriously, conditions did not 'ensure that this was invariably the case' [CVCP AAU report 1992: 13–14].

With regard to representation generally the time-scales and broad issues were similar in other institutions to those at Liverpool and Durham. The Students Union at Teesside Polytechnic expressed doubts in 1970 about the position of the president as the only student representative on the Board of Governors, and the first co-option of students to the Academic Board took place in 1974 [Executive 14 April 1970; SSLC 20 February 1974]. For a period from 1974 the Students Union withdrew its 'representation' in favour of attending as observers, in order not to be associated with procedures and decisions of which it disapproved. There were demands for more effective involvement in faculty boards. In 1974 two students attending the Arts and Social Sciences Faculty Board complained that they did not receive the agenda and papers in time to prepare for the meeting, and they did not obtain course outlines relating to new proposals until after the meeting, which was therefore 'largely a failure' [Executive 7 May 1974]. In 1978 the Academic Board established a 'formal standard structure' for faculty, departmental and course boards, each of which was to include elected student representatives [Academic Board 18 January 1978]. In 1980 the President of the Students Union reported on representation in terms which could well have been echoed by experience in other institutions:

> Major Polytechnic Committees on which we have representation include the Academic Board and Board of Governors plus a lot of others. We always attend these and have had some success . . . This, I feel, is still not good enough. We go to these meetings and argue for the issues we are concerned about (e.g. fees) but we never really go beyond this to establish ourselves as a major force in Polytechnic decision-making. For instance, things like course content, resource provision, staffing levels etc. are all things we have a say in but we are faced with the problem . . . that we don't really understand such issues. I know a lot about Social Studies and specific student issues but nothing else. The transitory nature of Students' Union officers is obviously one cause of this . . . but we really do need some formal structures for communicating with students in their departments.
>
> [Executive 4 February 1980]

The calendar of developments, also dictated largely by the student movement of the second half of the 1960s, was similar in the United States, though there are often no precise American equivalents to academic boards and senates, and comparison between American governing bodies and trustees and their British equivalents is not easy. At Penn in 1963 the President created an advisory University Council, taking over much of a committee structure previously controlled by Senate, and in 1968 the Council admitted 30 students (14 of them undergraduates) to its total membership of 100. Representation on an existing University Forum had been a base from which students secured membership of Council and its committees, and they became represented on a variety of committees concerned with campus affairs [21st Century Project, Office of the Provost 1969: 26–8]. Debate about the extent and purposes of student involvement of this kind continued into the 1970s, and one commentary described how student concern had spread 'beyond the football field, dormitory and glee club', to representation on 'scores of committees ranging from Research to Admissions'. Students had become defenders of the 'consultative and advisory styles of the Council system' [*ibid.* Clarke commentary 1970: 107–8]. An attempt in 1979 to secure student and faculty membership of the Trustees on an experimental basis failed, in spite of support by the University President [*ibid.* Task Force 1978: 6, Appendix III, 3–5]. Membership of Council remained important to the representation interest of the students' Undergraduate Assembly, which announced as one of its accomplishments for the year 1994–5 that it had obtained '50% more representation for undergraduates on University Council. This increase in representation on the University's main advisory body is the first increase in two decades' [UA leaflet 1995].

At both Penn and Penn State a central issue was often not that of representation so much as of forms of liaison or communication between the university and the student body. The University Council at Penn was created as advisory to the President, and there were other routes through which student opinion could be heard. At Penn State a joint University Student Advisory Board was created in 1971 in order to consult with the students on an organized basis. Twelve years later it was abolished by the administration to explore new forms of communication – according to the student newspaper, prompted to do so by the President of the Undergraduate Student Government because it was 'ineffective'. A new body was set up to meet with the University President once a month [Archival Colns, Inventory; *Daily Collegian* 9 September 1983: 1]. Representation on the Board of Trustees was secured, and also in 1983 the first woman student trustee was elected [*ibid.* 15 September 1993: 3]. In both universities the student body in the 1970s was attempting to work in the system of university governance, alongside efforts to improve the potency of the students' own organizations.

Given the differences of context and operation in the two countries, differences in student 'training' also appeared. American student affairs organizations frequently provide 'leadership development' programmes, aimed primarily at students taking on positions of responsibility in student government and other student organizations. At Penn State the Office of Student Activities offers consultations ('If you or your organization has a concern or an issue which you are unsure how to handle . . .'), leadership workshops and training ('We provide your organization with workshops on various leadership topics') and other 'special leadership projects for organizations on and off campus' [AT&T Center for Service Leadership, leaflet]. A course on student organization management is offered for students who are 'in a leadership position, or plan to be a leader in a student organization' [Student Affairs, Millar and Funk memo, spring 1995]. Training opportunities for their executive members are provided by some British students' unions, and the NUS has an annual residential event for newly elected sabbatical officers. The most frequent British training activity is for student representatives on course committees or their equivalents.

Course representative training has most commonly been provided by the students' unions themselves, sometimes with other inputs – including the academic registrar's office or, in the 1990s, by or sometimes under the impetus of the Enterprise in Higher Education organization on campus. Training is also often in collaboration with the NUS or using training materials produced by the NUS. At Chester College of Higher Education in the 1990s an extensive programme of training was undertaken jointly by the Student Enterprise Manager and the Students Union. At the University of Plymouth the Student Rights Officer embarked on a similar programme in 1993. One of the most sustained efforts was that of the Union of Students at Sheffield Hallam University, inviting the 400-plus course representatives to weekend and day training events, based around NUS and the Union's own materials, and also supporting course representatives with a flow of information. At the University of Durham an Enterprise/Union day seminar for academic course representatives in 1993 provided an opportunity, as did similar events elsewhere, to consider the reasons for and the nature of their involvement as representatives, to think about how to carry out their functions, and to share other new and experienced representatives' concerns about their aims, procedures and necessary skills.

Here, as at many other institutions, there were anxieties, within the Students Union and more generally, about the effectiveness of the course representative system – which could be attributed to the inexperience of the students, or to the failure of academic staff to take students and their views seriously. One course committee chairperson told us he had resigned because his staff colleagues 'closed ranks' against student criticism. Some students complained of implied or threatened victimization, others simply felt intimidated by the staff (which often meant the chair) and the procedures. In the 1980s the CNAA reported comments by visiting panels about the lack of serious consultation with students by departments and course leaders. In 1994 the Higher Education Quality Council, analysing the 69 reports on visits to institutions by its audit teams and those of its predecessor, the CVCP's Academic Audit Unit, reported such problems as the lack of a formal constitution, agendas and discussion documents not circulated in advance, meetings dominated by staff, and student disillusionment at recurring, unresolved problems. Audit teams had 'suggested to many universities that they needed to operate their staff/student liaison committees in a more professional way' (HEQC 1994b: 30–1). A study of student feedback and course representation in 1992 discovered that there were increasing difficulties in persuading students to act as course representatives, and as programmes became modular the concept of a 'course' had itself become elusive and other forms of dialogue with students were being sought. Although representatives tried to canvas student opinion as a preliminary to a course meeting, this was neither easy nor always the case (Silver 1992: 18–20). At one feedback session at the University of Central Lancashire 'many course reps commented on the lack of definition of their role and also that many students do not know who their course reps are or what they do' [Enterprise *News for Course Reps* [1994]]. Universities and colleges and their students' unions have in many instances attempted to remedy this situation by including explanations of the purposes and workings of the course representative system in their annual student handbooks, or in special publications.

Despite the difficulties, the principle of student representation at all levels of British academic administration and course or departmental processes began to be established from the end of the 1960s and became more systematic in subsequent decades. Student representation as such was not uniformly welcomed. At the end of the 1960s only Queen's University, Belfast, and Birkbeck College, London, had students on their Councils (NUS 1966), and though many were planning to accept the principle of representation, there were some, like those members of the Senate at Durham, who strongly resisted the idea. Students themselves, of course, had diverse objectives. Crouch looked at the categories of student demand and the possibilities in terms of consultation, representation and mass involvement or control, and dismissed the first and third (Crouch 1968). The Vice-Chancellor of the University of Essex thought that there had been progress, more student representation was needed, and it should be 'substantial' – a view with which the President of the NUS agreed: universities were (he recklessly suggested) the 'last great unreformed institutions of our time', and much of the change to date had been a 'façade' (Sloman 1970: 42–4; Straw 1970: 7, 27). The Secretary and President-Elect of NUS in 1968 quoted Bagshot to accuse the universities of 'consecrated obstruction' (Fisk 1968: 397).

Some universities in the late 1960s and early 1970s responded to events by producing their own working party reports. One that students particularly noted was that produced by the Grimond review body for the Council of the University of Birmingham which took serious account of the views of the Guild of Students and set out possible norms for student representation (University of Birmingham 1972). A substantial report of a working party containing equal numbers of students and staff at the University of York considered the role of students in the government of the University, noting that the response of York students to an appeal for evidence had been 'meagre in quantity, if valuable in quality. Conspicuously absent was even one submission from the hitherto most vocal and extreme critics of university decision-making: their views were therefore solicited by other (non-literary) means and taken fully into account'. Instead of proposing student membership of Council it recommended the formation of a committee, to include students, and drawing other members from Council, the Professorial Board and the General Academic Board [York 1968, in Select Committee vol. 7 1969: 142–79]. The most comprehensive study of developments in 'student relations' was that conducted by the House of Commons Select Committee on Education and Science, the report and appendices of which included considerable detail on existing representation, plans, reasons adduced for and against, and instances where none existed, or there were demands for more (House of Commons 1969b; 1969c).

Local and national developments and problems continued to be reported in the 1970s (see, for example, Jacks 1973; McLintock 1974). An example of what Fisk might have called 'consecrated obstruction' was that offered by a group of staff at the University of Hull who had recently surveyed student representation on university senates. The figures gave them 'much cause for concern . . . too many universities are giving too much student representation on Senate'. They suggested that changes in university organization could only be justified in order to provide the best possible education, and changes 'must be judged by this criterion. This position should be made abundantly clear immediately. Unless this is done, we believe that Senates will soon be composed of campus politicians rather than academics' (Bell *et al.* 1972: 45). Another such example would be that of Max Beloff who, when interviewed in 1973–4, was Professor of Government and Public Administration at the University of Oxford. He thought that a model of democracy was 'totally inappropriate to the university. The university is a community which is necessarily hierarchical . . . The university conceived as a model of democracy is outright rubbish'. He added that '[f]irst-rate students, unless psychologically disturbed, are never involved in student politics' (Beloff 1977: 155, 160).

It is clear from the institutional and more general literature of the 1970s that it took a long time for opposition to student representation to fade, or at least to become less public and vociferous. Important to the integration of the student voice in institutional procedures was the role of the CNAA, which consistently looked for evidence of student evaluation and feedback, and there were many CNAA institutions which took very seriously the opportunity to include students in course validation and review (Trent Polytechnic 1988; Barnett 1990a; Powney and Coyle 1990; Powney 1994). It is common currency among staff who experienced the role of the CNAA in relation to the colleges and polytechnics, that it was responsible for developing a student representative culture.

The trajectory of American development and debate is similar. Prior to the Second World War the student voice was rarely heard in any systematic way. By the end of the 1960s student representation was frequently being recognized as an inevitability, a right or simply good practice (Frankel 1968: 51–9). From the heat of the battle at Columbia University, Wallerstein, one of the most insightful of the academics commenting on the 1960s events and their implications, looked at arguments around representation as resting on conceptions of maturity and the measurement of its threshold, the nature of democratization in the modern world, and the implications of these and other perceptions of the position of students in the university. For the students the university was 'a public-service institution whose clients they are and from whom they are demanding a basic revision in the client–professional relationship'. Setting aside the particular issue of first year undergraduates, many under 18 and all in a period of transition, Wallerstein saw 'the child–adult' model needing to be abandoned in favour of a version of the 'client–professional relationship', in which the student is not a 'mere' client, but an apprentice in the professional community. Hence his conclusion that students 'have knowledge of and a direct interest in the conditions of their work and are therefore entitled to a say in establishing the social organization of the instructional process'. Hence also the need to find appropriate forms of participation, including representation on 'the organs of decision'. The governance of the university had 'thus become for the first time in a long time a major item on the agenda of society' (Wallerstein 1969: 72–104). This analysis and its emphasis on students as adults with roles in the workplace represents one thread of argument that runs through attempts to resolve the issue of student representation throughout the 1970s and 1980s.

For many in the 1970s adequate student representation was an important goal, but for many academics it was either inadvisable, or of little or ambivalent concern (Otten 1970; AAUP 1970). Students' representation on governing boards and trustees was patchy, and their presence often more symbolic than effective (Carnegie 1974; Hawes and Trux 1974). In 1980 an inter-collegiate conference of Ivy League students' associations was demanding representative university government and the appointment of student trustees (Gross and Shlomchik 1980: 63), and a study of undergraduates in 1987 found student involvement in campus governance 'almost nonexistent' (Boyer 1987: 244). In neither the United States nor the United Kingdom was the inheritance of involvement in campus government, what Wallerstein calls 'the social organization of the instruction process', as comprehensive and as effective as sometimes expected. Nor, in the changed climate of the 1980s and 1990s, was it necessarily as important to the student body being represented as it had been. In the United Kingdom representation in some cases declined as the size of controlling bodies was reduced, or the number of committees was drastically reduced for efficiency reasons. The tradition and strength of student representation remained widely secure, however. At Swansea in 1995, for example, students were represented on all major University committees, including five members on Council and eight on Senate. When the polytechnics were 'incorporated' as institutions released from control by the local authorities, and given degree-awarding powers with the demise of the CNAA, the position of students on governing bodies and academic boards sometimes became less secure. A temporarily successful attempt at Huddersfield in 1993 to remove elected academic staff and students from the Governing Body revived discussion about representation and accountability.

The story of student representation in British higher education can be told in part as a shift in emphasis from governing bodies and councils, senates and academic boards, to the role of students in monitoring and influencing institutional processes at the point at which they are most directly affected – the course committee, the board of studies, the department committee, the module feedback. For increasing numbers of students, however, a discussion of their 'experience' has to begin elsewhere.

6

The Experience

The Society for Research into Higher Education held a conference in 1978 on the previous 'decade of change', and called for papers in the expectation that the issues involved would have 'been the subject of great attention by those who survey, study, and speculate on such phenomena'. Few papers of this kind were received, and the editor of the conference papers explained that most of the papers, 'with certain honourable exceptions . . . speculate (data free research), review trends or call for research rather than record work actually carried out' (Armstrong 1979: 1). Not a great deal has changed. It is impossible to encompass the immense variety that has constituted the student experience over recent decades. Our sample simply points to feasible ways of sketching the changing landscape of students' activity, culture and attitudes. What is most easily approached is what is most commonly and most publicly shared – athletics, the bar, the disco, fashion, and so on. However, all of these and others immediately disaggregate. Experience differs by race, gender, social class, disability, and the infinite combination of personal characteristics – gregariousness or loneliness, religious belief or personal morality, conformism or eagerness to experiment. In addition, there are the diverse variables of place of residence, course, prior relationships or established tastes. We can only hint at some expressions of these complexities.

Over past decades there have been, in the United Kingdom, only occasional snapshots of student activity categorized in a limited number of ways – how they spend their time in terms of academic work, use of library, association with other students, entertainment, political activity or church attendance. American institutions and student organizations have more frequently surveyed their members, with very similar targets in mind – or, as we have seen, patterns of student behaviour of particular interest to student life personnel. The much publicized American literature of the 1980s and 1990s, portraying the 'decline' in student behaviour and commitment, has been 'data-free', personal reflections on current dilemmas. The material and sample on which our discussion is based is also a limited, but different, attempt to enter the changes in students' experience of the campus – through the often distorting lens of student records, or through the long memories of some on campus who have been closely involved with students outside the classroom. Let us take some examples of the latter.

Michael Belton, Administration and Building Services Manager of the Guild of Students, has been at the University of Liverpool for over 25 years. He describes the biggest change as student 'insecurity', a change from the early days when students had an air of confidence, even arrogance. In his first ten years at the University students were 'difficult to handle', thought they were 'top people', for whom a degree meant a good job. Now students are 'quieter', 'better persons'. Twenty-five years ago being at university in some way meant 'making a contribution'; nowadays students are more likely to be thinking about it as valuable for improving job prospects. They used to have pride in the Students Union; they do not have the same pride now. A quarter of the students have cars, a third receive a grant, and there is real difficulty for working-class students. Students are less elitist now. Since *in loco parentis* 'the kids have changed', are more willing to experiment. At age 16–18 they have had wider experience than students used to have.

Michael Gillett came in 1968 to what was then becoming Plymouth Polytechnic, later Polytechnic South-West when it merged with other institutions in the region, and then the University of Plymouth. He was a member of the mathematics department, becoming Head of Department in 1971, and eventually Deputy Vice-Chancellor (Resources). Some long-standing members of the Students Union commented on his supportive role, including when the Union went through a disastrous financial period in the 1980s. When he first came to the institution there were no student-led activities, the Principal's wife ran a Christmas party, and the institution was beginning to become more diverse, moving to CNAA degrees, establishing course committees, and attracting a more national constituency of students. There were few part-timers, and full-time numbers were growing slowly, but the students were very committed. The Students Union began to grow in the early 1970s: 'I was not conscious of it until the mid-70s'. It was always a very moderate Students Union, even in the 1980s. One 'uprising' had to do with a National Front student. There has been a greater level of participation in some respects than in the previous decade. Some societies are thriving – for example, exploring, offshore sailing, surfboarding – and the University has produced some international champions. Students have developed a growing commitment to their studies in recent years, and more serious learning goes together with a need for recreation. There has been a growing recognition that the Students Union provides additional experience. It has been a culture shock for students coming from school and classes of 20, to find themselves in groups of 50, 100 or even 250. They have felt the impact of 'course delivery changes, project-led, field work, seminars, practicals', and they are more prepared to express their views. 'We do not get politically highly motivated students, and political students are not a dominant force on the Executive.' There is poor attendance at meetings.

Henry Porter, writing in the *Guardian* in 1994, reflected on a return to the University of Manchester, where he had been a student 20 years before.

Superficially ('the same litter of handouts' outside the Union, another banner for a demonstration) things seemed not to have altered much, 'but look a little closer, spend just 10 minutes talking to any student or lecturer and you find that an enormous change has been wrought'. The main difference was encapsulated in the term 'pressure':

I don't remember us having any pressure whatsoever. While we bene-fited from pretty generous grants which were often, as in my case, topped up by parents, today's students are frequently forced to take part-time jobs and are compelled to borrow to cope with the diminish-ing grant. They get much less for their money. Tutorial classes, for instance, have doubled and sometimes tripled in size.

Lecturers now know their students less well. A discussion with eight stu-dents, most in their final year, showed that

there just isn't time on either side. About half of them said that they worked to make ends meet. One woman waited in a restaurant while another served behind a bar for 10 to 12 hours a week in order to earn about £36, which made the crucial difference in her life.

The issues of today, Porter discovered, 'are not about the miners or the removal of free school milk by a prime minister in the making, but the Criminal Justice Bill and, way ahead of everything else, student poverty'. A chance encounter for Porter as a student had meant he learned beekeep-ing, which he could never have done if he had had to work in a pub:

so much of the benefit of my three years came from the relatively relaxed conditions of the seventies, the time we had to ourselves, the attention that we got from tutors when we needed it, and even the weird encounters which all this relatively relaxed life enabled.

What he also found in 1994 was more crime, the increased availability and use of drugs, students needing more academic 'spoon-feeding'. The universit-ies were experiencing the effects of the enormous expansion of the 1980s, and of Margaret Thatcher: 'the Milk Snatcher's stern conviction that people should work harder and enjoy themselves less', in which she seemed to have been successful (Porter 1994: 2–3).

More laconic, but still revealing, were comments reported from the Uni-versity of Sussex. A still politically active alumnus of the University from the early 1970s took time off to visit it from a Labour Party conference in Brighton in 1995. In the 1970s he remembered the campus's public spaces being 'like one giant wall newspaper', advertising meetings and political activities. Now there was 'no evidence of political activity anywhere – posters for Christian Union, Industrial Society, sports clubs, but nothing political' – though he reflected that 'at least the students still look the same' (*THES* 20 October 1995: 4).

At the University of Pennsylvania a retrospective article published in 1973 indicated that the University was recovering from several decades of decline,

but now the undergraduates were 'bright, interesting, aggressive, and exciting to teach'. About a third were Jewish, 28 per cent Catholic, and the remainder were Protestant or of unknown religion. Students were finding a
location like Philadelphia, 'where the action is', attractive:

> Action of course refers to problems of inner cities: racism, poverty,
> education, and housing. Gone are the days when Penn students were
> more concerned about Saturday night dates, beer blasts, and which
> fraternity to pledge, when they involved themselves in Rowbottoms,
> a Pennsylvania way of blasting off steam (sometimes developing into
> pantie raids), or Skimmer, the annual crew race on the Schuylkill
> which became an excuse for excessive drinking and such high jinks
> as overturning trolleys, setting cars on fire, and dunking people into
> the river. Rowbottoms have nearly disappeared, and one celebrates
> Skimmer these days by attending a rock concert. Even fraternities have
> almost disappeared.
>
> (Goddard and Koons 1973: 227, 232)

Neither fraternities nor excessive drinking did disappear. One of the authors of this description, Linda Koons, was in 1995 Executive Assistant to
the Provost of the University, and reflected that in the late 1960s students
knew little about urban conditions and many of them were meeting black
people for the first time. In 1967 'men were still wearing suit jackets and
ties. By the following year they were wearing blue jeans and in bare feet.'
An interest in environmental conditions developed and students began to
want to do something for the surrounding community. 'More forums for
interaction now exist, issues get aired, students are more actively involved
in their departments, but problems of interaction with faculty remain.' The
undergraduate student body has become more diverse – 19 per cent are
Asian American and 30 per cent are minorities. Fraternities, which were
dying a couple of decades ago, have become 'stronger, more tolerant and
more involved in social issues'. Students on the whole are more conservative, anxious about jobs and making their way. They are both more indi-
vidualistic and wanting to do good. They take different tracks through the
institution and there are some tensions, for example between the Asian and
black students.

At Penn State University, Lee Upcraft, recently retired Assistant Vice-
President for Counseling Services and Program Assessment, had been at
the University since 1969. He had been Assistant Dean of Students, responsible for residence halls, for 12 years, and Assistant Vice-President for Counseling and Health Services. When he came to the University there was not
a lot of student involvement by comparison with other places. *In loco parentis*
was disappearing from 1967, and from 1970 men and women could see
each other privately – which meant there were some security problems, 'you
didn't know who was in the building'. Resident assistants were appointed –
paid students to sit at the desk, they lived with the students, were typically
junior and senior students who went through rigorous selection. Now there's

an increased tendency to solve disputes by violence, there is more of it, students are more volatile. Resident assistants have become more frequently involved in violence.

How are students the same? They still have the same 'combination of excitement and fear, know how to work, how to get on with a roommate, friends . . . they have the same feeling of belonging to a class, who they are, trying to establish their career definitions. There are the same student services, but there is an increased diversity of students – women, race, age.' How are they different? 'There's the diversity, how students view the purpose of education, careers, jobs.' Twenty years ago a percentage of them would say they were here to learn, were unsure. 'Students are less politically active, but they have a social conscience, do volunteer work.' Contact between students and faculty is rare in the students' first and second years. They have no 'adult influence' – there is more in small institutions. But students do not complain about the lack of contact and the large classes: 'Most students belong to something – they are under strong pressure to do so.' Since 1981 there's been a good job done for the disabled, with transportation and accommodation – 'there's still a lot to be desired but it's OK'. There has been 'a diminution in hard drugs and marijuana, but more alcohol. Seventy per cent of student crime, including assault, is alcohol-related'.

Also at Penn State, an article in the student *Daily Collegian* in 1983, under the title 'Fadtastic', attempted a comparison with previous decades:

> In the 1950s, college students across the nation amused themselves in a variety of ways: cruising, hoola hooping and stuffing themselves into phone booths. Beads, long hair and peace demonstrations were a big part of the 1960s. The 1970s brought us clackers, leisure suits and Watergate. Now the 1980s. It seems for the eighties, individuality is the key . . . Penn State students display a smorgasbord of varying tastes in fashion, fitness, music and fun.
>
> (Curry and Waldron 1983: 5)

Students on the whole are not as clearly aware of the changes over this period as are the academic and administrative staff who teach, work with and observe them. They have folk memories of what life used to be like, including student politics, dress codes, music and life-style. Specific categories of students are also aware of the pre-history of their present lives on campus. Women students, for example, are often individually and organizationally conscious, as we have seen, of the 'masculinity' that has survived the changes in the composition and culture of the student body. At the University of East Anglia women students in the late 1980s were creating their own organizations, to change the mores and rules which, in the words of one contributor to the Union *Handbook*, men 'made for themselves'. It was for women to change them, 'and by organising autonomously we give ourselves a platform from which to speak which is less intimidatory to stand on than being the lone voice in the wilderness whose struggle is useless'.

Events for women about women were unlikely to happen 'if it were left to the male dominated structures which run the Students' Union' [*Handbook* 1986/87: 19]. Here, as elsewhere, the feminist or assertive presence of women on the campus grew stronger, particularly in the 1980s. The story of women's experience of the campus in both Britain and the United States from the 1960s is one of a transition from an often all-female environment or one in which they had relatively clear-cut female roles. In the 1960s institutions and students' unions were, as we have seen, sometimes engaged in debate about whether female students should be allowed to wear slacks in lectures or in the refectory. At Durham, a joint meeting of the University Council and the Students' Representative Council in 1966 considered the question. The Vice-Chancellor reported that Senate was about to discuss the wearing of slacks at lectures: 'College meals would be a different matter' [SRC 6 December 1966].

Much of the American 'coed' tradition of previous decades continued into the 1950s and to a lesser extent the 1960s. At Penn in the 1950s men were 'men' and women were 'girls', women were pageant queens, were allowed to eat in a 'previously men-only enclave', and a campus restaurant trying to tempt more men to eat there advertised that 'Penn's prettiest coeds come to Mom's restaurant' (Silverman 1990: 49–50). A chronology of the history of women at Penn State, beginning in 1871, includes such items as:

Men and women share the same dining hall for the first time – 1957
Women are given keys to the residence halls so they may come and go as they please. Curfew is eliminated – 1969
In [an issue of *The Collegian*] an editorial headline proclaimed: Worst Thing About Apartment Life – Finding an Ugly Girl Living Next Door – 1971
Three women are escorted from the men's sauna in Rec Hall. There are no comparable facilities for women – 1973
The need for a Center for Women Students is identified and proposed for Penn State University – 1975
First woman is elected Undergraduate Student Government president – 1982
A study . . . dealing with the sexual harassment of students finds that nearly one of every four women students interviewed had experienced some form of sexual harassment during their time at Penn State – 1983
The Center for Women Students is opened – 1985
[GVF Women – general 21 June 1988]

The Center for Women Students was a division of Student Services, staffed by full-time professionals. In 1988 the Undergraduate Student Government also had a Department of Women's Concerns, run by students. The objectives of the former included advocacy, information, educational programmes and services. The focus of the latter was on sexual harassment, rape survival, job discrimination and affirmative action [*Daily Collegian* 26 August 1988: 6].

The issue of sexual harassment reported here in 1983 had become an issue of general concern by the 1980s. Students' union executives, student publications, student and institutional welfare committees, women's organizations and centres, addressed the issue consistently in the 1980s and 1990s. Harassment by staff and other students was reported, as were assaults on and off campus. In 1985 Plymouth Polytechnic Students Union considered the issue of women's fear of sexual assault and decided to provide a transport service to and from the Union building for women between 5 p.m. and midnight, and later on late bar nights [AGM 17 October 1985]. In Britain and the United States the provision of such minibus services for women was an important issue in the 1980s. In 1986 the Plymouth Students Union decided, in protest against sexism and offensive attitudes towards women, to elect a non-sabbatical women's officer to the Executive [*ibid.* 22 May 1986], and the election of a union officer specifically concerned with women's issues was a widespread feature of students' unions. The issue of security, of course, affects all students to some extent. Minibuses were often provided for men as well as women. An issue of the Liverpool Guild *Gazette* in 1994, reporting breaches of hall security, intruders and muggings, was headlined 'Are we safe?' [*Gazette* 20 October 1994: 1].

'Date rape' became a concern initially in the United States and then on British campuses, and this and similar occurrences reached institutions' disciplinary procedures and the courts. Across the USA in the 1990s the definition of acceptable codes of sexual relations, notably but not only between academic staff and their students, became an issue of major controversy, and codes of behaviour became more frequent on British campuses. This was true at Penn, as at many other American universities and colleges (the code at Antioch College, for example, attracted national interest). The campus experience of women students at Penn was the subject of a University committee report on 'consensual sexual relations', seeking to define the conditions in which these were permissible, and when they were not acceptable between teacher and student – given that academic judgement might be distorted [*Almanac* 7 February 1995: 2–3]. The proposed policy was to stand alongside the existing University policy on sexual harassment, which, often bracketed with other aspects of discrimination, was increasingly in the 1980s and 1990s also outlawed explicitly in the policies of British universities and colleges. Wolverhampton University policy on harassment defines it as:

> including sexist comments, unwelcome sexual advances, unnecessary touching, demands for sexual favours and sexual assault. The University believes harassment maintains existing inequalities of power and opportunity and results in:
> – making a job or study difficult to do.
> – creating an intimidating or hostile working or learning environment.

– affecting the health or safety of the individual, by causing stress.
– endangering career and job prospects.

[*Fix* 2 1994: 10]

With a similar definition, Cheltenham and Gloucester College of Higher Education adopted a policy which declared any form of sexual harassment to be 'totally unacceptable in any area or aspect of College life, whether directed at a student or member of staff', and set out detailed procedures for complaint and action [*Students Handbook 1992–1993*: 47–8]. With significant percentages of women students experiencing what was increasingly perceived as unacceptable harassment, such policies and procedures had by the 1990s become important features of the framework of campus life.

In the United States the 1960s student movement coincided with or related to the wider movement for civil rights, and tensions on campuses in many instances related to a raft of demands by black students, and to traditional racial divides, hostilities and discrimination. Campuses nation-wide were hearing and acting on the same kind of messages heard at the University of Pennsylvania. The Community Involvement Council at Penn, created by students in 1965, considered in 1968 that 'perhaps the most compelling social problem in America today is that of white racism', and a visiting speaker in 1969, the Rev. James Woodruff of the Black Liberation Movement, condemned American institutions as 'programed toward white folk' [*Daily Pennsylvanian* 1 August 1968: 5; UPF 8.5 54/1, DP 28 January 1969]. From the mid-1960s the campus experience of black Americans involved various and fluctuating measures of action to confront what was seen as institutional racism, to press for the recruitment of more black students, to provide black studies, to secure the appointment and tenure of black teachers, and to defend black students against discrimination. At Penn State confrontation in the late 1960s was primarily related to black students' demands along these lines. Other ethnic groups on campuses from the 1970s developed their own organizations and pursued their own aims. Many campuses began to witness the proliferation of student organizations or intensified cultural boundaries on the basis of ethnic or national origins. Although the general political atmosphere of campuses changed after the early 1970s, tensions resulting from real or perceived racism or other features of racial and ethnic relations recurred. At Penn in 1993, for example, racial tension was described by the Undergraduate Assembly as having 'reached an extreme level', and the University itself commented in 1995 on 'the widespread publicity of racial tensions on campus that resulted in several unfortunate incidents two years ago' [UA news release April 1993; *Almanac* 28 March 1995: 4]. In traditionally black institutions of higher education, and on other campuses where African American and ethnic groups, notably Hispanics, formed substantial minorities (and in some cases majorities), the issue of completion rates became prominent in the 1980s and 1990s: 'African Americans and Hispanics are more likely to enter college on the nontraditional path . . . African Americans and low-income students are the most "at-risk" in terms of dropping out of college' (Ottinger 1991: 1).

Overt and covert racism also became an issue on British campuses, and students' unions took up the cause of anti-racism in the 1980s especially. In some cases racism as such was the source of union action and support, as at Strathclyde where the welfare handbook invites students to come to the welfare service 'if you are suffering racist abuse'. In others anti-racism is seen as part of a general approach to discrimination, as at Liverpool, where the Guild has a constitutional policy aimed at 'combating and outlawing discrimination and harassment, whether it be directed against staff or students. Discrimination comes in a variety of forms, direct and indirect, personal and institutional' [*Handbook* 1994: 33]. Some students' unions have a non-sabbatical officer responsible for race issues, alongside other officers responsible for women's and other campaign areas. East Anglia, for example, has a race awareness officer, and since 1993 a Race Awareness Society has evolved [*Handbook* 1995/96: 23].

The experience of black and minority students on British campuses is, as in the United States, within a framework of race relations which goes beyond the bounds of the institution, but which is sensitive to student–student and student–staff interactions. Pressure for black studies or black tutorial staff has resulted on occasion from the concentration of black students in particular curriculum areas. Their demands and problems have often overlapped those of mature or part-time students, particularly in the larger urban polytechnics and universities, as well as in terms of grants, loans and student hardship. In 1994, nearly 42 per cent of black applicants to universities and colleges were over 25, compared with 13 per cent of white and 8 per cent of Asian applicants. In 1986 the Commission for Racial Equality found that most institutions had introduced or were introducing equal opportunities policies, but also found 'a tone of moral superiority or complacency plus ignorance of the issues'. Eight years later teachers' unions and others were providing evidence of persistent racial discrimination and abuse faced by black and ethnic minority students and staff (Younge 1995: 19).

About the experience of part-time students the available evidence is meagre, apart from research data on who they are, and their academic performance – mainly in the CNAA institutions and the Open University. The majority of part-time students are by definition mature students, non-resident, following a longer or different pattern of attendance, requiring a different pattern of support and services, and their roles on campus have necessarily been problematical. Something similar applies to students, full- and part-time, taking part in franchised courses in further education, a phenomenon that mushroomed particularly in the former polytechnics in the 1990s. Research on franchised and other partnership courses between higher and further education shows that they are aimed at students who tend to be local, mature, need to study part-time, have been under-achievers, have caring responsibilities and financial difficulties (Opacic 1996). Between 1991–92 and 1992–93 the number of franchised students increased from some 10,000 to almost 35,000. At Coventry University, for example, the numbers on such courses rose from about 200 in 1989–90 to 1,140 in 1991–2 and 2,349 in 1993–94 (*ibid.*) [*Strategic Plan 1994/95–1998/99*: 4]. In further education, with traditionally fewer students' unions and other amenities than in higher education, but on the first stage of a higher education programme, franchised students have – where geographically feasible – looked to the university students' union for a social environment, and these have attempted to provide support. Memoranda of co-operation between the two institutions have often, however, failed to take account of these implications, and many students' unions in higher education are unable to service franchised students because the union has not received additional funding for them in its block grant (Opacic 1996).

A discussion of part-time students which omits Open University students omits a student body which has grown from its first intake of 24,000 undergraduates, when the University became operational in 1971, to a total of some 130,000 undergraduate and postgraduate students in 1994. Our focus, however, is essentially on the relationship of students to changing campus and other conditions, outside formal teaching and learning. Although the students' lives relate to their academic experience, Open University students' experience of the University is through summer schools, the tutorial relationship, and student support networks. It is a special relationship, one which applies also to the growing number of other students on distance learning programmes.

The greatest difficulties, and sometimes the most severe limitations, in responding to campus opportunities are generally those relating to particular kinds of disability. We have seen how campuses respond to the potential and actual needs of students with disabilities. Broadly speaking, universities and colleges have recognized the possibilities and restrictions of their campuses, and students with, for example, motor, sight and hearing problems have increasingly found it possible to gain admission, register their problems and needs, and take advantage of residential, academic and social opportunities. Students' unions have recognized their own roles in supporting these students, and in responding to the defensive attitudes often adopted by institutions, by academic staff, and by other students. The Guild of Students at the University of Liverpool, for example, was at various points in the 1970s pressing for an improvement in facilities and passing resolutions on discrimination against the disabled. It published an article in 1987 which began:

No access to buildings, no access to education, no access to people. How are the disabled treated at Liverpool University. Surely the very lack of disabled students here says something in itself – there are in fact less than 20 at this university. By law, 3% of the staff SHOULD consist of people with disabilities. If this quota was extended to students then there should be well over 200 students with disabilities here AT LEAST. Why aren't there more?

Access issues concerned the Union building as much as the rest of the campus, and the Guild had been negligent in this respect. The article quoted a 1985 NUS conference resolution: 'our existing education system discriminates against people with disabilities of all types . . . students with disabilities and the issue of disability are the concern of ALL students' [*Guild and City Gazette* 11 May 1987: 8–9].

At Teesside in the 1970s and 1980s the Students Union was taking part in the Polytechnic's working parties, pointing out what was inadequate, pressing for action, setting up its own Disabled Students' Committee, and appointing its own disabled students officer. In 1975 a report to the Students Union executive quoted as 'no rash statement' a comment that 'not one thought has been given to disabled students in the planning and construction of these buildings', and drew attention to 13 major deficiencies in the physical lay-out of the campus and the buildings. A decade later the Union Council noted that 'there is only a minimum amount of assistance for disabled students at this Polytechnic', and that work on behalf of disabled students 'more often than not takes place without prior consultation with the students concerned and therefore does not necessarily meet their needs or priorities' [Council 9 October 1986]. The Disabled Student Officer was to ensure that disabled students' views were raised in the Union and the Polytechnic, to raise awareness of the issues and to initiate campaigns, to ensure that disabled students were not discriminated against and could take part fully in entertainment, sport and all Union facilities, and to monitor and develop appropriate policies in the Union and the Polytechnic [General Meeting, Constitution Revision 22 April 1989]. At the University of Glasgow the Students' Representative Council was explaining in 1995 that for various reasons access to some University buildings was restricted, though improvements had resulted from a student protest in 1990. The SRC and its Disabled Students' Interests Committee were campaigning for speedier improvements, in consultation with disabled students [*Welfare Handbook 1995*: 18]. Most institutions were making provision to advise students with disabilities not only about the resources of the campus but also about the availability of allowances, benefits and financial advice, in general and in relation to specific disabilities. In American institutions of higher education, as we have seen, under external and internal pressures from the 1970s in particular, access and amenities increased rapidly, and the voice of students with disabilities on campuses was heard with increasing strength. In many British institutions by the 1990s the context in which the experience of students with disabilities was defined included commitments to access and support. Disability had become a major part of the canon of equal opportunities.

These are some of the defining contexts of some groups of students entering higher education in recent decades. Students' early experience of higher education is governed by who they are, the structural and cultural patterns they enter, what strengths and problems they bring with them into the new environment – what we have described as the interaction of personal and institutional histories. Research reported at Plymouth

Polytechnic in 1975 had highlighted the greater difficulties faced by younger first year students, by those on courses with a lesser vocational bias, and by female students. Younger students particularly had entered higher education under greater pressure from teachers and parents than older students who had chosen to do so on their own initiative and were better motivated [*Spectrum* April 1975: 3]. A decade later, at a conference on 'The First Year Experience', researchers from Newcastle Polytechnic reported that students who

> only a few months previously were schoolchildren are expected, on entering higher education, to have developed and transformed miraculously into mature adults over the summer holidays. In all the interviews, comments such as: 'My school in no way prepared me for a University life', and 'I felt I needed to be older and more experienced to cope with the place', abound.
>
> [Downey and Woodley, reported in Liverpool *Guild and City Gazette* 7 October 1986: 2]

Questions of disorientation, difficulty of adjustment and loneliness have been a feature of the first year experience of some school leavers in a period when the increasing size of institutions has placed responsibility for addressing such problems on Student Services, and traditional pastoral roles of tutor and departments have been weakened or abandoned.

Students make the transition to higher education in a variety of contexts – academic, residential, students' union and others. The nature of the transition has changed, however, since the days when institutions were smaller, when supervisory and tutorial relationships were closer and on a smaller scale, and when the student body was more homogeneous. Outside the collegiate universities contact between students and tutors has become rarer or more perfunctory – even more so in American universities, where staff–student ratios have historically been very much greater. Numbers, modular curricula, multi-site institutions, and the increased pressures on both staff and students have led to the disappearance of some of the formal and informal points of contact. Examination pressures, which have changed as a combination of modules and a division into semesters has spread the load across the academic year, have also affected attitudes towards student life and responsibilities. In these situations students have a balance of activity to strike which may be very different from that of earlier generations of students. The balance struck is repeatedly described as working hard and playing hard – 'playing' often being associated with drinking. Students in general, and particularly mature students and those from families with no previous experience of higher education, are also described typically as studying harder than students in the past: 'they spend more time studying, more than I did at Birmingham' (Rhodes int.). They are in rapidly increasing numbers taking part-time jobs and the balance of academic work (and part-time jobs) and play for most students leaves little or no time or incentive for taking on the responsibilities of office or representation. Although the transition is different for mature students it may also involve a similar degree of stress, readjusting to study, reorganizing domestic commitments, awareness of younger students' different attitudes and priorities, reorientating from other kinds of lives. One former mature student in London, observing her successors, commented:

> Seventy-five per cent of the students here are mature, getting their second bite at an education, not from families with a tradition of going to the university, and also from various ethnic and cultural backgrounds. They live locally, have children, want to get involved but their main motivation is to get by – they've got to work hard. They haven't time to volunteer. Mature students take it more seriously, they are continually studying, don't take time off. You can't fit social life in with paid jobs and kids. It's tougher now than when I was a student here.
>
> (R. Watson int.)

The impact on students' union activities and facilities may be substantial. At Liverpool '[t]he Guild wants to attract more students to the precinct. This is made difficult by the increase in the number of mature students' (Lewis int.).

Over recent years students have, however, continued to find reason and time to belong. It is not possible to determine precisely in any one institution what proportion of students belong to or take part in the clubs and societies organized under the auspices of the students' union. Students' union presidents, administrators and others in Britain and the United States generally agreed, however, with the comment made to us at Penn State and reported above, that 'most students belong to something . . . they are under strong pressure to do so' (Upcraft int.), 'At least half the students belong to the societies, there's not much interest in politics, they're involved with their own society, don't care about the overall picture' (Weinstein int.). The Teesside estimate that 70–80 per cent of students take some part in Union 'activities' (Ebdon int.) was matched by an American survey in the 1970s which reported over 80 per cent of graduates as having participated in at least one of seven listed areas of college activity (Kapp 1979: xii). The numbers taking part in British unions are ambiguous, however. Is an evening in the bar 'taking part'? Does attendance at a sporting event count the same as being a member of the club? Even the numbers entering the students' union premises raise problems, and at institutions visited for this project estimates of the numbers using the union facilities could be estimated differently by different officers. Over recent decades, differently in institutions with different kinds of student intake and institutional culture, the popularity of particular sports and non-sports clubs and societies has waxed and waned, with expansion halting in the 1990s in the British case.

At the London School of Economics in 1933–4,

> during twenty-six weeks of the session fifty different clubs and societies have held between them nearly a thousand meetings a week, or seven

meetings on each of the five weekdays on which the School is in action. The fifty clubs and societies include twenty for different forms of athletics from Rugby football to folk-dancing; nineteen centring on some special interest from banking to music or religion, from India to the drama or the assistance of German refugees; seven (including University as well as School societies) of a political character; and four which appear to be purely social for particular groups of students.

The Director described this as 'prodigious' (Beveridge 1960: 38–9). In 1954 the Students' Association at Northampton College of Technology (later part of Nene College) had a handful of clubs – a dramatic society, a table tennis club, a discussion group ('free and frank and subjects are completely open'), a music club, a rhythm club, a science society and a touring club, plus a concert party, dances and a dance class (sports clubs, a Christian Union and a choral society would be organized if there was sufficient interest) [*Year Book* 1954–55]. How many clubs and societies were in existence in any institution, and how well supported they were, were clearly functions of the size and nature of the institution, and the composition of its student body. Into the 1960s and beyond it was at the larger institutions, with a substantial amount of hall of residence accommodation, that such organizations and their support were most extensive. At Liverpool in the late 1960s and early 1970s, in addition to the subject-related societies, the Guild had more than 50 'special interest' and political societies, including, at the beginning of the alphabet Acid, Africa, Anarchist, Anglican, Anglo-Turkish, Animal Welfare, Apathy, Arab, Archaeological, Association of Moderate Students and Astronomical, and at the end of the alphabet Scout and Guide, Seaborne, Sexual, Socialist, Southern Africa, United Nations Students Association, Wine, Women's Lib and World Development [Guild A. 032/60 Council 3 November 1969; A. 032/45 Finance Committee 22 October 1971]. At the same time Plymouth Polytechnic, with little campus residential accommodation, had a much smaller range of clubs and societies (and listed as 'inactive' its Conservative Society, Judo Club, Psychological Society, Radio Officers Association, Fencing Club and Debating Society). By 1977 the Plymouth student journal was listing 44 societies, just over half of which were for sports and athletics (given the location, these not surprisingly included Surf, Sailing, Sub-Aqua, Angling, Riding and Parachute Clubs). The only political society was the Socialist Society, and societies had appeared for Islamic Studies, Chinese Culture, and Malaysian Studies, as well as Hellenic Studies, a Christian Union, a Business Studies Society and an Engineering Society [*Fly* vol. 5, edn 1 1977]. Four years later the Polytechnic listed for a CNAA visit seven clubs and societies for 'group sports', 27 for 'solo sports', and 46 for 'non-sports'. The 'solo sports' continued to reflect the location and interests of the institution (adding to the previous list Canoe, Rifle, Windsurfing, Water Ski and others). 'Non-sports' continued to reflect the international nature of the student body, adding Nigeria, Bahai, Iranian, Muslim and Venezuelan, and including a Conservative and a Labour as well as a Socialist Society, some curriculum-related areas, including Social Work, Law and Architecture, and others which reflected the cultural interests of at least some students, including Anti-Nuclear, Environmental, Music and Arts, Real Ale and Photographic societies [Academic Board 21 January 1981].

At other polytechnics, with similar patterns of student enrolment, the range of societies in the 1960s and 1970s developed similarly, with sports and non-sports societies suiting the student body, curriculum and locality in similar ways. Amalgamations widened the character of these institutions, although in many cases the lack of campus residences by comparison with the universities meant a lower level of student participation. By the 1980s, however, the extent and range of student activities in polytechnics and universities had become similar, and what the newly named universities had on offer in the 1990s looked not unlike that in the older universities. In 1992 the Plymouth Students Union *Handbook* advertised 88 clubs and societies, split evenly between sport and interest groups. The Liverpool University Guild of Students in 1994 had 82 societies, and the Athletic Union, a standing committee of the Guild, had 45 clubs. The Guild societies probably represented a range similar to that of other older universities, and wider than that of some polytechnics which might not have the same array of subject-related societies (at Liverpool these included Veterinary, Medical Students and Hispanics). The list of political societies might differ across institutions and time, as Militant Labour or Student Liberal Democrat or Conservative might for various reasons disappear, go into abeyance, or reappear in an old or new guise. The Students Union at the University of Sussex predicted that for the session 1994–5, 40 clubs would operate under the aegis of the Sports Federation, nine under the Music Federation, nine under the Arts Federation, and 33 'others' – including Anti-Nazi League, Black, Islamic, Jewish, Lesbian, Gay and Bisexual, Final Frontier (SciFi Film) and Mandela Scholarship [*Alternative Prospectus 94 95*: 36–7] – all of them societies that could easily appear on the list at any other university. Standard items in such a list are the subject-related societies. Some societies relate to the ethnic or national identities of specific groups of students, including a Scottish National Association at Glasgow, and Welsh and Irish Societies at Liverpool. The list varies in response to student interests, and as the Sussex *Alternative Prospectus* tells its readers: 'If we don't have the Club or Society which interests you, FORM IT!' [*ibid.*: 36].

None of this describes the amount of interest displayed by students in these activities, though students' unions in all institutions lay down how many students are required for registration and eligibility for funding – generally between 15 and 30. This description also does not indicate the particular strengths and popularity of societies depending on the student profile, and the difference between formal membership and attendance in some cases. A political society may have the requisite number of members and never hold meetings, or it may have considerably larger audiences than its membership for speakers at some of its meetings. Movements and events outside higher education may also influence the extent of support for particular activities. A *Guardian Society* article in 1995 drew attention to the huge rise in the membership of organizations such as Greenpeace and Friends of the Earth in the late 1980s and 1990s, including the numbers of student and youth members. Amnesty International had grown from 1,300 student and youth members in 1988 to 15,000 in 1995 (Donaldson 1995: 9). The growth of support for environmental or socially conscious movements was reflected in the lists of organizations on university and college campuses, in less formal ways, in student activities conducted off campus, and in student membership of such organizations unrelated to their membership of campus-based societies. Societies started up or reactivated at the University of East Anglia in 1990–2 included Vegetarian and the Young European Movement [*Annual Report 1990/91*: 11].

This discussion also does not reflect the student experience of clubs and societies in smaller institutions than those we have illustrated, where it may be possible to sustain a small range of activities, such as drama and music, or societies related to the range of studies, such as social work and nursing, or education, or the performing arts. Here also outside movements or events may also for a time affect the focus of student activities, in relation to government policy, local issues, student finance, or some of the environmental and other issues. At Queen Margaret College in 1982–3 the CND group described itself as '200 strong, the biggest society in the college'. It had newly formed, was 'not as active as it could be, so next year we hope to attract active campaigners amongst our new members' [*Handbook 1982–3*: 10].

Something similar applies within a collegiate structure, where the majority of student societies are on a university-wide basis, but where activities may be generated within the colleges themselves. The Durham Students Union in 1970 was supporting 42 non-sport societies, the largest average attendances claimed being those of Anthropology (100), Chemical (125–150), French (100), Literary (147) and Music (160). For Change Ringers the number was 10, for Classical Guitar 25, Rock Music 46 and Science Fiction 30. Conservative had 36 and Socialist 30, Methodist 60 and Student Christian Movement 35 [Council 11 December 1970]. It is constantly claimed, however, that while at Durham students feel their 'prime loyalty is to the college. They are active in the college initially, then they graduate to University teams and other activities' (Holgate int.). For many students there is the possibility, strengthened by peer pressures, of committing themselves to a limited range of college activities. Some of these are inevitably social, given the attractions of the Junior Common Room and its facilities, including the bar, and the underlying social networks developed in the residential setting. Although not all students take part in college activities, the pressures to do so are strong (Stoker, Tooke, Halladay ints), and this is particularly clear in the case of sporting activities. College activities are attractive to students who supplement their academic commitments with an accessible and socially acceptable level of active or passive entertainment. What else students do at college level depends mainly on its traditions and external pressures imported by perhaps a small number of students. At Grey College, as at some others, discussion at the Junior Common Room general meetings in the 1970s and 1980s demonstrates the supreme importance of the Boat Club, but also other sports and drama. A proposal to form a college Campaign for Nuclear Disarmament Society in 1961 was greeted at a general meeting 'with loud uproar', and a demand that the college not be implicated 'in any demonstration of disobedience' [General Meeting 20 March 1961].

What some of these examples illustrate is the pressure on students to participate at hall of residence, college or university level. This is particularly, but not only, true in relation to sport: 'there is pressure to participate if you have any skill' (Halladay int.), and skill may often be more easily identifiable in sport and athletics than in the context of 'interest groups'. The fact, in the American setting, that most students are seen as belonging to something under a degree of peer pressure, suggests something about the gregariousness of American students and also about the felt need for some form of smaller-scale identification. In 1967–8 the Penn State *Student Handbook* listed, apart from sports organizations, 120 'student activities', grouping fraternities and sororities as one each. As in the British case, these included academically related organizations such as the Horticulture Club and Future Farmers of America, the Journalism Students Association and the Society of American Military Engineers, as well as other recognizable categories – national and ethnic (for example, Muslim Student Association and Chinese Student Club); a considerable range of interest and religious groups (including the Christian Science Organization, Eastern Orthodox Society, Young Democrats, Pep Band and Model United Nations); and organizations which reflected particular social traditions on campus (Block & Bridle Club, Hat Society Council, and the Rod and Coccus Club) [*Handbook 1967–1968*: 77–8]. A decade later the *Handbook* listed 120 'special interest organizations', plus 17 'music, communications, publications, and performing arts organizations', nine 'nationality organizations', 21 'religious and spiritual organizations', nine 'residence hall organizations', 29 'sports and recreation-related organizations', and a number of other 'executive, government and programming organizations and councils'. Organizations had proliferated in all the categories, and there was a separate listing of 70 fraternities and sororities [*Handbook 1976–77*: 20–5]. A four-page large newsprint *Penn State Student Organization Directory 1994–1995* listed a total of 455 organizations, including 82 fraternities and sororities, 27 nationality and ethnic organizations, 28 religious and spiritual organizations and 168 special interest groups. The last of these included a Monty Python Society, a Bridge Club, Dungeons and Dragons, and a Juggling Club. A host of other organizations addressed the interests of professional and social groups, the concerns of women and minorities, and opportunities to consider legal, political, economic, philosophical and other aspects of contemporary America. One clear aspect of the range of student societies and activities in both countries has been the sustained, and in some cases increased, interest in religion. The introduction to the *Penn State Directory* tells students that 'involvement in a student organization is the time spent on yourself'. This kind of involvement has been widely emphasized in recent decades, including by student organizations, as an essential ingredient of an undergraduate education, and as preparatory to successful careers and citizenship. A review of student life by the Undergraduate Assembly at Penn in 1986 desribed the University as

> a community of individuals who want to be exposed to intellectual, social, and cultural stimulation. A Penn education does not end in the classroom. The University and its city, Philadelphia, have a great deal to offer students . . . Non-academic life at Penn is of great importance.
> [UA *Year 1990: outlook on student life* 1986: 1]

Here, and in a considerable volume of student publications and activity in the 1980s and 1990s, the organized life of Penn students was influenced much more than at Penn State by the University's presence in a large American city, and the outreach function of student organizations has been influenced accordingly, as it has been in many British contexts.

The large number of sports clubs and the prominence of sports – a definition which sometimes includes snooker or chess as well as the traditional outdoor sports – are important aspects of campus life in Britain, the United States and other countries. American 'athletics' has for several decades been a major item of campus controversy, given the resources committed – in the view of some – to the detriment of 'academics', and the professional orientation, partly under pressure from alumni, partly because of the public glamour attached to successful participation in university and college leagues, and its importance for student recruitment. A review of these activities would take in not only the existence of the clubs, but also the nature of intra- and inter-institution games, the considerable physical provision on many campuses of everything from playing fields to climbing walls, from canoes to imitation ski slopes. Mapping the range of provision and activity as the number and size of institutions have grown over recent years would far exceed the possibilities of this discussion. Something similar applies to the role of the students' union across time in the provision of entertainments of various kinds. Student finances, off-campus competition from bars and clubs, and students' differential access to entertainment in different locations, have affected this picture profoundly since the 1960s and make provision and involvement difficult to survey. In the cases of both sport and entertainment it is also impossible to determine the extent of student support. Entertainment, for example, links closely to the social and cultural styles of individual students and categories of students. It relates to the existence in students' rooms of television sets and record or CD players, the functions of common rooms, halls and bars.

The prominence, throughout the history of higher education, of alcohol

as an element in the public image of student behaviour raises other difficulties in tracing student experience. Drinking is both a public and private
activity, and the prevalence of drinking becomes confused with the question of excessive drinking. The figures of alcohol consumption have to be
related over time to student numbers and other aspects of student activities.
The figures are not easy to interpret. In 1981 the 6,000 members of Glasgow University Union drank 10,000 pints of beer a week [242/2/59 *Glasgow
Herald* 6 February 1981]. In 1992–3 the Students Union at University
College London sold 462,000 pints of draught beer, 167,000 bottles of beer,
and 2,500 bottles of vodka (as well as 175,000 sandwiches and 225,000
packets of crisps) (Bates and Ibbotson 1994: 132). In the 1980s the bars at
the University of East Anglia Union of Students, managed by the University
until 1988, were consuming some 1,000 barrels of beer a year – almost
300,000 pints. In 1994–5 they sold 2,800 barrels, more than 800,000 pints
[Management Committee Notes for Guidance for applicants for Bars
Manager 1988; oral information]. Apart from the need to track the numbers of students in these institutions, other information has to be taken into
account. The Glasgow University Union has a large membership of former
students. The UCL and UEA bars are frequented by substantial numbers of
visitors from other colleges, and the UEA 1994–5 figures include sales at
the Waterfront, a city arts centre managed by the Union of Students. At the
University of Sheffield in 1993, according to a students' union report, 86.4
per cent of students surveyed used pubs and bars 'regularly', and 7.1 per
cent 'sometimes'. The most common expenditure on alcohol was £5 a week
or less (some 16 per cent spent nothing, 33 per cent spent under £5, 22 per
cent between £5 and £10, and 27 per cent more than £10) [Gerrard 1993a:
20, 24]. Students' union bars were everywhere widely recognized as the
most important focus of student socializing.

One of the problems in recent years has been the paradox of public,
university, college and students' union anti-drink campaigns, at the same
time as pressures to make bars more profitable – not by raising prices, but
by selling more, particularly beer. Apart from special events, such as real
ale festivals, students' unions make beer prices permanently competitive
in order to attract customers. At Durham in the 1980s, the University was
anxious about student drinking and conducted a study of what it considered the overly low price of alcohol in college bars. Students' unions in
some universities have successfully experimented with non-alcoholic bars.
Beer at often under two-thirds the price in public houses is obviously attractive to large numbers of students: 'a great many do get drunk, and by week
nine they're broke' (Weinstein int.). There are peer pressures to drink, and
the bar – rather than the political party or the campaign, the concert hall
or even the disco – has become for many students the balancing focus for
their studies, part-time jobs and tensions. Drinking and getting drunk are
for some students a personal and collective response to campus and social
pressures, and to some extent an acceptance of traditions associated in the
past, for example, with the rugby club or town-and-gown encounters in

local hostelries. It is impossible to tell how many students are teetotal, too poor to drink, only irregular drinkers, or more attracted to other forms of relaxation.

Drinking as part of the undergraduate rite of passage has an enormous international history, across, for example, the European universities from the Middle Ages to the twentieth century. In the United States the recent history is complicated by the raising of the legal drinking age to 21 in most states in the late 1980s. An Undergraduate Assembly report in 1989 at Penn, where suddenly 80 per cent of the students had become 'underage', commented on the change:

> In the past, social life at Penn centered mainly around alcohol. Often, students would socialize at alcohol-related functions such as keg parties in the Quad, fraternity parties, and attend various campus bars. But times have changed. The state of Pennsylvania's recent move toward tough alcohol restrictions has forced the University to abide by these rules leaving a void in the social lives of all underage students at Penn. The recent adoption of a more strict attitude toward underage drinking in the state of Pennsylvania has forced both the University and campus bars to become far more serious about preventing those under legal drinking age from entering an alcoholic environment.
>
> [*Report on Social Planning* 1989: 1–2]

Penn State was aware of a campus drinking problem in the mid-1970s, with a lot of 'hard partying' and more problem drinkers, at what had become a 'great, great drinking school' (Millar int.). At these and other institutions there were particular problems with first week drinking. Though the Penn 1989 report emphasized that fraternity parties could no longer admit students under 21, who were therefore debarred from 'what used to be a focal point of social life at Penn', and who were also denied admittance to campus bars, the times had not entirely changed. Many students falsified their IDs. Others were admitted illegally to fraternity parties (liable to draw the attention of the authorities or the police), or more often just drank illegally in the privacy of fraternity houses or dormitories. A Harvard School of Public Health study 'conducted at universities where drinking is common' found that 54 per cent of new students got drunk during their first week of college and '68 per cent went on drinking binges by the end of their first semester. A binge is defined as chugging at least four drinks in a row'. Freshers at Penn confirmed that this was their experience, including those who had previously drunk in high school. The problem was seen by some as generated by the fact that bars and parties were the only place to meet people [*Daily Pennsylvanian* 7 April 1995: 4].

If it is difficult to form a complete picture of the extent of under-age drinking, it is impossible to estimate the extent of drug abuse among students, in Britain or elsewhere. Cases of drug abuse which result in deaths or other dramas on campuses occasionally surface in the national press, as does occasional action by university or college authorities. It is generally considered that alcohol has become a greater problem than drug abuse, and while it is possible to sketch a picture of students and alcohol, the picture with regard to drugs is too elusive to be considered here.

Changes in campuses and students from the late 1960s have also been associated with other social changes which impinge directly on students. The increased level of crime and violence outside the campus has sometimes been matched on the campus, as has been true much longer of urban American campuses. A commentary on mugging in Manchester in 1995, for example, suggested that students

> are likely to be more at risk from crime than the general population. 'They are fairly young, often live in cheaper areas and aren't very security conscious – their parents will have dealt with security in the past. They are also seen as soft targets'.
> (Gallacher, reported in Nowicka 1995: 19)

Security has become much stronger on the campus itself, and, as we have seen, the provision of transport to off-campus halls of residence, or to and from outside entertainment events, is being more frequently provided by students' unions. The change in social attitudes generally has similarly been reflected among students. One observer at Penn State, for example, thought that student government had become more adversarial since the 1960s, student leaders did not respect one another, more students brought problems with them to the University, perhaps in the form of aggressiveness – students from broken homes, for example. There was more profanity by women students, more 'hate groups', and more violence between students (Millar int.). Similar trends have been observed on British campuses, including in the students' union. In an end-of-year report the Deputy President Education and Welfare at Durham in 1984 commented:

> At the very first DSU Council I attended I was struck by several things which I still feel are true. One was the lack of respect which people had for each other – exemplified by the needless antagonism between 'the Exec' and 'the hacks', uncalled for personal attacks on people with differing views.
> [Council 20 June 1984]

This, of course, is not entirely new, as the controversies and disputes of the 1960s or the fourteenth century would indicate, and it would not be possible to demonstrate how widely 'lack of respect' or 'more violence' prevail on campuses. There may be less overt hostility towards minorities or gays and lesbians, or towards other opinions, but it erupts often enough in the life of the campus to suggest that many would echo the view of the retiring Deputy President.

The discussion in this chapter, and to some extent previous chapters, has been essentially an attempt to explore some of the elements that have to be considered in any portrait of 'student culture', students' activity in the contexts in which it takes place, and diversified by the sub-groups in the student population. The latter are categorized not just by single criteria (male, older, etc.) but also by their contexts – notably types and distance of residence, course demands, staff–student relationships, students' union involvement, relationship to student services. What students bring with them to the campus are not just 'problems', but also elements which may help to define their place within the culture. A mature student at the University of Lancaster in 1975 wrote a diary, in which he described his surprise that other students expressed disbelief at the fact that he did not belong to a political party, club or society. He wrote at one point that he had noticed

> the way students place a particular emphasis on social activities as an escape from academic work. It's disquieting that students should feel this need to escape, and possibly suggests a fault either in the courses, or in the university organisation as a whole. Whatever the cause, there is a considerable disenchantment circulating.
>
> (Keylock 1975: 88)

Of the various directions in which these comments – simply by one mature student at one moment – may point, an interesting one is the sense of a student culture built at least partly on reaction against what is not seen as part of the student's 'own' culture, on degrees of uncertainty or unhappiness, on what we have discussed as counterbalancing academic work. Although the experience may help to shape attitudes, the experience does not begin in a vacuum.

How this works out in practice is, as we have also suggested, both an individual and a collective set of decisions and outcomes, and we have stressed the importance of taking account of different categories of students in order to avoid the over-emphasis on students' common roles of some earlier writing on students. This is not to deny the commonalities that do exist. Researchers have over the past quarter-century found degrees of consensus among entering students regarding their expectations and their perceptions of the balance of their commitments and responsibilities – though research conducted in Australia in the late 1960s for example would be no more than a starting point for examining the impact of later changes (Katz and Arbib 1971). Within the concept of 'student culture' it is possible to trace common behaviours, what one piece of American research approaches through students' levels of activity, involvement, most common and least common experiences (Baird 1990). Pursuing student 'sub-cultures' in the 1960s – for example, with a view to relating type of accommodation to features of student social and academic life (Warr 1964; Albrow 1966) – remains a difficult exercise, but is a reminder of the kaleidoscopic contents of the concept of a culture. The *Times Higher Education Supplement* looked in 1991 at what it labelled 'Student culture in decline', commenting on the legacies of past radicalisms and fashions: 'these stereotypes have left echoes behind – in the popular imagination certainly and arguably in the belief that there is a pattern to student life, a distinctive student culture. That belief may already be unsafe and will become unsafer as the system accelerates towards mass access' (*THES* 20 September 1991: 14). A determination of such patterns, and judgements about the nature of their continuity or decline, can rarely be grounded in 'hard' data. Who and where students are, what they do, how they define themselves individually or collectively, and with what effects, are visible in some of the directions we have taken. There are others.

7

Opinions and Attitudes

In 1979 at the University of Strathclyde an Extraordinary General Meeting was held to debate a motion of no confidence in the President. One disgruntled student complained that it was 'diabolical that Association Members do not come to Meetings. Even today, out of 6400 students, only about 350 were present' [AGM 12 December 1979]. In some places over the past two decades that number and percentage of students attending meetings might have been considered less than diabolical. Students' union meetings, their agendas, their officers' reports, their protests and campaigns do not necessarily reflect the opinions of the membership at large, who on many or most of the topics being debated may have had no opinion at all. What has been debated and decided since the 1970s does, however, give some indication of the interests of at least the more committed or vociferous students, but also of the mood and outlook of students more widely. The conduct of meetings, the causes espoused by students' unions and their constituents, the range of union activities, the eruption of demonstrations and sit-ins, the dominant ideologies, tell a great deal about the 'apathy' of students and the decline of student radicalism after the events of the late 1960s and early 1970s.

What has appeared on agendas of executives or councils or general meetings, what resolutions were adopted, what action was taken, inevitably depend on the political composition of the student body, or the persistence of individual students or factions. Students' union records provide interesting and complex invitations to interpret. The Guild of Students Council at Liverpool, for instance, in October 1975 was proposing to boycott Spanish goods, deploring the encouragement of students to live at home as a consequence of the government's education cuts, protesting against show trials and political prisoners in Chile, and proclaiming the need for a successful rent strike. A month later it censured its own Executive for failing to gain the active support of more than 10 per cent of the students in halls of residence for the rent strike, deplored the overworking and underpaying of junior hospital doctors, and the reactionary nature of the management of Sayers Bakeries in Liverpool which had dismissed 36 members of staff. It was concerned about the badminton courts, apartheid, the National Front, and the age of consent for homosexual acts. In February 1976, however, Council noted: '(1) The lack of enthusiasm generated in the Union. (2) The need to make the Union a Social Union. (3) The size and the popularity of Camra [Campaign for Real Ale]. (4) The drawing power of real and non-keg beers' [Council 13 October 1975, 21 November 1975, 9 February 1976].

Students' union concerns shifted after the 1960s from political causes to campus- and student-oriented causes, but national and international issues and campaigns did not disappear. In the 1970s students' unions at Rolle College (a teachers' college which was to become part of the University of Plymouth) and the universities of Durham and Liverpool were addressing issues relating to human rights in, for example, Chile, Argentina and South Africa, the war in Vietnam, Ireland, and national policy debates about racism, gay rights and abortion. In the 1980s Strathclyde, Liverpool and Teesside were concerned with South Africa and aboriginal rights in Australia, a united Ireland, the nuclear deterrent, arms sales, furs, banks, the National Health Service, lesbian and gay rights, the poll tax and education cuts. In the 1990s many of these issues remained on the agenda, plus, for example, the Gulf War and a campaign against the Swiss food giant, Nestlé. Agenda items were often responses to public events or issues. In 1989 the Liverpool Guild Council responded to the Hillsborough football disaster, identity cards for football fans, salaries action by the Association of University Teachers, homelessness and racism.

Alongside these kinds of agenda items, however, the shift towards more domestic issues is clear. At Rolle College in the 1970s prominent and often persistent concerns included the College's future, teacher unemployment and the College's academic structure. Liverpool was concerned about the standard of food and catering and the lack of a family planning service. Durham and Teesside unions were concerned about library provision – Teesside because of the lack of seating facilities, poor soundproofing, lighting, maintenance work during term time, lack of provision for the physically disabled, library closure on Saturday afternoons and in vacations, poor security for bags and cases, and insufficient numbers of main texts [Council 14 January 1975]. Durham was also planning Durham Against Racism, and action on the matter of a crèche and students with disabilities. A report to the Teesside Union in 1974 listed the weaknesses of the previous year, beginning with: 'Student apathy and non-involvement in the Union and in NUS campaigns' [Executive 23 September 1974], laying much of the blame on the Union itself. At Queen Margaret College the Association's Council decided to hold a referendum on 'the best way to get the opinion of the general students over the issue of evacuation' in any future bomb scare [CSA 2 October 1973], and issues discussed included cigarette machines and counter sales, football machines, nursery facilities and childcare, telephones, diaries, Christmas cards, grants, the refectory, contraceptive machines and a road safety petition. Many of these kinds of issues were, of course, addressed in other unions.

A typical late 1970s council agenda is one at Strathclyde in November 1979, which, apart from a number of international and other causes, contained the following:

> the sale of soft drinks; amendments to bye-laws; elections; NUS Universities Sector Conference; reports on Boards of Studies; student accommodation in blocks of flats; a Week of Action against education cuts and overseas students' fees; the appointment of a senior member of the University staff 'responsible for needs of the handicapped students on campus'; a 25 per cent student failure rate ('grave concern was expressed by the students on this matter'); the Union's serious financial position (the University had not received fees from the Scottish Education Department); the installation of a stamp machine; a TV repair; difficulty of withdrawing from the Bank of Scotland over South Africa because of the financial position; affiliation to the Scottish Council of Civil Liberties; a Children's Christmas Party; a week of activities 'to increase awareness among students of the facilities which the Athletic Club offers'.
>
> [Council 20 November 1979]

In the 1980s Strathclyde was commenting on 'the lack of organised student participation in academic issues which affect them in the University' [EGM 17 October 1984]. Student loans and grants, rents and everything concerning students' finances were recurrent issues in union meetings during the decade, as was Aids, alongside issues already familiar from the 1970s – for example, nurseries, food and accommodation. In 1988 a report was presented to the Plymouth Union Executive under the agenda heading 'Campaigns', and listing 30 'items which affect students', beginning and ending:

1 The decor – ongoing process.
2 Sporting Clubs and Societies – Brought up at Governing Body.
3 All-Weather pitch – scrapped.
4 The merger – Seale Hayne (College of Agriculture) – see what response from their Exec.

. . .

25 Student Loans – Demo's for end of February. No final decision.
26 Student Survey Problems – Welfare communications.
27 Block Grant – Decision withheld until end of February.
28 'Beyond the powers' – Ultra Vires – always keep within bounds.
29 New Poly's Corporate Structure – Logo – not appreciated.
30 Non-Alcoholic Drinks Promotion – Stock now in bar.

[Executive 13 December 1988]

In 1987 at Nene College general meetings discussed street lighting, a library lift and ramps for disabled students. A typical late 1980s Executive Committee agenda would be one at Teesside in 1987, which included as items:

A ban on a student who had sexually harassed two female students; a policy paper on complaints and grievances; a decision that the film society should not show as intended a sexist film; representation on the local Campaign for Racial Equality; request for the use of a Union minibus for an international camp by Hartlepool Volunteer Development Agency; a grant towards participation in ski-ing championships; the installation of a photocopier; representation on the Union's disciplinary committee; the operation of the racial harassment sub-committee; a proposal for a health surgery and the publication of a pamphlet on health; a week of action on student financial support.

[Executive 20 January 1987]

There were comments in the 1990s about the 'apolitical' or 'apathetic' nature of the union membership at very many institutions, and a typical issue that surfaced throughout the United Kingdom was that of 'blind' or anonymous marking, an issue pursued by unions strongly and persistently. This kind of issue probably did reflect student opinion widely, as an Academic Audit Unit team discovered when it visited the University of Durham in 1992: 'During discussions with students it also became clear that there was substantial enthusiasm for blind marking of examination papers . . . The audit team welcomed the fact that the issue was being discussed between the Students' Union and the University' (CVCP AAU report July 1992: 9). Also in 1992, there was at Plymouth, as at other places, some staff resistance to anonymous marking, and a Union paper argued that

while there is evidence to support and reject the call for anonymous marking by doing so it is not only an important equal opportunity statement, guards against gender, racial or any other form of bias, but additionally PROTECTS the integrity of Academics lifting all reasonable doubt from the Poly, and urged the Union to keep the issue alive.

[OGM 28 May 1992]

University of Wales Swansea Students Union included anonymous marking under Equal Opportunities in its *Handbook* in 1993. Giving each student a number to substitute for a name would stop bias in marking, 'be it overt or subconscious'. Studies had shown that women and minorities did some 10 per cent better when marked this way: 'Any progressive, modern academic institution committed to equal opportunities should readily adopt this form of marking – or what do they have to fear?' One department had already adopted anonymous marking, and others were willing to follow [*Handbook 1993–1994*: 3.22]. Liverpool in 1993–4 was also involved with anonymous marking, and with environmental issues as they affected the University – recycling, vegetarian meals, energy conservation, diesel, toilet paper and a 'Green Charter'. What had emerged from the 1970s was an increased and often dominant concern with more immediate student issues, regarding campus amenities, academic affairs, and students' grants, loans and living conditions (these three linked issues fairly uniformly shared across institutions and often linked to campaigns co-ordinated by the NUS). Student life, emphasized a students' union president, was 'far less political than it used to be' (Ebdon int.). A former president at the same institution commented sadly: 'The students won't storm the barricades for themselves, let alone Chile or wherever' (White int.). Asked in 1989 how often they attended Union meetings, 8 per cent of students at the University of Sheffield said 'regularly', 17 per cent said 'occasionally', 23 per cent 'rarely', and 52 per cent 'never' [Sheffield/Gallup 1989: 4].

Occasionally, from the 1970s onwards, student politics of a new kind resulted in what superficially looked like the earlier student activism. Sit-ins, occupations and demonstrations took place, but almost entirely around the issues that concerned students directly – grants, rents, accommodation, government education cuts and other government policies such as the poll tax. These tended to be less confrontational on campus than in the 1960s, given that they were directed primarily against government policy, though sometimes against the institution and its acquiescence in implementing the policy. The action was more obviously symbolic. Students' unions and their officers were constantly engaged in dialogue around all of these issues with vice-chancellors and principals, committees and other senior administrators. Even where underlying relations were cordial and constructive the job of 'representing' the students and their current interests could be frustrating. Two successive Students Union presidents at Oxford Brookes University, for example, pursued with the University the idea of awarding credit to students for

> extra-curricular learning, learning that resulted from working part-time, in the community or as a student representative . . . In my year as President, it was the issue that produced the most un-student-centred thinking. Many staff's attitude was so insulting to the students that had to work . . . we kept pushing the issue forwards, as did many staff, but it got nowhere.
>
> (Brierley 1995: 4)

Her successor spoke of her frustration in carrying on with this policy:

> these proposals seem to have got lost along the way . . . if there's something like crediting the learning by student representatives, that nobody immediately warms to or takes ownership of it's simply farmed off to two or three or four committees or working parties.
>
> (Weinstein 1995: 5)

The latter considered her presidency to have been an exercise in diplomacy, often pressing students' union policies which were unpopular with the University, and being made to 'feel temporary' (Weinstein int.). As one commentator points out, students' unions had by the 1970s made themselves 'a presence to be reckoned with', and the relationship with the institution therefore meant that 'many union presidents find themselves forced into "tough" negotiating stances', regardless of their formal political positions (Arblaster 1979: 25).

This picture of British students' unions applies to some extent to American student governments, where a similar changing balance was taking place between political causes relating to American foreign policy (Cambodia, South African divestment, Chile, Central America, and so on), causes concerning minority and other rights in general (Aids, gay and lesbian, environmental) and campus-specific issues (loss of sports amenities, fraternities, campus security, library hours, parking). The issues at Penn State in the 1970s included bus services, heating, telephones, parking, the disciplinc system, assaults on women, and police use of binoculars 'to apprehend window pot marijuana growers'. Themes such as racism, Aids, homelessness and harassment persisted. The question of 'representing' the views of tens of thousands of students has been different from that in the UK mainly in relation to scale, but the somewhat different position of student government and activities in relation to their institutions also raises other issues. In the 1980s and 1990s there has been a greater element of confrontation in these relations than in the British case over some of these causes, including over issues of 'political correctness'. There has also been a similar, and longer-standing commitment to the commercial viability of union facilities.

Whether British students' union officers, when promoting, implementing or negotiating policies, have reflected majority or minority opinion, in their roles as caretakers of student social amenities and activities in general they have acted more clearly on behalf of the great majority of students (though part-time, mature or ethnic minority students may sometimes doubt this to be the case). If students were seeing the union as 'a service provider' (Tregoning int.), and if the union's facilities were basic to its financial calculations, union officers and staffs were responsible and accountable for something increasingly central to the definition of unions as 'social organizations' and commercial enterprises. Decreased funding of the unions from public sources made it, as we have seen, essential for them to supplement these funds in other ways in order to sustain their activities. They were driven, in the 1990s particularly, to develop their entrepreneurial roles. Their management structure or ethos changed in order to reflect the commercial approach, though not equally or simultaneously in all institutions.

One of the pioneers of the successful new students' union commercialism was at the University of Sheffield, described in the *THES* as one which 'blends economic success with campaigning politics'. In 1982 the Union made a profit of £30,000; five years later it made £100,000 on its trading activities, including its travel office, nine eating outlets, five bars, a print shop, a retail shop, a cinema, a bank, an insurance office and a launderette. In so doing it had at the same time 'consolidated its strong record of political campaigning' and ensured the loyalty of its members, 'nearly all of whom are involved in one or other of the union's myriad activities'. This was in addition to its grant from the University – £719,000 in 1988. Realizing that the government's education cuts in 1981 would drastically affect the union, 'officers decided to embark on a long-term programme of investment with the aim of ploughing the profit back into the union's welfare and political activities' – for example, its women's minibus service at night. In the late 1980s it was aiming to expand its counselling centre, provided a nursery, an overseas students' bureau, a community action programme, and an athletics office. Its campaigns in 1987–8 included protests against the Education Bill, the poll tax, student loans, changes in social security regulations, and Aids awareness (Griffiths 1988: 7). The Edinburgh University Students' Association in 1984–5 administered five buildings and three other premises within the University, and received £605,000 from the University – and had a turnover of £3.8 million (Eight Scottish University Student Bodies 1985: 29). In the early 1990s the preparation of Nene College Students Union business plan included a customer profile, a review of the operation of the bars, redecoration, canteen prices and product range, and other possible sources of income [Management Committee 16 December 1991, 7 February 1994, 21 February 1994]. We have previously noted the commercial operations of unions at East Anglia and Strathclyde, and all of these and others have been attempts to keep alive the traditional mix of clubs and societies, campaigning and policy-oriented structures and processes, the representation of the student body in dealings with the university or college, and students' social needs.

These developments were responses to the public financing and market-oriented policies of the 1980s and 1990s. Students themselves across this period were often described in interviews as 'Thatcher's children'. Radical students returning to their old universities might now include a management consultant or lawyer, an accountant or an advertising executive, or, further afield, in Germany someone active in the Green Party, or in the United States a Reaganite economist or a Wall Street broker (Johnson 1988: 13; Belsey and MacLeod 1993; Beckett 1994: 5). They would find students more conservative politically than they had been. The Students Union President at Plymouth in 1994, who had first been a student there in 1986–7 and previously President in 1988–9, described the students as more middle-class, generally not politically active, not as interested in the Students Union, failing to turn up to committees of which they were members, less interested even in sports, and wanting to be paid for things they did (Horton int.). Council and general meeting minutes frequently recorded the lack of a quorum. Student events were reported in the press under titles such as 'March of the moderates' (*The Guardian Education*, 30 January 1996: 4). One students' union president described students as 'less proactive than in the '70s and '80s – for example, over the poll tax. They have other things to worry about, they don't march in London, they prefer their books and their friends' (Parker int.). Another said:

> These are first generation Thatcher's children, they do very little campaigning on grants and so forth. The University is refurbishing a residential block and rents will go up from £42.50 to £50, but students

don't seem anxious. We got lighting in Singleton Park after a vigil, but only 40 volunteers turned up.

(Chambers int.)

The word 'apathy' was frequently used in interviews, though students were also seen as 'caring', rather than espousing conventional politics, and this has clearly also been the case in the United States. Students had been turned off formal politics but cared about specific issues (Mathews 1993; Hodges 1995). A sit-in at Penn in 1978, the first since the Vietnam War, was over an attempt to eliminate hockey, gymnastics, badminton and other programmes and curtail the professional theatre programme. The agreement which ended the sit-in gave the students several things – the reinstatement of gymnastics, badminton and golf programmes and the transfer of hockey players to other programmes, fund-raising by the University to assure the future of the professional theatre programme, the delaying of midterm examinations, improvements in provision for ethnic minority students, and the re-establishment of a task force on university governance [UPA4 349/1; UPA8 298/1]. 'The emphasis, it seems', said one press comment, 'has shifted from broad-based social and political issues to a more practical set of concerns', with a particular emphasis on a greater student voice in administrative decisions [UPA4 349/6].

Claims of the 'end of apathy' occasionally surfaced, in Britain as elsewhere, and the 1970s and 1980s did continue from time to time to have their boycotts of lectures (at Liverpool, over education cuts), occupations (at Teesside over overseas student fees, at Queen Margaret College in protest against cuts and the devaluing of teacher education), and active campaigns (at Glasgow and elsewhere against refectory prices, cuts in grants, and a variety of what were often called 'bread and butter issues'). In the United States new forms of activism took shape, including well-organized lobbying, collective bargaining and various ways of working with the system for change rather than confronting it (Beeler 1979; 1985). What analysts perceived in students from the end of the 1970s was a mixture of conservative politics and liberal personal attitudes, the latter being concerned with 'life-style questions', personal morality and freedoms, resulting very often in new forms of pressure groups and local activism (Altbach 1979: 609–17; Altbach and Cohen 1990: 33). American controversy over 'political correctness' was a serious issue on some campuses in the 1980s and 1990s, provoking conflict between students and faculty, administration and other students, over the interpretation of everything from sexual relations to the history of slavery, and the effect on free speech. This was, however, basically what was generally considered a relatively quiet period. 'Thatcher's children' in Britain were paralleled by the 'me-generation' in the United States, the generation whose horizons generally ended where self-interest plus an element of social conscience also ended.

'Thatcher's children' showed 'a degree of selfishness' (Halladay int.) and were 'passive consumers' (Baldwin int.). Their American equivalents were the product of a period of the much analysed dominant individualism which 'lies at the very core of American culture' (Bellah *et al.* 1985: 142), a 'competitive individualism, narcissistic preoccupation with self' (Lasch 1978: xv), which had been briefly breached in some of the ideology and action of the 1960s. Students were now the first generation – as one of them is reported as explaining – who 'won't do better than our parents', they were 'drifting and unfocused' (Cage 1993: A27–8). This was a 'socially liberal generation' whose liberalism was 'rooted in issues of personal freedom; that is, the right of individuals to pursue their own lives without the encumbrance of external restrictions. The emphasis here is upon "me", not upon "us"' (Levine 1980: 84–5). From interviews with students Riesman concluded:

> Although it is easy to exaggerate the proportion of students who in any epoch enjoyed 'learning for its own sake,' both women and men today are often involuntary captives, needing a credential to go on to postbaccalaureate training and doing the necessary work grimly and anxiously rather than with any sense of pleasure in learning.
>
> (Riesman 1980: 90)

By 1974 *Time* was describing a new spirit on American campuses. Not since the 1950s had students been 'so highly oriented toward careers and financial security. Deeply worried about an economy that is fraught with future uncertainties, overwhelmingly concerned with preparing for lucrative and satisfying jobs, today's college students can be fairly characterized as the Self-Centered Generation' (Segall and Pickett 1979: 42). Dramatic changes reported in surveys of students in the 1970s and 1980s, confirming the view of students as 'the self-centered generation', included changes in their personal values or 'life goals', and of these the one which had shown 'the strongest upward trend is "being very well-off financially"' (Astin 1991: 129–31).

Again, making allowances for differences between the two countries, the American verdicts also apply roughly to British students under similar pressures in the same period. Commentators in both countries therefore saw students as paradoxically both pleasure-seeking and extremely serious. An evaluation of the University of Durham's Enterprise programme in 1993 indicated that 'many student comments still show the sad perception that their degree programme is an endurance test, with one damn thing following another in similar guise' (Slee 1994: 24), and these could well have been the American students about whom Riesman had commented. Endurance test or not, students have certainly found it necessary to be serious (with or without pleasure) about their progress and outcomes, for the social and economic reasons suggested by *Time* and others. Whether taking part in 'vocationally relevant' courses or activities sponsored under government-funded Enterprise in Higher Education projects, some of them student-led, or in more clearly employment-oriented courses, students have much more widely than in previous generations seen a need to include employment explicitly among their aims. As we have seen in other connections, there is a general view among students' union presidents and others that students are more focused on obtaining a degree and getting into a job – 'they need to get their heads down' (Rixon int.) – and therefore less interested in taking union office. The house manager of one of Glasgow's union buildings reflected on her 25 years there ('just the fact that I've been here 25 years speaks volumes') and described students as 'not so politically inclined now. Students are apathetic and think student government is a waste of time' (Ingleton int.). There is evidence that employers are 'worried about a new breed of swots emerging from university without having done much except study' (MacLeod, citing a report by Lee Harvey, *The Guardian*, 22 August 1994: 4). Demands on careers services have increased considerably, and the services have attempted – sometimes with Enterprise support – to introduce careers planning into courses.

An apparently contrary trend, important in preserving a perspective on at least a significant fraction of students, has been the operation of Student Community Action groups in Britain and 'volunteerism' or 'service learning' in the United States. There are 130 constituted SCA groups (not all bearing that name) in the UK, 50 or so more than in the mid-1980s. The total number of students taking part in these groups' volunteer activities is difficult to gauge, since it varies during any given year and from one year to the next – and there are 'community action' involvements by students through other channels. At Durham in 1993 there were roughly 1,000 students engaged in SCA activities, regularly giving at least one hour a week; 300–400 of them were giving at least three hours a week (Thurston int.). Glasgow Volunteer Service averages about 500 regular student volunteers a year, and Swansea SCA over 400. In some of these cases, as at Durham, SCA is regularly the largest organized student society, and in the majority of cases it is part of the students' union.

When an attempt was being made at Durham to build up SCA activities in 1991, the student chair visited Swansea SCA, which was 'the model' (Thurston int.). Swansea SCA had been born in 1966, and by the 1990s was one of only a handful of SCA organizations with full-time, permanent staff. It receives financial aid from commercial and philanthropic sources, from individuals (including members of academic staff) and the National Lottery, and is supported by the Students Union and the University – though as a registered charity it is independent of both of the latter. Its 400-plus volunteers take part in the evenings and at weekends in a considerable range of activities, initiated by community organizations and services and by the students themselves – in the latter case, for example, work with the homeless. Students run clubs, weekends away and other activities for children of lone parents, hospitalized children and children with learning difficulties. They work with elderly people, schools and people of all ages with special needs. They record material for the blind, arrange shopping with students who have mobility problems, learn sign language in order to work with deaf children, train to help witnesses through the Witness Service, drive vehicles for a range of projects, and take part in a Nightline and first aid activities. Although now more comprehensive and systematic, the range of student community activities at Swansea has remained similar throughout its 30 years of existence [*Project Handbook* and leaflets] (Bevan 1966). The motives of students for committing themselves to regular involvements of this kind include contributing something useful, a search for companionship, the attraction of off-campus activities, the continuation of previous experience of volunteer activities, doing something different, facing a different challenge, and the value of the experience for future employment. The project emphasizes confidence building and an awareness of the issues and processes involved, and the organizers and students are resistant to the idea of 'accrediting' the activity as in some institutions (and notably in the United States) – 'the students are not lovers of certificates'. The strongest motivation is probably simply one of wanting to do it and helping to make a change (Knight int.).

These kinds of activities are to be found elsewhere, but there are also other components and emphases. Traditions of student community involvement, or community service, are linked in some cases to the settlement movement, but also to student 'rags'. The latter aimed to raise money for charitable causes, perhaps suggested a student conscience about the existence of poverty, but need not involve students in other forms of action. The modern community action movement grew in the 1960s out of two concerns. The first was the public image of students and 'town–gown' relations. The Liverpool Guild *Gazette* reflected the former in 1967 when it considered the popular image of students as 'feckless ne'er-do-well's wasting the public's money on wild orgies of self-indulgence', and reported that organized 'community service' by students was rapidly changing the image. Liverpool students were becoming involved in helping to promote racial integration, visiting lonely old people, decorating and gardening for the aged and disabled, constructing an adventure playground in Toxteth, promoting Shelter, and organizing entertainment for the underprivileged and pre-school playgroups [*Gazette* 12 December 1967: 6–7]. The Guild decided in 1969 to establish a Community Services Committee and in following years involvement with the local community was often seen as one of the Guild's priorities. Students at East Anglia had in 1964 created a Voluntary Service Unit, with an aim of breaking down social barriers; by helping, for example, at a local mental home, with meals on wheels, and redecorating a blind old lady's bedroom (all work already begun), the work of VSU could 'help prevent the University from becoming an isolated, narrow-minded community' [*Handbook* 1964–5]. From 1969 at Durham there was tension between support for traditional rag activity and a new form of community action. The Students Representative Council in 1969 simultaneously discussed town–gown relations and moving away from the rag towards community action [Council 15 October 1969]. Into the 1980s Durham students were discussing the need for stronger community links [e.g. Council 20 June 1984, 24 October 1984]. Poor town–gown relations continued at Durham, as at some other university towns, into the 1990s and remained a context for SCA activities (*THES* 18 December 1992: 8) [*Palatinate* 19 November 1993: 1].

The second reason for the growth of community action – as distinct from the more neutral version of 'community service' – was as an offshoot from or alternative to other forms of student activism. Action in Birmingham in 1969, also deliberately moving away from the 'rag' tradition, turned to an analysis of the effects of hypothermia and living conditions among the aged, in Manchester to work with gypsies against harassment and persecution, in Bristol to work for the mentally ill (Barr 1972: *passim*; Holman 1972: 187–94). Such activities were debated within the NUS, leading to the establishment of a pilot NUS Student Community Action running from 1971 to 1974. The NUS was faced with the search for an acceptable definition of community action (having rejected 'service'), that would imply empowering the groups in the community with whom students would work: 'A major task of STUDENT Community action must, therefore, be to struggle against the prevailing values of the academy, which is at the service of those with rather than without power' (Phillips 1974: 1–2). The report on the NUS pilot indicated how students were in fact working with the powerless on, for example, homelessness and housing, illiteracy, claimants and welfare rights, addiction, offenders, and mental health. In Liverpool Student Community Action meshed in with the positive discrimination element in government-funded Urban Aid and Educational Priority Area programmes (*ibid.*: 4–14). The report summarized accounts of SCA activity at ten institutions, including for example, Bangor, Heriot-Watt, Loughborough, Sheffield and a number of colleges of education. Numbers participating in these local groups ranged from 20–30 to 300–500, and included references to camping trips for children, squatters, motorway research, a community relations centre, a community festival, and an overnight shelter for the homeless (*ibid.*: 21–2). Following this report in 1974 the NUS decided to finance a continued SCANUS project with full-time workers. Initial scepticism about NUS involvement with a possibly less than radical movement had been largely overcome. Although local debate about the purposes of action, whether to fill gaps in the welfare services, to 'help', to 'raise consciousness', or to 'promote change', did not disappear, the emphasis was predominantly on working with and improving conditions for the disadvantaged and powerless, but not on reversing the social power structure.

Characteristic of the movement in the 1980s was the Students' Union statement at Brighton Polytechnic that it extended 'its services to the local population. The Community Action Group provides a two-way link between students and less fortunate members of the community: a practical involvement that is highly beneficial to both parties' (Brighton Polytechnic 1985: 88). An article published by the Association of Community Workers, asking 'What has community action to do with students?', surveyed their typical activities 'across an enormous span' – work with the elderly, the mentally handicapped, young children, a PHAB club (for physically handicapped and able-bodied people), prison visiting, work with a welfare rights group or a women's refuge, and links with a variety of local community organizations (Aiken 1984: 2). Plymouth Polytechnic SCA was in the mid-1980s sending delegates to or taking part in working parties on disability awareness, anti-racist action, women in SCA and others, some of these being regional or NUS-organized activities [E/GM/2/86–87]. The tendency, through SCA, for students to work with other community organizations was widespread. In the 1990s Swansea SCA was working closely with many other voluntary organizations in the town and surrounding area (Knight int.). Collaboration with other institutions and organizations was very often initiated by other bodies – at East Anglia, for example, hospitals and Help the Aged, which established the frameworks of student involvement (Patyal int.). Glasgow Student Volunteer Service in 1995–6 had links with well over 100 community organizations, some local, some regional, some Scotland-wide [Annual Report 1995/96]. Community Action at Strathclyde (which had started life in 1967 as Strathclyde Voluntary Service) included among its projects work with the Scottish Association of Youth Clubs, the Greater Glasgow Health Board, Strathclyde Regional Social Work Department, Barnardos, the Samaritans, and fund-raising for Alzheimers Scotland [*Crust* 1980: 12; *CACTUS Project Handbook* 1993–1994]. Many of the SCA groups worked with school tutoring programmes, sponsored locally, by British Petroleum or by Community Service Volunteers.

All of these SCA activities are supported by national networks and a national organization which have replaced the NUS machinery, which was abandoned by NUS in 1977 under financial constraints. An SCA National Committee, SCANC, was set up in 1980, and this in turn established the Student Community Action Development Unit, SCADU, the following year. SCADU provides support services for local groups, circulates information relevant to the voluntary sector, offers consultancy visits, and organizes working groups and conferences – in such fields as women in SCA, anti-racism, disability and community arts. It provides training and education facilities, and is a source of publications and forms of dissemination of experience and good practice in work by student volunteers. It receives core funding from the Voluntary Services Unit of the Home Office, and has received grants and donations from a wide variety of industrial companies and charitable trusts [*SCADU Review 1993–1995*: *passim*; leaflets]. Although the ideological underpinning of the 1960s movement is no longer dominant in SCADU and the local groups, it remains a self-conscious movement, anxious to base volunteering on concerns about the society to which it contributes. SCADU, for example, declares that it aims

> to support students to question their practice: it is not simply an issue of doing, it is also about *how* students do their volunteering. SCADU exists to encourage students to enquire into their values, process and methods of their voluntary activity,

including an awareness of the existence of oppression [*Annual Report 1991–1993*]. All of this has to bear in mind, of course, the difficulties we have considered with regard to students' financial and other preoccupations. Student volunteers are 'much less concerned with radical left-wing politics'. Recruiting volunteers has become more difficult, because of 'student poverty, lack of time, course structures, modularization, [the division of the year into] semesters, and part-time attendance' (Drake int.).

The volunteer movement in American higher education (as well as in high schools) has had features which parallel the movement in the United Kingdom, but has inevitably in some respects been markedly different. A letter to the President of the University of Pennsylvania in the early 1980s, from an 87-year-old correspondent, emphasized that she considered 'one of the most encouraging trends in American life is the rebirth of volunteerism' [Hackney papers, box 129, 1980–3]. This 'rebirth' of an important feature of American life was taking shape significantly and rapidly in education. Campus Compact, driven by the presidents of a number of elite American universities in the mid-1980s, was intended to accelerate the already established trend towards student volunteer activity. Public institutions also became involved, and a survey of Compact campuses in 1986 (67 of 102 responded) showed 10–20 per cent of students taking part in volunteer activities, but within two years the picture had changed. Of 5,100 Yale undergraduates, 2,200 were involved in community service work, and more than 60 per cent of Harvard's students were apparently involved (an increase from 33 per cent in 1983) (Theus 1988: 31). At Penn students had since 1964 been 'quietly engaged in community service projects', including tutoring school students, helping to run hospital emergency rooms and providing companionship for psychiatric patients (Goddard and Koons 1973: 245). From some 400 volunteers in 1967–8, the number had grown to between 1,500 and 2,000 of the 8,700 full-time undergraduates in 1986, and the emphasis had shifted from protest activity to 'social issues, such as homelessness, poverty and educational opportunity' [*Daily Pennsylvanian* 1 August 1968: 5; UPF 8.5 204/10 18 March 1986]. In the mid-1990s there were between 4,000 and 5,000 volunteers, and one of the leaders of the 1960s radical community involvement movement, now Director of Penn's Center for Community Partnerships, describes the change as one from protest to 'a sense of belonging', a student search for a sense of purpose and mission in changed circumstances, from turmoil to group identity and a willingness to act as a bridge to the community (Harkavy int.). The Director of the Program for Student-Community Involvement in 1995 thought that 'the great majority of Penn students are involved in community service, occasional or regular' (Grossman int.).

An important factor in the growth of volunteerism at both high school and higher education levels has sometimes been the built-in requirement of voluntary service for graduation, and the development of courses focused on 'service learning' which carry academic credit. The Center for Community Partnerships at Penn in 1995 listed more than 30 such courses which involved some form of community service, often working with students in various kinds of schools and other aspects of the West Philadelphia urban revitalization programme [CCP 14 March 1995]. Birmingham-Southern College, Alabama, with some 1,500 students, in the mid-1980s had ten students engaged in volunteer activity; this figure rose to over 500 by the end of the decade. At Oberlin College, Ohio, with almost 3,000 students, the numbers participating rose over a two-year period from 59 to over 300 students, and the college had by the end of the 1980s begun to offer credit-bearing courses in such settings as a shelter for the homeless, a battered women's home, and a low-income Hispanic neighbourhood (Levine and Hirsch 1991: 123–4). At Penn State the Assistant Director of Student Activities estimated in 1995 that roughly a quarter of the students were engaged in volunteer activities – and given the geographical location of the university in a rural area of the state, students were engaged in activities as far afield as Harrisburg, or elsewhere during vacations (J.M. Curley int.). The student newspaper had the previous year described community service as 'becoming one of the hottest trends on college campuses across the state – and Penn State is no exception. University organizations have seen a dramatic increase in student volunteers over the past few years.' The paper quoted the Assistant Director: 'In the '80s, students were driven to succeed and to concentrate on their own issues, but we are now seeing students with a broader perspective' [*Weekly Collegian* 2 September 1994: 2].

The American experience was therefore broadly similar to the British in seeing a growth among students during the 1980s and 1990s in particular of forms of social rather than political activism, though an element of the single-issue politics we have discussed has also been present. The kinds of activities undertaken by American student volunteers have been not unlike those undertaken by British students. The activity has been both responsive to social concerns and student-generated (though in the American context with a strong element of co-ordination or support from university or college administration). There are, for reasons we have also discussed in other contexts, important differences between the national role of SCADU and the kind of role played by Campus Compact in the United States. The latter is 'a project of the Education Commission of the States', and there are state-wide organizations run by associations of universities and colleges. In 1993–4 there were nationally 475 member campuses (unlike SCADU, which has member student organizations), and in Pennsylvania the state organization was established by 24 institutions, with an Executive Committee of Member Presidents [Pennsylvania Campus Compact 1994: 1]. In 1992–3 the national Compact estimated that undergraduates at its member campuses contributed some 17 million hours of service, and that 58 per cent of the institutions were providing academic credit for service related to a course (Bearman and Kilgore 1993: 1–2). The growth of student volunteerism in the United States was more dynamic in the 1980s and 1990s than in Britain, but the American movement also had to face limiting factors. Not all campuses with student volunteer organizations were affiliated to the Compact, but the 475 members in 1993–4 represented less than a sixth of the total of four- and two-year colleges and universities. There was a similar growth in the United States of student part-time employment, economic pressure, a need to focus on academic study, and a decrease in commitment to extra-curricular activities (Walker int.). Nevertheless, even taking account of differences in the extent of participation and the reasons for the differences, the involvement is an important indicator of changes in the opinions and attitudes of significant numbers of students. A 1987 Gallup Poll on 100 randomly selected American campuses asked students whether they were involved in any 'charity or social service activities' of various listed kinds, and 35 per cent answered 'yes' (Theus 1988: 28). At a SCADU conference of 140 volunteers in 1995 the students were asked why they volunteered. Small percentages responded in terms of an enjoyable use of free time or promoting equality, 16 per cent wanted to meet new people in the university and the community, 25 per cent wanted to gain transferable skills and experience, and the largest response, 29 per cent, was 'to make a difference, change society, because it is useful, worthwhile and necessary' [SCADU SCA Volunteering report 1996].

8

'Then it's Worse'

Times, conditions and outlooks have changed. An Oxford graduate reflected in 1949 that as an undergraduate he and his fellow students 'hadn't a clue' what the outside world that awaited them would be like (Davies 1949). They simply did not give it a thought, and that was undoubtedly true of very many students in other universities then and in subsequent decades. For most students in the 1980s and 1990s, however, the employment market became a more imminent and harsher reality, of which they were aware much earlier in their student experience. The reality of their condition as students had also profoundly changed. For a recently retired senior adviser of students in a Scottish faculty of science in 1995 the change was clear: students in the 1960s had been 'reasonably well off', because they had their grants and vacation employment, and they would not have thought of taking part-time jobs during term (Thomson int.), the last point being echoed in other interviews. Some mature students in the 1960s and 1970s supplemented their grants with holiday work, 'often going back to our old trades and old employers . . . it took me years after leaving Art college before I earned anything like as much as I had as a student' (McLean 1992: 5). Many mature students, of course, did not have trades to return to, had families, and were under other pressures.

When the NUS gave evidence to the Robbins Committee in 1961 its leaders emphasized how much opposition there was – which they shared – to a vocational trend in higher education, encouraged by industry: 'Many students think that the emphasis on vocational training has now become much too insistent throughout higher education.' Closer links between industry and higher education had, 'in some cases, begun to distort the national pattern of higher education' (NUS 1963: 219, 231). Since the job market was a relatively open one at this time, the emphasis of the NUS and others was on a broad liberal, general and personal education which avoided both specialized and vocational concerns. In these and other respects, especially in the late 1980s and 1990s, students have encountered a basically different situation, in which the impact of the prospective job market and the students' own level of funding has been considerable. 'Hardship' and anxiety about their futures everywhere also became integral vocabularies in students' lives, and their meanings and implications became an incscapable feature of the reality of a large proportion of students. They also grew in importance for those considering whether to enter higher education.

A student counsellor in Wales commented in 1996:

> Students' expectations are different. They have more financial problems. They come in saying 'I'm broke' and they're desperate for financial support. Half of the major problems that come to me have to do with being broke and the throw-back on their lives. Many of them give up. Many of them take at least half-time jobs. Fifteen or so years ago students might take the odd Saturday job, they had benefits, including housing benefit in the vacations, now they have nothing, not even free prescriptions. They're not eating, they're not warm, they get to need more prescriptions ... They don't realize how bad it is before they come, they know former students perhaps for whom it was different. Then there's the Welsh ethic, 'don't borrow'. They don't realize the extent of the bills – their parents used to pay. They are lonely, homesick, they go out and drink, get into debt, and the banks arc only too willing to give them a loan. At the start it doesn't seem too bad, then when they've spent the loan it's worse. They can't afford what they would like to enjoy. Even the ones who don't smoke or drink are not managing. A reporter asked me if they were getting three square meals a day, and I had to explain they are not even getting one. And now the mature student's allowance for new students has been stopped.
>
> (Gowen int.)

In the late 1980s and early 1990s the government withdrew various other benefits, including Income Support and Unemployment Benefit in the shorter vacations and then in the summer vacation. The value of students' grants had been decreasing in real terms from 1979, and from the beginning of the 1990s top-up loans were introduced, followed by a systematic reduction in the level of grants (Deacon 1994; Pilkington 1994). Grants, loans, debt, hardship, part-time jobs and dropping out had become central topics of discussion about and among students. A study of four Welsh institutions of higher education in 1992–3 concluded that though Welsh students were not as much in debt as the UK average,

> they are still considerably in debt. It seemed to affect students regardless of age or sex. Thus debt is as much a part of student life as queuing in the canteen or taking exams. Perhaps student lifestyles to an extent influence debt ... When it comes to a choice between buying 'that textbook' or 'that meal' it is evident which is going to come first. The idea that students can devote their spare time to studying instead of seeking employment is fast becoming a thing of the past.
>
> (Deacon 1994: 44)

A formal government scheme of student loans – distinct from the traditional system of bank loans – was new to British higher education. We are not concerned with its operation and changes, though to many students the scale and conditions of available loans became increasingly important in the balance with other sources of income. Of parallel importance was the balance of students' overall income against the pressures of expenditure, and finally there was the impact on students as students. A survey by the student newspaper at Liverpool in 1992 found that 64 per cent of students were in debt, compared with 52 per cent in 1990 before grants were frozen and loans were introduced [*Gazette* 21 February 1992]. By 1993, some 31 per cent of Deacon's sample of students in Wales had taken out a loan under the scheme (Deacon 1994: 37). A *Guardian*/Gallup survey of over 2,000 final year students in 49 universities in November 1993 found that 32 per cent had top-up loans, and 42 per cent had a bank loan or overdraft – some of these, of course, being the same students. A study of the same sample (1,400 responded) in July 1994 showed figures of 67 per cent and 63 per cent, respectively (*The Guardian*/Gallup vol. 1 1993: 19; vol. 2 1994: 11). A study at the University of Newcastle in 1992 found that 57 per cent owed money either to student loan companies, banks and credit agencies, or to friends and relatives: 'the percentage of students with debts rose from forty per cent among students in their first year to sixty-six per cent of those in their second year and eighty per cent of those in their third year, even though each of these years was only a third advanced at the time of the survey' (McCarthy and Humphrey 1995: 82). In 1993, 13 per cent of second year students and 29.8 per cent of students at Sheffield had debts between £1,001 and 2,000 [SUSU 1993: 3]. The *Guardian*/Gallup survey asked students how they felt about their living standards. Those 'living comfortably' on their present finances represented 14 per cent of the sample, 37 per cent were 'coping', 31 per cent were 'finding it difficult' and 18 per cent were 'finding it very difficult' (*The Guardian*/Gallup vol. 1 1993: 18).

Substantial numbers of students are resistant to taking out large loans, or loans at all. Of Deacon's Welsh sample in 1993, 69 per cent had taken out no loan. Of these about half at that time did not need one (for example, because of parental support), and 28 per cent relied on part-time work or did not believe in loans (Deacon 1994: 37). As the level of grant was cut, the numbers of students taking out loans, and the amount borrowed, also increased. By 1995–6 the grant had been cut to £2,340 for students living in London, and £1,885 for students living elsewhere (less for those living at home). In 1996 half of students eligible applied for loans, and those who did were graduating with an average debt estimated by Barclays Bank to be £2,293 (Jones 1996: 31). The average conceals wide disparities. The NUS had the previous year calculated that the average spent on accommodation in London was £1,857 over a 38-week term, the figure outside London being £1,516. Some halls of residence costs were much higher. Food averaged roughly £1,000, with transport costs varying between £610 in London and an average of £185 elsewhere (Hunter 1995: 33). These three items, plus leisure, were the largest items of expenditure, with accommodation accounting for by far the greatest share. Expenditure on drink came third, after that on food. What Deacon calls 'student lifestyles' do, of course, influence the levels of expenditure and debt, and participation in student leisure activities in the available venues for socialization does, as we have seen earlier, represent an important element in student life. In Britain and the United States, as we have also seen, drink has traditionally been a component of the transition to the ambiguous status of studenthood. The stresses associated with students' changed contexts, on and off campus, also feature in this and other aspects of students' leisure activities.

The profile of students' lives as affected by changes in their current finances and future expectations has attracted such press descriptions as 'Bachelor of debts' (Insley 1995: 8). The University of Glasgow's Director of Residential, Catering and Business Services told a conference in 1994 that the University needed

> to come to terms with the changing culture in which students find themselves – we need to come to terms with the culture of debt and the effects of student poverty on the one hand, and the widening gap between rich and poor students on the other, on academic performance and educational opportunities.
>
> (Johnson 1994)

One Scottish students' union president in 1993 described student poverty as being 'out of control' (McLaughlin int.). Student hardship has become a complex issue. It has, with increasing conviction on the part of students' union officers, university welfare personnel, vice-chancellors and others, become a central part of the description of large numbers of students. Poorer students are described as deterred from entering, or there is a 'widening gap' among students, or they are found to be missing meals, or responding uncertainly and unhappily to a problematic and unexpected situation. Those in need have in the 1980s and 1990s often found it difficult to ask for money from parents who were themselves confronting problems of redundancy or other financial pressures, and did not realize students' economic and social situation. The impact is seen clearly by institutional and students' union welfare services, and there is no doubt from the institutions visited that the increase in hardship-related problems encountered by these services has outstripped the rise in overall student numbers. Welfare services have more and more faced the effects of 'real student poverty' (Phelps int.), in nutritional or mental health terms, inability to cope with course demands and financial worries, directly or indirectly expressed. Vice-chancellors and university and college senior boards and committees were in the mid-1990s publicly voicing their concern about student poverty and its effects, and a CVCP deputation to the Secretary of State in 1995, led by the Vice-Chancellor of Oxford Brookes University, 'expressed deep concern about the financial hardship faced by many students in general and disappointment that the Government had done nothing to address this problem' [Oxford Brookes On Stream 5 December 1995: 1]. Many of the students affected struggled through to graduation, while others dropped out of higher education. The CVCP reported in January 1996 that 54,000 first year students had already left their courses, 10 per cent more than in the previous year, and almost 60 per cent of these had left for 'non-academic reasons'. Students from underprivileged backgrounds and mature students were most likely to leave their courses (Jones 1996: 31; Richards and Thomson 1996: 1). Finances are not the only 'non-academic' reason for dropping out in the first or other years, but the connection was perceived at all levels of higher education as a real one. One pro-vice-chancellor offered a perspective by suggesting that many students had never had enough money, and the position was 'only worse'. In his time as a student, on a full grant, he had felt he was 'doing all right', but the change was now very marked: 'students' financial problems are really acute'. Dropping out in the 1960s was 'unheard of', but now it happened (Lloyd int.).

Closely allied to issues of debt and hardship, as the value and level of grants fell during the 1980s and 1990s, was the rapid increase in part-time paid work in term time. The figures vary but are consistently high. In Wales in 1992–3, 38 per cent of full-time students undertook paid employment (Deacon 1994: 38), and at Oxford Brookes 57 per cent did so regularly during term, reflecting what its Vice-Chancellor called 'a widespread national phenomenon' (Booth 1993: 1). Barclays Bank estimated that 14 per cent of new students in 1995 had part-time jobs for an average of 11 hours a week *in their first term* (Jones 1996: 31). The Union Treasurer at the University of Wales Swansea described in 1966 the 'enormous number of enquiries for part-time work at the bar' (Cawdell int.). A survey of students at Strathclyde in 1992 found 27 per cent of students with a term-time job (90 per cent had tried to obtain a summer job and 62 per cent had succeeded) [*Strathclyde Telegraph* 15 September 1992]. The number of hours of paid work undertaken by students also varied considerably, but the range of 15–20 hours a week is perhaps the most common, with some working 25 or more. In December 1993 at Queen Margaret College students in applied consumer studies were described as being 'broke at this time of year, were working extra time at supermarkets etc., working unsociable hours . . . two mature students are working overnight in an old people's home' (Galloway int.).

The effects of this increase in part-time jobs have been marked. At Oxford Brookes the conclusion reached by the research was that these students 'tend to get poorer marks as a result, and that over 250 each year could be gaining a degree one class lower than they deserve' (Booth 1993: 1). Those students working evenings and particularly at weekends at Queen Margaret College were unable to take advantage of IT facilities (Galloway int.), and students sometimes changed their electives to fit in with their employment patterns (Baldwin int.). Students' voluntary activities at Strathclyde had declined because of part-time work (Day int.). In an informal survey at Swansea Institute staff quoted students as acknowledging that 'their work had considerable effect on their studies' and 'a number of students have identified the impact of part-time work on their studies. We find that a large number of students are unable to give their studies the required effort outside classes' [Academic Quality Unit 1996]. A lecturer in the Department of Politics at the University of Leeds received a note from a student in 1995:

'I write to inform you of the reasons for my absence from the past two tutorials. Due to financial struggles I took a part-time job on Monday nights causing myself to be in an extreme state of tiredness the following day. The matter has now been rectified in that I have been allowed to change my nights of work.' During the day I have seen three other students about their poor attendance and in each case the reasons given have been financial difficulty leading to the taking up of casual work to make ends meet. In two cases young men are working three or four nights a week till 3.30 am, with consequent effects on their performance.

These were well-motivated, bright students with 'exemplary' school records, 'stressed and close to tears' (Charlton 1995: 30). These situations do not apply to all students – it is probable, for example, that fewer students on teacher education courses take part-time employment, though some certainly do. The extent of the practice is influenced not only by the social and economic position of students, but also by the availability of part-time work – on and off campus. Some universities or students' unions in the 1990s began to establish part-time job agencies, recognizing the inescapable need of some students, though some staff – including the writer of the above letter – have argued that this is an abdication of responsibility for the students' education.

High levels of part-time employment among full-time students have for a long time been a feature of much American higher education. A survey of 400 students attending a meeting of the National Student Association in 1965 found that 56 per cent of them worked for an average of 14 hours a week, their most likely jobs being office clerk, food service worker, sales clerk, tutor or instructor's assistant, library assistant [Penn UPF 8.5 202/1 February 1966: 43]. In the mid-1980s it was estimated that nationally approximately 40 per cent of full-time college students 'work at some sort of job for an average of 20 hours a week' (summer jobs were excluded from the calculation) (Newman 1985: 71, 186). In 1988, 60–70 per cent of undergraduates were reported as having part-time jobs, this being described as the 'major detractor' from a full experience of college (McCartan 1988: 11), and a research summary two years later set out the following analysis of the American position:

- More traditional college students – full-time students aged 16 to 24 – are working today than 15 or 20 years ago. The proportion has risen significantly from 35 per cent in 1972 to 46.5 per cent in 1988.
- Sixty-two per cent of students of all ages are working.
- Full-time students who are employed are working on average 20

hours a week. Almost one out of five is working 30 hours or more, and one out of 10 is working 35 hours or more, the equivalent of a full-time job.

• Traditional college-age students tend to be clustered in food service, sales and clerical jobs rather than technical or professional positions.

The most significant increase was with regard to female students – from 39 per cent in 1972 to 56 per cent in 1988 (Hexter 1990: 1–2). These figures are not always directly comparable – for example, students on 'co-operative' or 'work/study' programmes are sometimes included, and in one case above the figures include older high school students. What is clear, however, is that the figures are generally accompanied partly by an acknowledgement of the value of the experience gained, but equally by faculty complaints that students' jobs have an adverse effect on studies and extra-curricular activities: 'job schedules constrain a teacher's ability to confer with students out of class, to arrange field trips or group projects, even to count on student time in the library' (McCartan 1988: 11). It is difficult to relate the American experience to the more recent British trend for a number of reasons. The motivation is not always the same – Newman suggests, for example, that the percentage working is roughly the same for all family income categories up to about $50,000 a year (Newman 1985: 71). Not only for reasons to do with part-time employment, though significantly so, large percentages of American students do not graduate within 'normal' time-frames, drop out and later re-enter, or never graduate. The existence of part-time jobs on campus is not only part of the campus culture, but has also been promoted in the past by federal grants to help provide such jobs for students from low-income families. It is arguable that British students are entering a similar campus culture to one long familiar to American students, but at all levels of British higher education the trend has been identified with the deteriorating financial position of students, and its impact on the students' studies and campus lives. Universities, complained one union officer, are fully aware of students' money worries, but do not recognize sufficiently 'the effect on student life' (Cawdell int.).

Discussions of student stress couple these issues concerning finance with those concerning anxieties about degree results and future jobs or access to postgraduate courses. There has been an important change in this respect since the 1970s and early 1980s, when graduate employment prospects were already becoming more difficult. In 1984 the President of the NUS, discussing attacks on the level of grants, confronted the existing (but not necessarily the continuing) passivity of students:

Today's students worry about their degrees because they had to fight to get into college in the first place, at a time when demand for higher education is at record levels. And they worry about their future prospects because students can no longer be sure of a well-paid job at the end of three years, with graduate unemployment running at around 10 per cent during recent years and graduate earning prospects lower than ever in real terms.

(Woolas 1984: 53)

The changes since 1984 include the opening of access, but also concerns in the 1990s about entering the culture of debt and for students in higher education the fight to stay. An awareness of fluctuations in the employment market has become a more permanent feature of the student outlook. This awareness of itself does not necessarily mean a level of serious study, since it is possible to turn aside from the anxiety and treat the undergraduate experience as an 'unreal' period to be enjoyed while it lasts. Coupled with the other kinds of difficulty we have discussed, however, this has generally not proved to be the case. What we have witnessed in various ways in this discussion is the emergence of a stronger pressure to achieve, a deeper concern about qualifying in a way which will ensure employment and a career. Two findings in the *Guardian*/Gallup survey are of interest. First, 71 per cent of students thought they had a 'very good' (13 per cent) or 'fairly good' (58 per cent) chance of obtaining a job they wanted when leaving university. Twenty-four per cent thought the prospect 'fairly poor' or 'very poor' (2 per cent already had a job). The largest category, 'fairly good', may conceal a wide variety of levels of optimism, wishful thinking or anxiety. The interesting second finding, however, is that 73 per cent (very close to the previous 'very good'-plus-'fairly good' total) expected to graduate with a first or upper second class degree. None expected to fail (*The Guardian* vol. 1, 1993: 7, 9). It may be surmised that there is a connection between these two findings, with students working seriously enough for a good degree to expect or hope this to be a passport to reasonable employment. Students 'spend more time on course work, they can't afford to mess about, the degree is not an open door' (Cawdell int.).

Getting 'their head down', taking their studies seriously, 'working hard and playing hard', and all the other similar judgements reported in previous chapters, are not unrelated to these findings, to the focus on succeeding, given fewer jobs, more graduates and a depressed or uncertain graduate employment market. Whether struggling to enter or to stay in higher education, the outcome has been similar. As the Students' Association at Heriot-Watt put it in 1985, when a place at university was becoming 'more valuable, students tend to work much harder and longer with the remainder of their time spent in purely social pursuits, rather than organisational activities' (Eight Scottish University Student Bodies 1985: 46). It was becoming more important to finish, not to fail, to do reasonably well. Modular and semesterized structures intensified the pressures. A high percentage knew that they needed to work for a good degree. Over the time-scales we have discussed, and paradoxically in spite of the problems, American commentators have also frequently alluded to an increased commitment by many students to achieving, in order to obtain the grades, the final outcomes and therefore the well-rewarded jobs to which they have aspired. In 1978, reflecting on changes over the previous decade, 24 per cent of college presidents thought students 'serious about their studies' and another 14 per cent thought them simply 'more serious' (Stadtman 1980: 22). In a discussion of attempts to reintroduce forms of *in loco parentis* in the late 1980s and early 1990s, new hall of residence restrictions on overnight guests formed part of the analysis, and the University of South Carolina was asked if institutions were trying to control morality? A spokesperson answered: 'part of it is prompted by today's students, who are much more serious. They are looking for an academically conducive environment' (Thomas 1991: 36). In the United States, as in the United Kingdom, it is difficult to generalize on this as on other issues, but there are strong grounds for seeing the 1980s and 1990s as a time when, with their motivation shaped by a number of important social and economic factors, students encountered the increased stresses of changed lives and pressures to achieve.

Reference needs to be made, finally in this connection, to two aspects of student 'seriousness' in the 1980s and 1990s, the first of which applies with greater force to the United States. A by-product of a number of factors, but most recently including the pressures we have discussed, has been the growth of plagiarism and other forms of cheating. The history of American higher education is peppered with discussions of cheating, often in the nineteenth century treated by students as part of an unceasing battle against their teachers; Veysey remarks on 'the widespread persistence of cheating in examinations, with little sense of personal wrongdoing', with a black market in written themes that was 'a major industry' (Veysey 1970: 299). Only in the early twentieth century did the Yale faculty try to clamp down on cheating, 'which had always been considered by the students a perfectly legitimate way to stay in college' (Kelley 1974: 311–12). Cheating, including at some of the most prestigious American institutions, has become a prominent public issue in the 1980s and 1990s particularly, and American institutions and student organizations have addressed it directly, primarily through the development of 'honor codes' or codes of academic integrity. At Bucknell University, a private university in Pennsylvania, for example, the Student Government drew up a 'Student Code of Conduct', which was to 'be a student created document', and the aim was to 'have all cases judged by a board of students, [and] assure that all cases are treated on an equal basis, with a clear definition of possible penalties'. Students signing the code pledged 'to uphold the principles of academic honesty' [SG Student Affairs Committee (1987–8)].

The Penn example of a university Code identifies as academic dishonesty: cheating ('using unauthorized aids'), plagiarizing, fabricating information, multiple submission of a piece of work for credit in more than one course, and writing a paper for someone else. The Code emphasizes student and faculty responsibility for adhering to 'the highest standards of truth and honesty' [*Almanac* 30 March 1993: 3]. Penn's experience of cheating in the 1970s and 1980s was persistent. The alumna who wrote to the University in 1976 about her experiences was forthright:

There is flagrant cheating in courses. Term papers are bought. People cheat outrightly in tests. Fraternities are said to keep old papers on file for their members to 'refer' to. This is a difficult problem to deal with. One ruthless way, which other schools have used (Princeton), is to have a severe honor code which holds a student who does not report another student who cheats punishable. Thus, students like myself who knew of other students cheating, but felt guilty about reporting them, would feel obligated to do so.

[A4 348/7 Mitchell 8 January 1976]

In 1988 the Student Committee on Undergraduate Education produced a report on *Academic Integrity at Penn*. It described the lack of academic integrity as resulting from 'a variety of culprits including society's current emphasis on credentials and grades as opposed to education and knowledge, the general moral ills of the 1980's, and students' self-imposed academic pressure'. A SCUE poll had shown that 46.1 per cent of undergraduates surveyed had 'personally observed someone violate the Code of Academic Integrity'. A narrow majority of students were aware of the existence of the Code, most believed it to be ineffective, and only 55.3 per cent had read it. Fifty-two per cent of students surveyed thought that 'it is easy to cheat at the University'. Fifty-eight per cent (described as a 'heartening result') thought that the student body should 'have some authority to discipline cheaters'. All of this highlighted 'the severe nature of the academic integrity problem at the University'. The report suggested five possible categories of students who cheat – 'chronic cheaters who perpetually con the system'; those who cheated because of 'their own grade-competitiveness and time constraints'; some who simply did not know that action such as plagiarism was cheating; others who 'cannot think of a compelling reason not to do so'; and those who had 'no respect for the professor or found the subject not worthwhile' [UPS 58, SCUE 1988].

Penn's experience was no different from that of many other universities, including the most prestigious. Studies in the 1970s showed that, for example, 30 per cent of undergraduates at Stanford had cheated at least once; 43 per cent at Amherst had cheated on an examination or paper; 30 per cent at Johns Hopkins had cheated by their senior year (the University had an honor code); and 50–60 per cent at Dartmouth College and the University of Michigan had violated their honor codes at least once (Levine 1980: 66–7). There is no need here to go into the varied and imaginative ways of cheating used in these and other institutions. The important point was made in an analysis of student life in 28 American institutions shortly after these reports:

if there is one area in which students are in total agreement, it is the observation that academic dishonesty on campus is widespread. Perhaps more surprisingly, much of the cheating is done quite openly, without shame or guilt and with little fear of repercussions.

(DeCoster and Mable 1981: 30)

A historian of American campus life presented a slightly different picture in 1987:

> Students report mixed feelings about cheating. On the one hand, it violates the code of fair play among them: the cheater creates an unfair advantage for himself vis-a-vis other students, especially serious when grading is on a curve. Yet some also admire one who wrests a high grade from a professor. Cheating, in fact, only extends the normal transaction of the classroom. A few dramatic cases have surfaced in which students have stolen exams from professors' offices or trash baskets, but students find legal channels to achieve the same ends. Files of back exams, once the guarded treasures of fraternity houses, are, in this more democratic age, kept by counseling centers.
>
> (Horowitz 1987: 270)

Whatever the motives or morality involved, the point here is that they have been at least exacerbated by the competitive environment, and the perceived need to succeed by whatever means.

The extent of cheating in British universities and colleges is not similarly documented, and it is the particular example of plagiarism which is most often identified as a problem, though it is likely that traditional institutional and degree structures have minimized it. It has not surfaced as a significant feature of the campuses visited for this study, and the literature of British higher education reveals little in the way of evidence. Minor plagiarism in course assignments has generally been dealt with under course and institutional procedures, and more serious cases have surfaced at examination boards and in consultation with external examiners. One senior administrator thought that given the 'pressures to achieve there is more plagiarism', but elsewhere it was seen as a rare occurrence. Course documentation regularly explains to students what plagiarism is and warns against it, and in many cases universities and colleges underline the importance of the issue in their student handbooks. The University of Plymouth, for instance, has a Code of Practice on the Prevention of Academic Dishonesty, which emphasizes that the University and external bodies 'see any academic dishonesty as a serious offence'. The list of dishonest practices includes trying to obtain an advance copy of an unseen examination, plagiarizing by copying someone else's work or not acknowledging it, falsifying data, sitting an examination on behalf of another student, copying from another student during an examination or taking notes, scripts or other material into it [*Student Handbook 1995/96*: 5]. The University of North London tells students: 'Work which is submitted for assessment must be your own and unaided; copying from the work of another student, from a book or article is an assessment offence, and will be treated seriously' [*Student Guide 1995*: 8]. The warnings and the temptations have existed in British institutions as in the United States, and growth in the scale and complexity of courses, as well as in the pressures we have discussed, may have contributed to some increase in the problem. It has not normally been perceived as 'widespread'.

The second issue relating to student 'seriousness' is that of course relevance, since students' choice and perception of courses and employment-related interests and activities mesh in with other aspects of their lives as students. These issues have become more prominent for large numbers of students, though for students in professional areas the employment relationship of their studies has always been a real one. The relationship ranges from the explicit preparation of students for specific, regulated forms of employment, to various kinds of diffuse links with employment, and to courses which are not designed in relation to employment needs but may produce characteristics important to employers (Burnhill and McPherson 1983: 255–6; Silver and Brennan 1988: 41–52). The 'vocational' has always been a confused concept, and students outside the most rigidly regulated category have often had ambivalent attitudes towards it. Preparation for the 'liberal' professions, if perceived as vocational preparation at all, has historically had a different status from that for practical and other 'occupations'. 'Vocationalism' came to be interpreted almost inevitably as 'narrow' vocationalism, and associated in higher education with pressures to provide human resources for industry, commerce and the newer professions. Student resistance to excessive emphasis on specialization and preparation for employment was expressed, as we have seen, to the Robbins Committee, though there were, and still are, considerable subject differences. In 1970 at the universities of Sussex and Essex 'physical science students showed most tendency to favour specialist approaches, and students in literature, languages and the humanities were most favourable to broader educational ideals' (Oxtoby and Smith 1970: 98–9). An extensive study across higher education in 1969–73 showed students of English to have 'no doubt that their subject was non vocational and they were happy with that', and students in business studies and mechanical engineering – however disappointed with the content of their courses – were focused, in the former case, on the 'occupational benefits', and in the latter case on certification (Brennan and Percy 1976: 138–41). The impact of developments from the 1970s was to blur, or at least to attempt to blur, the distinctions between the vocational and the non-vocational.

British and American institutions responded to the changing situation by increasing the vocational choices and content available to students. In the UK in some cases this might mean access to (or a requirement of) employment-relevant modules, most commonly in information technology. Many institutions, faculties and courses also moved to a greater emphasis on employability, skills and competences, and capability, in an effort to extend subject areas of all kinds into the development of students' personal transferable skills. Numeracy, communication skills, working in groups, problem-solving, keyboard skills, were no longer the prerogative of a particular range of subjects, or of preparation for particular employments. Student resistance to 'the vocational' began in the 1980s and 1990s to be replaced by an acceptance of 'personal development' as an integral part of programmes of study. There was at the same time the appearance in students' unions of an interpretation of their activities in general, and their training activities in particular, as important development opportunities for students, additional to what formal academic programmes could offer. Hence the interest in some places in recognizing in some way the developmental experience of students as organizers, representatives or community activists. The Enterprise in Higher Education programme, announced in 1987, had a variety of implications for students which relate to this whole area of student 'seriousness'.

Under the programme successfully bidding institutions of higher education were being offered up to £1 million each spread over five years. The government's aim was to encourage the production of graduates who wanted to work in industry and who had 'developed a flair for enterprise'. The Manpower Services Commission launched the initiative 'to develop more enterprising graduates, who are aware of the needs of industry and commerce, who have had some direct experience of the world of work and who will leave higher education better prepared for adult and working life' (quoted in Richards 1987: 3). The programme as interpreted and implemented by universities and colleges reflected those objectives, though in ways which had not been forecast. Much of the EHE-supported activity focused on curriculum change and the involvement of employers but much also related to other aspects of students' lives on and off campus – student representative training, community action, film production, publishing, support for careers education, equal opportunities, multi-site students' union co-ordination, and so on. The emphasis, including through the appointment in many institutions of student enterprise managers, was on active student involvement in a variety of ways. The Enterprise Development Officer at the University of Glasgow, summarizing the experience of the first 11 EHE institutions, commented that 'there have always been enterprising students, just as there always will be apathetic students. But there is a change in the air – a significant shift in balance, as students become more active participants in higher education' (Sinclair 1993: 18). Student enterprise managers and others talked frequently about the impact of EHE on 'changing student culture', 'student participation' and 'empowering students'. EHE at Cheltenham and Gloucester published a report on EHE and Student Empowerment, based on experience at universities and colleges where student profiling, student tutoring in schools, training and other activities were expressly connected with the concept of student empowerment alongside aspects of curricular and other innovation (Cheltenham and Gloucester [1994]).

Enterprise activities at the University of Liverpool included funding to survey the needs and aspirations of mature students; funding for halls of residence students and staff to produce a video on 'opportunities available for personal development outside the curriculum'; a production of Shaffer's *Equus* by students and townspeople, for performance in local venues, as well as workshops in schools; support for a Student Community Action training programme for its management team and volunteers; and a project working with local advice agencies and Guild of Students officers to provide information on safer drinking, drug-taking and sex, with the long-term aim of setting up a working party of volunteers to monitor trends in the student population. A 'Students and the Community' week of activities supported by EHE included art exhibitions and workshops, with local artists, poetry readings and concerts, aimed at breaking down barriers between students and the local community [EHE *Annual Report* 1992–3: 5–6; 1993–5: Appendix 5; *Networks* March 1994].

At the University of Humberside the Enterprise Unit ran skills workshops on leadership development, assertiveness skills, how to find vacation work, group work, working in committees, time management and coping with conflict. Enterprise at the University of Central Lancashire decided to focus on 'personal development planning' as a major theme, and when the University validated an Enterprise elective on 'Planning your career' it immediately attracted 200 second year students. The aims of Enterprise at this university included the following: 'All higher education programmes will enable students to acquire and develop enterprise skills including a capacity to solve problems and implement solutions with confidence, flexibility and imagination', and 'There will be a significant shift towards student-centred learning' [*Annual Review 1992–3*: 8, 11, 16]. Here as elsewhere 'empowering students' was made an explicit and major theme, and 'student-centred learning' was already at this stage becoming a central feature of Enterprise planning and activity, nationally. The Enterpise Centre at the University of Edinburgh established a Student Executive Group to be responsible for a separate budget, allocating funds for student projects up to a maximum of £500 per project. As a result, from five student-led projects in the first three years, 14 were funded in the first six months of the fourth year. These included publications; 'vocational skills', for example, through holding a Scottish Student Video Festival, an Amateur Radio Society and theatre workshops; and a range of other activities. Guidance packs and training materials were produced for class representatives, some 200 of whom attended three training sessions in 1992. A project was developed to place students in local community agencies, of benefit to departments, the agencies and the students themselves [*Focus* nos 15, 17, 22, 1993; *Annual Report* 1991–2: 9].

In three rounds of funding, 56 EHE contracts were issued, involving 67 institutions (some contracts were with consortia) (Wright 1992: 205–6). In each annual report institutions had to indicate, among other data, how many students had been involved. In some cases, as with student-led projects, the extent of the involvement is clear. In others, as with changes in curriculum content, the development of profiles and records of achievement, and 'student-centred learning' developments, the extent of the involvement is not always clear. 'Empowerment' meant different things, and although some students' union resistance to EHE on the basis of its initial rhetoric did not disappear, Student Enterprise and Enterprise units generally, as at Liverpool and Edinburgh, worked well with students' unions and their sub- or related bodies, particularly Student Community Action. EHE has in many ways introduced or strengthened what have become continuing features of students' academic and campus life.

Neither Enterprise nor part-time employment, vocational choices nor the pressures of hardship, did affect all students, or those whom they affected equally. They are indicative of changes, some of them major changes for many, in students' perceptions of their roles and possibilities, their culture and identities, in the 1980s and 1990s particularly. Much of what we have described and discussed for earlier decades remained, but what it meant to be a student was no longer quite the same.

9

'Community'?

We have been concerned in this book with establishing a topography of students, their lives and roles. In addition to reflecting on this endeavour, we need to return to two other themes. The first of these is the relationship of students to their university or college 'community' – a discussion embedded in our consideration, for example, of students as 'adolescents' and questions of representation. The second theme is concerned with the images, metaphors or models of students which have pervaded our entire discussion – what it has meant and means to be a student.

In exploring the changing situation, experience and responses of students over recent decades we have largely bypassed their programmes of study, what and how they learn, requirements and choices, assessment, outcomes – all of which are changing aspects of being a student. Being a student, however, has always meant something more, and we have focused on aspects of the 'something more'. It has always been this that has framed images of and attitudes towards students – whether, over decades and centuries, those of growing up, asserting privileges and freedoms, resisting and opposing, leading or following cultural, social and political trends, or visibly taking maximum advantage of an ambiguous 'interim' before independence. Our picture of what has gone into being a student since the 1960s is not everyone's picture. Our focus has been British, but we have called on the help of American sources for various reasons. The boundaries of studenthood are not national, and at our starting point in the late 1960s American student experience had enormous international resonance. American higher education is also more self-analytical, better documented, and though it is different in so many ways there are important parallels, and the accumulation of information and analysis and opinion provides guidelines, if not for conclusions, at least for reflection.

The dangers in drawing our kind of topography are many. Pennsylvania is not Massachusetts or California. We have constructed maps without engaging with many serious controversies – other people's maps. In some cases we have not just disregarded them, we have rejected them. Let us take an American example. In 1968 Jacques Barzun, prominent cultural historian and commentator on education, drew a relatively understanding, even

sympathetic, picture of mid-1960s students rebelling against the university
(Barzun 1968: ch. 3). The following year he published a critical and start-
lingly clear exposé of students, who were projecting the university back to
the Middle Ages:

> by organizing hatred . . . by assaulting and imprisoning their teachers,
> dividing faculties into factions, turning weak heads into cowards and
> demagogues, ignoring the grave and legitimate causes for reform, ad-
> vocating the bearing of arms on campus, and preferring 'confronta-
> tion' to getting their own way, hostile students have ushered in the
> reactionary university of the future, medieval model.
>
> (reprinted in Barzun 1991: 191)

Reprinting that essay, Barzun added a new essay and more than two decades of anger at these continuing features of American higher education.
It is important to convey the full tenor of the argument, which begins:

> It can be assumed that many of the college-bound arrive on cam-
> pus with other things in mind than to drink and take drugs, cheat on
> exams, and commit gang rapes, though they soon come across oppor-
> tunities as well as examples of such behavior. But other forms of self-
> expression that have little to do with education also exist, and these
> become part of the student's life as spectator or participant, because
> condoned and often encouraged by the authorities . . . This worsened
> state of the campus is familiar to every concerned parent and every
> reader of the news. A law in Wisconsin requires every college to inform
> prospective students of its crime rate for the preceding year. But be-
> fore this battlefield condition became general, guerrilla attitudes had
> set in. The first casualty was free speech. Whether members of the
> faculty or guest speakers, persons known or supected of harboring the
> wrong views on the issues of the day were denied a hearing, often in
> tumultuous and offensive fashion.

This was a form of democracy that worked 'by verbal onslaught and physical
disruption, the small group coercing the large community into submission'.
From Dartmouth to Berkeley what was satisfied was 'malice, vanity, revenge,
and kindred feelings. The Montagues and Capulets were at least paying
each other back for the death of relatives.' The weapons were vandalism,
demands for resignations, sit-ins and strikes, group slurs, 'imputed inequality
of treatment – outcroppings of Chauvinism, male and female, black and
white, sex type A and sex type B' (Barzun 1991: 177–8). Barzun's specific
examples are real enough, but his overall topography is the product of a
hysterical attempt to present it as the only important guide to the contemporary campus and its students. Other attacks on political correctness have
done something similar, and there have been other ways of presenting a
disturbing picture of the modern American student, notably that of Bloom
in *The Closing of the American Mind*, with its explicit sub-title *How Higher*

Education Has Failed Democracy and Impoverished the Souls of Today's Students (Bloom 1987).

A Committee on University Life at the University of Pennsylvania acknowledged the existence of problems and reported that

> institutions of higher learning across the United States are troubled by what they see as the 'declining quality of campus life', by proliferating incidents of racial and sexual harassment, bigotry and incivility, by a disappearance of the community that serves, at least in retrospect, to have characterized American universities of an earlier era.

In more measured terms than those of Barzun, the Committee related these incidents to the racial polarization and economic inequality of American society, and the fragmentation of universities and student life. A diverse student population was 'overwhelmed and often threatened by the scale and unfamiliarity of campus society' and retreated into groups 'that reproduce their own backgrounds and special interests'. The issue was not the 'incidents' but the difficulty of building community in a diverse society on and off the campus. It was not the incidents that were common, but the trend for a 'genuinely diverse community life' to become 'fragmentation and separation that does little to mitigate the sense of unfamiliarity, insecurity and, often, marginality that many of its members feel' [*Almanac* 16 October 1990: 5]. Carnegie studies of *Campus Life* and *College: The Undergraduate Experience in America* (Carnegie 1987; 1990) conveyed none of Barzun's focus or animus.

The point is not that there is no truth in Barzun's picture and that 'political correctness' pressures and incidents of the kind that anger him do not occur, but that his picture is unrecognizable in the United States as a general statement, and on British campuses it reflects nothing but the rarest and most isolated examples. His problem is not unlike ours. Who is left out of the picture? Is this *the* picture? What is 'typical', worth mentioning or emphasizing? How deep do attitudes run? Barzun has, however, chosen a way of presenting a map that cannot be reconciled with the way we have chosen. His generalizations about the 'state of the campus', 'the students' life', and the large community 'under submission' contain threads of reality presented as the whole tapestry. We can make passing reference to such an onslaught, but cannot incorporate it. Our silence on some other kinds of map drawn in Britain and the United States may indicate something similar, or more likely – as we believe – that most writers on higher education have either nothing to say about students or nothing on a level that can be easily related to their lives and roles.

In the American sources on which we have drawn we have, however, found work with which it has been important to engage. There are many examples in the literature on 1960s student activism, picturing students in relation to the scale and nature of their institutions, that are relevant to the situation of British students as their institutions of the 1980s and 1990s have begun to look more like their American counterparts. A vivid example is the report of a commission at Berkeley which in 1965–6 looked, among other things, at 'the challenging conditions of size and scale that confront our university community'. It approached the question by describing aspects of the student body, one of the largest and most diverse in the United States. In 1965 there were nearly 27,000 students, including 10,000 graduates. Two-thirds were men, and over 2,000 were from abroad. Students were divided among 14 schools and colleges and faced the complexity 'inherent in the organization and purpose of the University'. After four years, of the more than 12,000 students in the College of Letters and Science who entered in 1961, half had left. Of those who did graduate, 38 per cent had done half or more of their work in other institutions. Amidst this enormous turnover of students on campus, new students did not find a 'tight-knit college community'. Of the 30 per cent of students living more than ten minutes' walk away from the campus most spent between two and six hours a week commuting. Their pattern of life was like 'going to a daily job':

> In such a large student body with widely scattered residences and a high rate of turnover, it is hardly suprising that many students feel alone in a community of strangers. In the April 1965 survey, almost two thirds of the students felt the University to be an 'impersonal institution' . . . A dearth of close student contacts has its effect on the informal intellectual life of the campus . . . Many Berkeley students find their friendships limited to a few intimates. For many of those who remain at the University, solitude or social intercourse with a few associates, which began as a necessity, ends by becoming a way of life . . . a unified college community cannot be found here.

These conditions had given rise to the popularity of the 'factory' metaphor – the University did not fit students' expectations of what a college should be, 'and in their disappointment, they find "factory" an apt description . . . where identical articles are mass-produced and workers are treated impersonally' (University of California at Berkeley 1968: 12–16). British students do not yet drop out or transfer to the same extent as in this picture, but in increasing numbers they transfer within large institutions with modular structures, at the end of each module. At the beginning of every semester they encounter a crowd of new faces, there is little opportunity for sustained intellectual life, they have little or no real contact with tutors or other academic staff, they migrate to accommodation, may have few intimates and commute. Students in many institutions, old and new, 'do not feel that this is a university, it is not what they expected' (R. Watson int.). The cameo picture of Berkeley students in the mid-1960s is not unlike that of British students in the mid-1990s. The Berkeley report emphasizes that the experience was unlike that in small colleges, and the same is true in the British case, though with closures and amalgamations the number of small colleges declined dramatically from the mid-1970s.

    Our discussion has also pointed to a paradox which emerges from the considerable differences in student constituencies, backgrounds and responses to changed campus, financial and other contexts. Bloom and other critics of American higher education present a picture of students with inferior academic background, poor understanding of the purpose of higher education, a lack of interest in books, no literary or classical tradition, a lack of commitment to learning outside the prescribed curriculum and texts, immersion in the musical and other fashions of popular culture, and an inability to establish other than superficial relationships. They are 'nice' but they are 'uncivilized' when they enter higher education (Bloom 1987: Pt 1 *passim*, 341). Bloom's concern is primarily with 'tradition' and 'background', not with contexts and explanations. We have pointed, on the other hand, in the United States but especially in Britain to various senses in which students are seen as more serious, and the paradox lies in the emphasis. Even if the characteristics described by Bloom do apply, students may still be committed to their studies and outcomes. The imagery which surrounds students, however, draws more heavily on the negative and the critical. It also draws on the shadowy memories of public events long past or on more recent isolated incidents.

In reviewing recent student political attitudes, however, we have been aware in both countries of much publicized incidents and events, but we have had to be cautious about how 'representative' or indicative they have been. One important aspect of such a review is that there *are* legacies of times long past. For example, in a radio interview in the early 1970s Lord Ashby referred back to Sir Walter Moberly's comment that a university may teach students how to make bombs or cathedrals, 'but it will not teach them which of the two objects they ought to make'. Ashby's reflection was that:

> Moberly's complaint is less and less justified. My generation, and that of people twenty years younger than myself, has been immensely affected by the great protest movement of youth. It has done us good. Today, anyone teaching the technology of either bombs or cathedral building would have to justify the making of bombs and, for that matter, the building of cathedrals . . . at least now the teacher knows how to pursue Moberly's dilemma, because the students won't let him run away from it. To that extent we have shifted a little way in a good direction.
>
> (Ashby 1977: 293)

Any teacher knows that it is in fact possible to 'run away', and not all students are willing to put on the pressure to justify. Pressures, in any case, come from other directions, inside and outside the institution. There is an important element of truth, however, in Ashby's reflection. There is no continuous legacy from the 'great protest movement', but there are aspects of openness and challenge that have remained. The single-issue politics of the 1980s and 1990s has retained some of the moral sensibility with which Ashby was concerned, even though it can be argued that it is capable of running over into excesses of political correctness. Perhaps another paradox, therefore, is in the continuities that may be traced in this way, alongside the obvious changes in student attitudes and activities that we have explored. Students, commented an article in *Time* in 1974, were 'far more intent on using their college education as a means of entering the American system than as preparation for reforming it' (Segall and Pickett 1979: 120). They may not have fully accepted the system they were to enter, or have entirely lost the capacity for reform, but the nature of the 'protest movement' has markedly altered, and the extent of students' ability to influence their elders 'in a good direction' has become significantly different. Students and their teachers and institutions have both had to respond to pressures from elsewhere.

A paradox of a different kind is that at the same time as students have looked for a degree of independence and individuality, they have also become subject to the anonymities associated with size and fragmentation. Central to our discussion has been the tension for school leavers between the campus youth culture and the reaching out for adulthood. The discussion about these tensions is not of recent origin, but it has acquired a new urgency. There is a growing literature on the academic experience of mature and part-time students, but there is still in the imagery of the 1990s a failure to approach anywhere near the heart of the changes and tensions. In an analysis of the role of teachers and taught internationally, Kitzinger in 1991 rightly pointed out that it was part of the Anglo-Saxon tradition that 'college educators should not only teach skills but also act as midwives to post-adolescent self-discovery'. The weakness of the tradition, he suggests, is that it fails to take account of different opportunities for students to have these kinds of relationships in British or other institutions. He argues for the merits of a year working abroad before settling to university studies, because

> I strongly doubt that boys and girls straight out of school are the best material for even our most academic higher education today: they mostly lack the maturity and the sense of perspective to benefit to the full from even the most insular syllabi.
>
> (Kitzinger 1991: 39, 42)

There is a lot to be said, and it has long been said, about the merits of an intervening year between school and higher education, but these formulations raise interesting issues. College educators in most institutions, certainly by 1991, did not have the traditional opportunities to engage seriously in midwifery for post-adolescents. Their roles had been translated into student welfare and other services. 'Boys and girls' is redolent of the old imagery, and even though Kitzinger's discussion takes in the polytechnics as well as the universities of 1990 it is strongly suggestive of the 'most academic' higher education tradition. Students are 'material', and there is no sense of what the institution itself may do for 'maturity and the sense of perspective to benefit'. We have pointed to the difficulties in which students find themselves in the modern, large campus, but there are not dissimilar difficulties for students who have worked abroad, and for mature students.

Kitzinger's imagery is not influenced by students' responses to the variety
of campuses, by such activities as Student Community Action (most of whose
volunteers are unlikely to have spent a year out after school), and by attempts
to overcome notions of students as inert, inevitably unadult material ('raw
material' or partly processed material being fed into the average redbrick
university, according to the former vice-chancellor of an Australian university)
(Rowe 1960: 247).

The paradox in these examples depends on where one begins – with the
particular uncomfortable case or the need to reinvigorate a tradition, with
academic difficulties resulting from part-time employment or from a lack of
'civilization'. The commentator on higher education, particularly when the
comments are policy-related, finds it necessary to generalize from the frag-
ment of impression and truth on which the larger picture is based – and
in doing so it is easy to replace students by fragments of students. Take
a British news item about American students in 1995, focusing on the provision of residential accommodation and the level of university-provided
and student-provided facilities. At Purdue University, Indiana, a survey of
a sample of 6,000 college rooms found 3,000 answering machines, more
than 5,000 televisions, close to 4,200 compact refrigerators, about 2,000
microwaves, and just under 3,000 video recorders:

> A growing number of United States students will be greeted this au-
> tumn with the kind of creature comforts usually aimed at business
> travellers: cable television, fitness centres, and semi-private bathrooms
> ... 'Our students are consumers and they have been raised on fast
> food and microwave ovens ... they are sophisticated consumers', says
> John Sautter, Purdue's residence halls director.

The creature comforts are part of the competition between universities,
and the article reports university officers elsewhere as arguing that accommodation has to be at a high level in order to attract and retain students.
Purdue's halls of residence marketing team were preparing a video to go
out to high schools on the theme: 'Experience the ease' (Cornwell 1995:
8). This, it is suggested, 'says it all about the needs of the modern American
student', and though it does not in fact say 'all' it says a great deal. The
difficulty lies in relating information such as this to an acceptable, coherent
'picture' of students. All of this has in some way to be related to students'
other expectations and experience of the campus, their involvement in
volunteer or other activity, their response to pressures from students who
wish to detach them from 'the ease', the role of communal facilities and
activities which run counter to that of the televisions and video recorders,
the nature of student interactions, the students who do not have this level
of technology, and how the university as 'academe' approaches students as
sophisticated consumers. This last example, however, leads particularly to
the difficult discussion of the terms in which it is possible to continue to
speak of the college and university as a 'community'. So, of course, do references to the university as factory, student diversity or the issues associated

with institutional or class size and course or departmental fragmentation. A question posed by a Penn task force on governance in 1968–70 has been expressed in various guises across the years that follow: 'Is the University only a "community of scholars"? Who are and, by hypothesis, are not, its citizens?' [21st Century Project, report 1970: 11].

Traditional versions of the concept of the university or college as a community contained exclusions that we have seen, women in some cases or students generally in others. The basis of the concept also shifted across these decades. A discussion of 'community' in the 1940s or 1950s would have been about student residence, staff–student relationships, tutorials, extra-curricular activities, and the dangers of increasing institutional size. In the 1960s or 1970s it would have been about the rights and responsibilities of students, authority, participation and representation, the provision of student services, changes to the curriculum, anxieties about diversity within and among institutions, and increases in student numbers and in the size and number of institutions. Across all of these decades there would have been discussion of the aims of universities (and from the 1960s the new vocabulary of 'higher education'), values, change, and the presence of tensions or conflicts in academe. There would have been growing attention to the influence of the state and to the meanings of autonomy and accountability, the problems of community maintenance or community building in changing economic and political circumstances, and the increasingly complex map of knowledge. The vocabulary would have been that of redbrick and plateglass, collegiality, status, and the outcomes of policy or the lack of policy or system – what Livingstone in 1948, discussing the 'casual English way', thought might be the subject of a book called 'Drift' (Livingstone 1948: 13). In all of these discussions and in those which go back centuries beyond the 1940s, 'community' was a place, with citizens and denizens, and issues which focused on aspects of living and teaching and learning there – the chapel, the canteen, the playing field, the regulations, the lecture, and eventually the car park. Since the 1970s the profound changes we have discussed have to a large degree silenced understandings and discussions of community. Physical, social and intellectual fragmentation have made it difficult not only to answer the Penn question 'Who are the citizens?', but also to listen to the question.

'Community', in 1990s Britain as at 1960s Berkeley, seemed a long way from what higher education had become, and from the agenda of debate. It was a long way from the experience of students, and from the reflections of those who had been students.

> At Manchester in the early 1970s we had one-to-one tutorials, and until the 1980s it and others were 'real universities'. Now a tutorial might be for eight or ten or twelve people, and for a seminar there might be 30. Mass higher education is OK but not if it's without funds. It's not possible to have the same view of education.
>
> (Tregoning int.)

The biggest attitude change from 25 years ago is that students at college used to have a damn good time, qualify, and then get a job. Now jobs are scarcer, now they're going for good results because of the job market, they're determined.

(Gowen int.)

The university role for students has changed. My ambition was simply to go to university. Now it's 'I'll go for a degree and move on.' They don't identify, don't know what to believe in. They drink, work, leave, and don't enjoy. They don't get enough out of it. It's a question of making the money last. They don't throw themselves into it.

(Cawdell int.)

The rhetoric, and for many students reality, had had something to do with 'belonging' in relatively small communities, or being able to take full advantage of union activities, or the Free Trade Hall, or a shared sense of access to people and ideas and fun. For the Scottish Union of Students in 1961, '[i]deally, the members of individual Colleges and Universities should form close-knit communities, the students being the junior members, the staff the senior' (SUS 1963: 887). The Cambridge college was not only a compact community but 'until recent times [it] was the social and personal expression of the unity of knowledge' (Jeffery 1950: 14). This latter symbolism has been the most persistent aspect of community expressed as 'a community of scholars' or an 'academic community'. An Anglo-American conference on *Students and Universities* in 1969 suggested that 'the academic community was a way of organizing a set of personal relationships, of contriving an equilibrium of conflicts, so as to promote an imaginative grasp on living knowledge' (Herrman 1969: 14). The strength of the compact institution lay precisely in the opportunity, even the necessity, of organizing, contriving and promoting in these ways. The feature of the university historically was that it did so in ways different from those in other forms of community or social organization. The early history of the universities as communities was honed in its relationships with the surrounding society ('ville, principauté, Etat, Chrétienté') and other, possibly competing forms of community ('ordres religieux, métiers, communes, etc.') (Verger 1983: 22).

The nature of the 'community of scholars' or 'academic community' in its modern setting has become an important but elusive concept (Damrosch 1995; Barnett 1990b; 1994). Even the modest growth of the years immediately following the Second World War could be interpreted as damaging to traditional understandings, or at least as raising awkward questions. The Students Representative Council at the University of Durham held a three-day residential conference in 1947 for new students, inviting some distinguished speakers to consider the question 'What is a university?', in the conviction that 'a university is essentially a community of persons consciously sharing in a common pursuit', and needing the kind of personal welcome the conference was intended to be (Morris 1947: 513). The American college or university of the nineteenth and early twentieth centuries was as much an exemplar of such a community as was the Oxford or Cambridge college. 'The traditional academic institution', said a former Secretary of the Department of Health, Education, and Welfare in 1965,

> was a community. Those who spent time there knew they were members of a community. It had a 'personality' that could be described and loved – or laughed at. Undergraduates were often marked for life by its style and spirit. And the community was to a very considerable degree what its members wanted it to be. In short, it was autonomous.
>
> (Gardner 1968: 6–7)

Despite its limitations, difficulties and shortcomings the community could be seen to have personality, an equilibrium of conflicts, a close-knit identity.

Growth and size did not necessarily destroy such characteristics, and many modern institutions sought to organize themselves in ways which reproduced these sorts of relationships – with collegiate sub-structures within the university in the cases of York or California at Santa Cruz. The model in such cases was Oxford and Cambridge and their tradition of close student–staff relations through the residential and tutorial systems. These have had a strong tradition of corporate life within colleges, each of which, in the words of the Franks Commission of Inquiry on Oxford, 'is not just a well-endowed hall of residence', but welds together residence and teaching. It provides 'more than bed and board: it has also to be the centre for the intellectual activities which are the chief purpose for which the young men and women are at the university at all' (University of Oxford 1966: 100–1). The college has in one sense been 'corporate', with these characteristics, but in another it has been a well-defined hierarchy with understood responsibilities and relationships. The Franks Report talks of the fellow or scholar having rooms in college which generate the atmosphere of a family: 'His own pupils come to him for tuition. He is aware of them not as the blurred outlines of an audience but as sharply defined characters sitting by his fireplace' (*ibid*.: 98). This at least has been the tradition, struggling to survive in new circumstances. The symbolism of the fireplace may no longer be appropriate, but the relationship it suggests remains. Moberly, 17 years before Franks, was dismissive of the 'dubious and transitory worth' of the collegiate, 'family' relationship:

> The family has tended to be patriarchal; it has, very markedly, been a society of unequals. The teacher has been regarded as being *in loco parentis*, the student *in statu pupillari*. They have differed as adult and adolescent, superior and subordinate, director and directed.

He quotes the Statutes of Trinity College, Cambridge: 'We decree and ordain that all inferiors behave themselves towards their superiors in a submissive and reverent manner' (Moberly 1949: 202). The college community was historically built on the combination of hierarchy, discipline, the family and the fireplace (and, we may add, the dining hall, not the cafeteria).

It was an important model, and the Robbins Report in 1963 was still able to draw some general conclusions from it about higher education institutions, which were 'not merely places of instruction. They are communities'. The merit of the collegiate system was that it enabled 'senior and junior members' to have contact with comparative ease, and this united them in 'a common way of life'. Robbins recommended that efforts should be made in other institutions to provide for such contact, not to develop 'closed academic communities with staff and students forming a kind of world within a world'. Some staff should live within a reasonable distance from their work, and facilities should be provided by the institution 'so that teachers can not only meet pupils but also entertain them' (CHE *Report* 1963: 193–4). Students were still 'pupils' (*in statu pupillari*), and the envisaged communities were still of a kind that enabled hospitality to be a central feature of the discussion. These aspects of the Oxbridge-type college applied also in the first half of the twentieth century to the teacher training colleges (as they were called until the 1960s) which shared a common pursuit and which were small enough to emphasize the virtues of the 'family' atmosphere. The Oxbridge college has retained its combined residential and teaching characteristics, but other college-based universities are closer to a model of clustered halls of residence, only sometimes and sketchily associated with tutorial support. The problem we have seen in relation to a concept of community is that of the 'other institutions' for which Robbins made recommendations. Where staff live, what facilities are provided, the numbers of students for whom they have any teaching or tutorial responsibility, the opportunity for 'entertainment', the ease of contact – all of these have in the great majority of cases ceased to be relevant features of mass higher education.

Laments for the passing of the community have become increasingly common since the 1970s, and have pointed in different directions. Academic staff loyalties are torn between their institution and the national or international 'community of scholars' of which they often feel more a part. Students see different kinds of fragmentation, and among students themselves what we have described frequently represents an extremely low level of community feeling. The relationships with teaching staff are even less tenuous than when Robbins was advocating their improvement. Ashby in 1973 bluntly talked of

> the cant about scholars and students united in the pursuit of truth for its own sake . . . If 'community' means a cosy consensus about common interests, the modern university is not a community. It is only toward the other end of the spectrum of meaning – the community defined as people with a diversity of interests and goals working on the same campus, sharing the same central heating and catering facilities – that the word is appropriate. Even so, it may be less of a community than (say) a brewery . . . Universities today are communities only in an attenuated sense of the word.
>
> (Ashby 1973: 60)

They have lost their personality, and their fireplace. The community is no longer one of scholars united by class, privilege and a good cellar. It is not necessarily the university of school leavers, united by athletics, residence, the expectation of an honours degree and good employment prospects. It is not necessarily the unity of commitment to the subject, the single honours, the discipline, the 'course'. Some of these have remained for some students in some places, but they are no longer the common core of definitions of the university or college community. Students may be influenced before entry by old images of community held by their teachers or other elders, and may find themselves having to adjust not only to a new but also to an unexpected environment.

The history of what it has meant to be, or to fail to be, students in a community over recent decades relates to many of the features we have discussed. In the late 1960s and early 1970s the argument centred on the willingness of the institution to admit students into its governance. Whatever other overtones the students' battles may have had, their attempt to redefine the community so as to incorporate students was central. The Select Committee Report on *Student Relations* in 1969 did not accept the NUS view that students had 'a *right* to participate in the running of an academic community', but accepted that comment and criticism by all its members were a right, 'and if this right is to be exercised effectively by junior members there ought to be formally established ways for them to become involved in decisions which affect their education'. By a detour, therefore, the Committee came to the recommendation that joint consultation was essential at faculty and departmental levels, and that student representation on governing bodies and academic boards or their equivalents should be accepted (House of Commons 1969a: 121, 153).

A transatlantic conference discussion of The Meaning of an Academic Community in 1970 agreed that all members of the community had a right to share in its governance and that there were areas of particular common interest to all – discipline, the curriculum, the appointment, promotion and dismissal of staff, and 'general governance', including financial and academic priorities (Clarke 1970: 14–15). The conference membership included a number of British vice-chancellors and other senior university and other figures, and officers of students' unions and the NUS, as well as American and Canadian presidents, vice-chancellors and students. One person present was Professor Max Beloff from Oxford, and it is unlikely that he acquiesced readily in the conference conclusions. In the radio interview shortly afterwards from which we have quoted, Beloff argued strongly against treating the university as 'a democratic community'. Students were interested in participation as a slogan, but did not make use of it once they had obtained it. The good students, the future 'essential cadres of an advanced society – do not take part in any of this. First-rate students, unless psychologically disturbed, are never involved in student politics' (Beloff 1977: 155, 159–60). Beloff was not alone in resisting participation, just as Ashby was not alone in searching for formulas by which to accept it. The conceptual confusions disguise the difficulty of coming to terms with those changes in higher education which were challenging the traditional position of the student in both the academic community and the wider campus or cultural community – these being the tissue enabling students to pursue their studies and make sense of their direction and purpose.

Apart from the question of representation there were other aspects of 1960s student activism which helped to question the adequacy of old notions of community. In the United States particularly, students questioned the validity of assumptions about the university's disinterested search for truth, given its commitment, for example, to military research (see, for example, Nelkin 1972). Maxine Greene described students as having 'exposed the anachronistic nature of the claims made by certain academics that the university remains, beneath the turbulent surfaces, "a community of scholars"'. They had gathered evidence about the millions of dollars received, for example, by the University of California for work on nuclear explosives, and about Massachusetts Institute of Technology and Johns Hopkins University as major military/aerospace corporations. It was students who had first raised such questions as the morality of racial segregation in public places in college communities, the propriety of secret military and espionage research, and the responsibilities of academic institutions within their immediate communities (Greene 1970: 20–1, also drawing on K.B. Clark, 'Learning from students').

Students also challenged the fragmentation of the university, the decline of a sense of community. Penn's Student Committee on Undergraduate Education addressed the issue of 'segmentation' of the campus, between faculty and students, and between both and the administration. This made 'meaningful student–faculty contact almost impossible, when, ideally, continual and stimulating dialogue between student and teacher is a necessary criterion for a dynamic and fulfilling intellectual community' [21st Century Project, SCUE report 1966: 10]. In this as in other cases in American and British institutions, the student challenge at least provoked a need to debate the issues, and to promote structures in which they could be addressed. The point is that community was in various forms a concern of students, and interest was frequently expressed in the fact that it was in the sit-ins and occupations of the late 1960s and early 1970s that for the first time many of them encountered a meaningful sense of community. This was something, Hoggart suggests, which their 'predominantly middle-class homes had not given them' (Hoggart 1979: 4), and Ashby quotes a student who had taken part in the occupation of a building by hundreds of normal, law-abiding students – it was

'one of the deepest experiences of my life. We were packed in those rooms and corridors with hardly room to breathe, talking the whole night through. We came to no agreement but it was a great experience just the same.' This hunger for a community spirit, followed by a pathetic satisfaction with such an ephemeral and impoverished experience

of communal life at a sit-in, is a symptom for me that something very
important is missing from the environment of the university where it
occurred.

It was something which happened at places like Harvard and Cambridge as
well as 'less fortunate universities' (Ashby 1973: 64–5).

The question was to be how far it was possible to rescue or adapt forms of
community which it had still been possible to identify and propound in the
1960s and 1970s. When universities became 'pluralistic "non-organisations"',
how much diversity of values, purposes and activities could they tolerate?
(Duke 1992: 64). How well could they respond to the combination of greatly
and rapidly expanding numbers and the diversity of their populations? As
the old model of a community disappeared on campuses around the world,
how well could they develop new models? The Penn Report on university life
in 1990 saw the recruitment of diverse students as a beginning, from which
a commitment to building community and celebrating diversity by making
it central to campus life was needed. It quoted from a Brown University
report on minority life which argued a distinction between *diversity*, 'in which
individuals from various groups are merely present', and *pluralism*, in which
individuals and groups maintain their identities but come together in a
community enriched by its members' differences and similarities. It would
not be surprising if 'building pluralism is not easy; in its difficulty lies its
very importance' [*Almanac* 16 October 1990: 5]. The pluralisms are not
only those of race and ethnicity, but also of age and experience, gender, disability, and the spectrum of characteristics which define the student body
of the modern university.

There is a need in some, perhaps particularly younger, students across
this range for shared independence, just as in others there is a need to
submerge their experience and independence in some form of supporting
and encouraging environment. In the past many have resolved their mix
of needs in small, sometimes monotechnic (teacher education, performing
arts, etc.) colleges, and in the scramble for rationalization since the 1970s
the opportunities to do so have diminished. The main difficulty has been
how to remodel the urban, often predominantly commuter, institution, in
order to address the issues of diversity and pluralism, to meet the expectations of students, to do more than submit to the mounting pressures to
define them in simple terms as learners and customers. Student Services,
learner guidance and support, induction programmes, the amenities and
activities of the students' union, have been some of the moves towards a
solution (the last of these ill understood by government). In the presence
of the forces of fragmentation and 'segmentation', numbers, modules, the
diversities we have portrayed, and student hardship, they have been necessary but inevitably insufficient. The issues surrounding the nature of a
university or college community have been to a large extent suppressed by
other, immediate, partial concerns of institutions and their constituencies.

If the traditional notion of a community is no longer available for most

of higher education, the basic issue is whether the question will become
more or less acute, and whether institutions and higher education generally
have begun adequately to shape or will need to invent major, different
responses. The question applies acutely to students on franchised courses,
and will do so increasingly to students who transfer credit between institutions. The question does not relate only to the kind of campuses and students we have had primarily in mind for most of this discussion. We have
excluded Open University, essentially 'non-campus', students from the discussion, but they raise an important question that relates to these concerns.
Not only is the Open University the largest university in the United Kingdom, but its operations have been reflected in the development of distance
learning for some students in other institutions, ranging from such large
institutions as the University of Wolverhampton, with more than 20,000
students, to small institutions like the Maryvale Institute of Religious Education or the Glasgow Bible College, with only one or two courses at undergraduate or master's level. Distance learning has become a feature of higher
education provision in a wide variety of countries, and as computer and
telecommunications technologies develop it is inevitable that larger constituencies of students should emerge who, like Open University students,
do not have the consistent relationship with a campus that is the feature of
full- and other part-time students.

The technologies which will affect this discussion of the relationship
between students and the campus are already widely in place, developing
rapidly, or prefigured in a variety of ways. The shape of the student population is open, for example, to the influence of video conferencing and the
spectrum of uses of computers, satellites and communications technology,
which are not merely of use on the campus but may have other repercussions. These include increased access by students whose contact with the
campus in the past has been minimal to some of what the campus has
traditionally provided, the adaptation of the campus itself, and the development of universities which – like the Open University – do not depend on
such a conventional campus. The issue of the future of the student relationship to campus life is therefore both one of changes in the concept of
student life, and possibly one of an increasing proportion of students who
do not share in it as in the past. The issue looks different from different
kinds of institution – from those committed to collegiate experience, from
small 'total institutions' or from multi-campus urban universities which have
in recent decades struggled to find or provide an adequate supply of accommodation. Whether residence remains so significant an element in
the operation and planning of higher education will be an important question if significant percentages of students cannot afford to occupy campus
or private accommodation, and have the option of obtaining qualifications
from their place of work, home or other centres using the new technologies. In these cases the relationships of students to one another would follow the pattern of technological interchange developing in society at large.

Given student, institutional, family, employer and other expectations of the campus 'community' in the past, the question is a serious one. It has implications for students' unions, and for aspects of teaching and learning which have been assumed to be a vital part of higher education. The tutorial relationship has already been substantially undermined, but there are questions about the future conduct or viability of the seminar, the individual or group presentation, group projects and peer learning, and student–staff and student–student interactions of many kinds. What will be the responses of departmental and discipline cultures? The existing experience of distance learning has messages for this changing situation, since for off-campus students in various categories there is an issue of sustaining motivation and achievement which may or may not be answered by the student 'ownership' of technology-based learning. There is an issue about face-to-face tutorial contact, summer schools and student self-support groups, and about the relevance of campus resources to new needs, given not only the distance of students but also the widening choices available to them between courses but also between institutions nationally and internationally. The trend is now and will continue to be towards even less homogeneity of students and of their relationships with the campus. The point about this technological pespective is not that it invalidates a discussion of community, but that it underlines how far the discussion has to go beyond its old parameters. 'Participation' applies to the large numbers of students who will remain full-time and campus-based for the foreseeable future, but in other ways also to students who do not fall within those definitions.

A Carnegie discussion of *Campus Life* has suggested six principles which define what a college and university should be. It is an educationally *purposeful* community with shared academic goals; an *open* community where freedom of expression is protected; a *just* community, where the sacredness of the person is honoured and diversity aggressively pursued; a *disciplined* community, where individuals accept obligations to the group, and behaviour is guided by well-defined governance procedures; a *caring* community, encouraging service to others; and a *celebrative* community, where tradition and change are shared (Carnegie 1990: 7–8 and *passim*). This has been a valuable contribution to debate about the campus, but as a set of principles. It has to be translated also into the experience and needs of the commuter student and the distance learning student, the students' union and student government, the factors which affect the ability of students to benefit from the community, and their attitudes and activities. The discussion of principles has to be in dialogue with the realities of students' lives.

10

Students as . . .

A discussion of community returns us to a focus on the ways students are perceived within the institution and outside. Neither 'the student' nor 'the institution' is homogeneous and the images rest on complex expectations and attitudes. Students have been and are seen as many things. At the time we took as our starting point, the end of the 1960s, C.H. Wilson, Principal of the University of Glasgow, commented with some care on interpretations of the student's status. Some aspects of student life had basic continuities – 'the crowds, the lecture halls, the voices and the conversations, the tumult of ideas and sensations, the alternating moods of exhilaration and boredom'. What change had taken place, however, in the status of 'the student as such'?

> Within the university his status was time out of mind that of pupil and learner, junior member and apprentice of the academy whose graduate he desired to become. In such societies the authority of the teacher was qualified by the acceptance that all the members were adult and all engaged in the pursuit of knowledge. At its best there was a felt equality of consideration throughout the body and the attitudes of persons to each other aimed at being tolerant and humane. Since no one was there who hadn't chosen to come and since the society operated by a widespread devolution of responsibilities there were established expectations for teacher and student alike. The one could count on the authority he needed to teach his discipline, and the other on the care and interest of those who taught him.

That was within the university, and though it neglects the difficulties and conflicts that regularly troubled the surfaces of these 'societies', it is a sharp outline of the relationships of the old community in which students were seen as interchangeably pupils, learners, junior members and apprentices, with the rights and responsibilities that went with this status (and increasingly 'her' as well as 'him'). To the world outside:

> the student was a phenomenon *sui generis* but an ancient and familiar one. Students were that portion of the young men and women of the

community who by accident of fortune or desert had been given a 'time between' school and work which was to be used for learning and for professional training. They and their universities operated on a sort of special license . . . they were treated with a special indulgence and not made strictly subject to the same norms of conduct as were applied to most other people.

(Wilson [1970]: 4–6)

It is from this special dispensation, and from what gave rise to and followed from it, that students were seen also as privileged or irresponsible or worse, depending on the time and the circumstances – rowdy, drunken, licentious, and so on. Wilson was aware of the profound changes particularly in public perceptions of students, and though he saw opinion moving 'away from the traditional view of the student', and though he had views as to what should be rescued or preserved, what was replacing the traditional view was not at all clear.

Half a decade later, the President Emeritus of York University, Canada, whom we have quoted, essayed a historical approach to the question of what the role of the university student was. His elaborate question was whether the student was an apprentice, working closely with a master; a ward of the university, placed by parents or society in its custody; a client of the university, involved in a professional relationship; a customer, purchasing services; or a member of the university, with the rights and obligations of one of its citizens. Or did the relationship incorporate aspects of all of these? (Ross 1976: 67). The list itself constitutes a kind of history, moving from the student as medieval apprentice to the student as late twentieth-century customer. It goes via the *in loco parentis* situation in which students were placed, through the professional relationship in which students as adult were seen by Wilson in Glasgow or argued for by Wallerstein amidst the turmoils of Columbia (Wallerstein 1969: 92). Historians and sociologists have similarly developed typologies of kinds of students, some of them representing changing characteristics of students over time – collegiate, vocational, academic and nonconformist (Clark and Trow 1966) or college men, outsiders and rebels (Horowitz 1987). Many of the labels have survived, others have been interred, as was the concept of the student as child, with the collapse of *in statu pupillari*. The notion of the student as apprentice was conceivable when students were preparing for the old 'liberal' professions which included the academic, but became obsolete as the destinations for graduates widened and mass higher education developed other characteristics.

We have largely bypassed aspects of students' lives which have become so significant a part of modern student mythologies – the promiscuities, misbehaviours, idiocies, illegalities, and so on. It has been sufficient for our purposes to suggest the ambiguities of adolescence, education for responsibility without having responsibility. Whatever the pressures on full-time students, there inevitably also remains something of the sense of a 'time between'. Making allowance for these features of many students' lives, it is difficult to judge how substantially students differ from large numbers of the rest of society. The complex balances between the academic and extra-curricular lives of students, in the immense variety of campus and sub-campus cultures, also make it difficult to arrive at a suitable imagery. There may, for example, continue to be perceptions of students as members, but there are widely different ways of categorizing membership – from junior partner (a commercial adaptation of the old apprentice) to regular customer paying an admission fee (the swimming or golf club). There are ambivalent views of students within the academy on the part of some academics as pressures grow on them to fulfil research or other requirements which turn students from guests (welcome guests as financial survival depends on them) almost to intruders or nuisances or distractions from other priorities.

In the competitive, market-oriented higher education of the United States, involving both state-funded and private institutions, in the conditions of the nineteenth and twentieth centuries the view of a student from the academy or from the students themselves came to include at least a large element of the student as customer or, as one former student described it, as commodity. Students were 'marketable goods', and if students were dissatisfied they could be directed elsewhere: 'like soap, one can shop for the institution that works best. If dissatisfied with one brand, one can always turn to its eager competitors' (Siegel 1967: 219). As British public higher education has been driven towards the market the dominant imagery has also become that of the consumer, customer and purchaser.

Consumerism in American higher education in the 1970s was a recognition of the tradition of consumer issues and the demand to protect the student-as-consumer from misleading claims by institutions in the higher education market-place. The student-as-consumer was not new, what was new was the demand to regulate the conditions of consumption and the emergence of a national debate about regulation of the rights of 'citizen-students' – and the alliance of students and federal pressures against recalcitrant institutions (Stark *et al.* 1977: 15–28). The consumer was seen to hold an important degree of power, and a new concern emerged to assess the impact of mass consumerism on the institutions of higher education. One way of perceiving the power of students was to blame the faculty and the institutions for 'capitulation to the bazaar; not the barbarity of student demands, but the seductiveness of student coffers' (Riesman 1980: chs 4, 9; Farago 1982: 714). In these conditions what was emerging was an increasingly 'intelligent' or 'calculating' consumer (Penn and Franks 1982: 28), a result of trends evident from the early 1980s and in the consumer rights activities of Ralph Nader. These were rights being advanced by students, expressing their demands in ways different from those of the 1960s, and targeted on asserting their power as consumers in the market-place.

This consumerism, superimposed upon the traditional view of the student-as-customer, preceded the British interest in the student-as-consumer which resulted essentially from government financing policy. It had become important for institutions to recruit and to retain students, and for these and other reasons student judgements about the quality of their courses had similarly become important to their parent institutions. 'Student feedback' related to concerns other than those of gratifying the consumer, though the latter played an important part. The Department of Education and Science commended as good practice those places which had established 'customer care units' (DES 1991: 7). Explanations of the rapid spread of student feedback mechanisms in the 1980s do lie in institutions' interest in the attitudes and judgements of their 'consumers', as well as in information needed for generalized accountability purposes and for specific external scrutinies, and in satisfying themselves that they were operating effectively in the marketplace. The Nuffield project on research and innovation in the early 1970s was already indicating a range of attempts to establish effective staff–student committees, feedback procedures and other ways of involving students in academic affairs (Nuffield 1973–4). Following a strong American interest in the evaluation of teachers, the British versions followed with a different emphasis – on course quality and student 'satisfaction' with their courses and institutional environments – and efforts were made by those conducting the processes to separate information needed for course monitoring and improvement, and that needed for institutional management. In some cases efforts were also made to construct the research instruments on the basis of student involvement in establishing the questions to be addressed. The mechanisms used included primarily questionnaires and various kinds of structured group feedback strategies, conducted by teaching staff within their modules or courses, or by specialist units set up within the institution. From the students' point of view there were sometimes serious issues – that of 'questionnaire overload', lack of feedback *to* students on the outcomes of their expression of opinions, or failure to link this process with the operation of course committees (Silver 1992: *passim*). At one end of a spectrum it was possible to see feedback as simply management data, and at the other end to see responses to courses and level of satisfaction as part of the process of student empowerment alongside other student roles in quality assurance (Harvey and Burrows 1992).

Students as consumers had become central to discussions of the identity and status of students, and this could be taken to imply a passive or active image of students. 'Consumers' also linked to 'customers', and both pointed to the idea of consumer or customer rights. Customers had a right to open and honest information, to the delivery of what was promised, to appropriate forms of service. In the United States this meant consumer (student) protection, Congressional policies on 'truth-in-advertising', consumer-oriented regulations and 'student consumer information'. Students were seen in this respect as citizens of the wider community where consumer protection applied, and like other citizens students had the right as consumers to 'gain satisfaction for grievances' by appropriate, including legal, means (Stark *et al.* 1977: 3, 18–21; Penn and Franks 1982). In Britain the outcome of this kind of interpretation was the government's *Charter for Higher Education* in 1993, part of the government's commitment to citizens' charters. It explained how universities and colleges would respond to the needs of the customers of higher education:

> This Charter explains the standards of service that students, employers and the general public can expect from universities and colleges and other bodies involved in higher education in England . . . Customers of universities and colleges also have responsibilities and the Charter reminds you of some of them. But the focus is on the meeting of *your* legitimate needs. If you are not satisfied with the service you receive, the Charter explains what you can do to get it put right.
>
> (DFE 1993: 1–2)

For the government the student, like anyone else, was now called the customer, just as announcements on railway stations had come to address 'customers' not 'passengers'. A Charter 'movement' offered related and different perspectives. The NUS issued its own *Student Charter* in 1992, acknowledging the importance of students' needs and rights and advocating measures by which 'students are empowered to seek the type of education they require', and the quality of education in which they themselves invest (NUS 1992: 1–6, *passim*). Charters produced by individual institutions – usually by working parties involving senior academic and administrative staff and students – underlined such features as students' academic and other entitlements, representation and participation in decision-making, students' union organization, and responsibilities. The University of Wales Swansea *Student Charter* defines its purpose as setting out the general principles which determine 'the relationship between you, the student, and other members of the university community', and information about services. It includes a statement about 'fair governance': 'The university is committed to open and fair academic structures and its governance procedures should reflect the ethos of a partnership between students and other members of its academic community' [Swansea 1994: 1–2]. An analysis of charters by the NUS concluded that they fell into two categories – 'minimalistic charters', which were bland, offering little challenge to the institution, and 'developmental charters', which saw the charter as part of an ongoing process and about genuine change (NUS [1994]). The consumer–customer definition of students had produced opportunities to review the relationships involved, and to emphasize different aspects of the expectations and rights of the different parties involved.

Underlying all of this were the changes in the funding of British students, the move to diminish the state's role in funding both institutions and students – at the same time as increasing student numbers. The debate about student loans revolved around ways in which students could contribute to their education – by loans to replace part or all of the grant, by a graduate tax, or by some other means. What these financial decisions did was move the British student towards the American model of the student as the purchaser of an education, just as modularization and credit transfer had moved the British student towards the established American model of the discriminating consumer. The benefit of American and British consumerism was the emphasis on students' rights, the possibility of outcomes that could improve their academic and campus lives. Fundamental outcomes, however, depended on other factors, affecting the funding and policies of institutions, and the roles and attitudes of students' other partners in the enterprise. The weakness of the focus on the student as consumer or customer or purchaser was that it could point to the crudest possible interpretation of what it means to be a student, and what is meant by a higher education.

In their contemporary setting there are reservations to be expressed about all of these interpretations of studenthood, and particularly about the approach by government, by institutions and by students themselves, to their roles as consumers and customers. Students, or others through the students, do of course buy education, but the purchase is not of education as a *product*, but of education as a *process* in which the students actively participate – to the extent that one Swedish commentary discusses 'students as colleagues' (Bjorklund 1995: 15–17). The purchaser model tends to evade the constructive, participative role of the student. Even at its best the model contains elements of the student as outsider, of a separation between the provider and the recipient. If the student buys rights as a result of the purchase, however, the central right is that of becoming a member, a participant – a member with greater need and power to contribute than the apprentice in the guild or the weekend user of the golf course. The niceties of exactly how equal a student member can be in the academic community or partnership are not important here. What the student has acquired as part of the legacy we have discussed is the right to influence, to propose, to oppose, to make effective representations, to promote change, to encounter frameworks and opportunities within which to create an education – which is, and always has been, a great deal more than a formal academic process. The student enters as a member in the fullest sense, and thereby becomes a participant in creating the process of education in its fullest sense. Whatever shape higher education processes may take amidst new changes, it is to these considerations of students in their communities that institutions and all concerned with them will need more seriously to return.

Appendix I: Interviews

Cheltenham and Gloucester College of Higher Education
Andy Howard: Student Enterprise Manager   22.3.93

University of Durham
Dr Jeremy M. Black: Lecturer in History; Director, Research
    Foundation and Society of Fellows   18.10.93
Nicola Boud: Senior Durham Students Union representative;
    third year student, College of St Hild and St Bede; active in
    Student Community Action   18.10.93
Simon Evenson: President, Grey College Junior Common Room   15.10.93
Jane Grieve: Enterprise Bureau, St John's College; former student;
    tutor   17.11.93
Eric Halladay: Principal, St Chad's College; former Master, Grey
    College   5.11.93
Dr Margaret Harvey: Lecturer in History   18.10.93
Dr Sidney Holgate: former Master, Grey College   2.11.93
Lesley MacDonald: Director, Enterprise project   8.10.93
V.A. McIntyre: Director, Careers Advisory Service   5.11.93
Bernard Robertson: Development Manager; Governing Body
    member   18.11.93
Dr Peter Slee: Director, Marketing and Corporate Communications;
    former Director and evaluator, Enterprise project   2.11.93
Ian M. Stewart: Deputy Secretary   11.10.93
Samuel G.C. Stoker: Principal, St Cuthbert's Society   18.11.93
Adam Thurston: third year student, College of St Hild and St Bede;
    Chair, Student Community Action   5.11.93
Susie Tooke: Research Assistant; recent student; Community Action
    and Welfare Office   7.12.93
Victor Watts: Master, Grey College; Lecturer in English   26.11.93
Jon Walsh: President, Durham Students Union; former President,
    Junior Common Room, Van Mildert College   7.12.93

University of East Anglia
Paranjit Patyal: postgraduate research student; former Student
    Community Action organizer   7.11.95
Bill Rhodes: Central Services Manager, Union of Students   7.11.95

University of Glasgow

Tim Geering: Board member, Glasgow University Union; Convenor of
    Debates; second year student; graduate of St Andrews University   5.9.95
Ann Ingleston: House Manager, Queen Margaret Union   7.9.95
Stephen H. Johnson: Director of Residential, Catering and Business
    Services   6.9.95
Moira Mackay: Assistant Archivist; former University student   7.9.95
Kerry Mackenzie: Assistant Development Officer, Student Volunteer
    Service   6.9.95
Lawrence Reynolds: Assistant Clerk of Senate and Clerk of Faculties   5.9.95
Stephen Rixon: President, Queen Margaret Union   7.9.95
Dr Robert Y. Thompson: recently retired Senior Lecturer in
    Biochemistry; former Court Assessor; Senior Adviser of Studies,
    Faculty of Science Studies   7.9.95
Gill Watt: Education and Research Officer, Students' Representative
    Council   6.9.95

University of Humberside

Alisa Lopez-Mendez: Digital Student Enterprise Officer; recent
    graduate   10.2.94

University of Liverpool

Michael Belton: Head of Administration and Business Services, Guild
    of Students   9.3.95
Rachel Curley: President, Guild of Students   9.3.95
Neil Lewis: Senior Assistant Registrar and Personnel Officer; former
    Secretary, Guild of Students   9.3.95
Emma Watson: Student Development Manager; former Student
    Enterprise Manager   9.3.95

National Union of Students

Sofija Opacic: Research Officer   29.3.95

Nene College of Higher Education

Dr Michael J. Daniel: Assistant Director (Academic Quality)   31.1.96
Howard Parkinson: General Manager, Students Union   18.3.94
Chris Tann: Vice-President, Students Union   18.3.94

University of North London

Mark Watson: Chair, Mature Students Society; Acting President,
    Students Union   28.5.93
Ruth Watson: Student Employer Links Coordinator; former UNL
    student and Student Enterprise Coordinator   19.1.96

Oxford Brookes University

Nicki Weinstein: recent President, Students' Union   27.9.95

University of Pennsylvania

Dan Debicella: Chair, Undergraduate Assembly   7.4.95
David Grossman: Director, Program for Student-Community
    Involvement   6.4.95

Dr Ira Harkavy: Director, Center for Community Partnerships 21.4.95
Linda C. Koons: Executive Assistant to the President 7.4.95
Francine F. Walker: Director, Student Life Activities and Facilities 3.4.95

Pennsylvania State University
Judith M. Curley: Assistant Director, Student Activities 17.4.95
J. Thomas Eakin: Assistant Vice President, Student Programs 12.4.95
Brenda Hameister: Director of Services for the Disabled 17.4.95
Mike King: President, Undergraduate Student Government 18.4.95
Dr Stan Latta: Associate Director, Student Life 14.4.95
A. Craig Millar: Associate Vice President for Student Affairs 10.4.95
Leon Stout: University Archivist 10.4.95
Dr Lee Upcraft: Associate of the Center for the Study of Higher
    Education; recently retired Assistant Vice President for
    Counseling Services and Program Assessment 10.4.95,
    13.4.95

University of Plymouth
Jeff Butel: Director, Enterprise in Higher Education 8.3.94
Professor Les Ebdon: Deputy Vice-Chancellor (Academic) 5.3.93
Dr Michael Gillett: Deputy Vice-Chancellor (Resources) 16.6.94
Carol Harris: Student Rights Officer, Students Union 8.3.94
James Herring: President, Students Union, Exmouth Campus; four
    sites co-ordinator 4.3.93
Matthew Horton: President, Students Union; also previous period as
    President 16.6.94
Ivan Sidgreaves: Dean of Academic Services 10.6.94
Terry Warne: Mature Students Officer 8.3.94

Queen Margaret College, Edinburgh
Penny Aitken: Librarian 2.12.93
Jon Baldwin: Director of Modular and Access Courses 2.12.93
Tom Begg: Lecturer, Department of Applied Consumer Studies;
    College historian 1.12.93
Alison Galloway: Lecturer, Department of Applied Consumer Studies 2.12.93
David Henderson: Head Janitor 2.12.93
Johnny McLaughlin: President, Students' Association 1.12.93
Christine Skinner: Senior Lecturer, Department of Speech Therapy 2.12.93

Strathclyde University
Mike Day: Membership Services Manager, Students' Association;
    formerly NUS Training Officer 7.9.95
Liam McMonagle: President, Students' Association 11.9.95

Student Community Action Development Unit
Kelly Drake: Director 29.1.96

University of Wales Swansea
Robert Barnes: Academic Registrar and Director of Registry 15.1.96
Duncan Cawdell: Treasurer, Students Union 16.1.96
Adam Chambers: President, Students Union 16.1.96

Jonathan Ivens: Project Support Worker, Swansea Student
    Community Action   16.1.96
Christine Knight: Development Worker, Swansea Student Community
    Action   16.1.96
Professor Alan Lloyd: Pro-Vice Chancellor (Academic Affairs)   15.1.96
Nick Tregoning: General Manager, Students Union   16.1.96

Swansea Institute of Higher Education
Ken Ellis: Senior Lecturer, Swansea Business School; Student Union
    Staff Treasurer   17.1.96
Lesley Gowen: Senior Student Counsellor   17.1.96
Professor Ken Jones: Dean of Education   17.1.96
Jill Nicholls: Equal Opportunities Officer   17.1.96
Dermot Parker: President, Student Union   17.1.96

University of Teesside
Ben Ebdon: General Secretary, Students' Union   25.11.93
Morgan McClintock: University Secretary   24.11.93
Barbara McGuinness: Chair, University and Student Support
    Committee   22.11.93
Gus Pennington: Director, Enterprise project and Education
    Development Service   15.11.93
Mark White: Head of Academic and Administrative Performance;
    twice President, Teesside Polytechnic Students' Union   24.11.93

Appendix II: Archival and Primary Sources

Minute books unless otherwise stated; sub-headings in italics indicate location.

Bucknell University
Student Government
– Student Code of Conduct [1988]

University of Central Lancashire
Enterprise Unit
– Annual Review 1992–3
– *News for Course Reps*
Planning and Performance Analysis Office
– Annual Review of Student Satisfaction, 1993 Survey, 1994 Survey

Cheltenham and Gloucester College of Higher Education
Student Services
– *Students Handbook 1992–1993*
Enterprise in Higher Education
– *Equal Opportunities in Higher Education: EHE and Student Empowerment*
– *EHE Five Year Report* (3 Parts), 1995
Central administration
– *Whose Course is it Anyway? Your Guide to Student Participation in Academic Quality*
  (joint publication with Students Union)

Chester College
Students' Union
– Set Representative Handbook, information and training material (jointly with
  Student Enterprise)

University of Durham
Old Shire Hall
– Senate 1968–9 – 1987–8 (20 vols)
– Joint Committee of the Senate and DSU 1970–87
– Colleges Committee 1985–8
– Colleges Board 1990–3
– *Calendar*, 1973–4

- CVCP Academic Audit Unit, *Report on an Academic Audit of the University of Durham*, 1992
Careers Advisory Service
- *Annual Report of the Director 1991–1992*
Enterprise Bureau
- Joint Management Committee, 1989–93
- Annual Report 1992
- Directory of EHE-funded Projects 1992–3
- The Enterprise Bureau with St John's College, *Training for Success: Course Guide 1993–1994*
Grey College
- JCR General Meetings 1959–63, 1971–5, 1975–84
- JCR Executive Committee 1962–7
- *Grey College Handbook 1993–94*
Durham Students Union
- Students' Representative Council 1964–6, 1966–7, 1967–9, 1969–70
- Council 1970–1, 1978, 1979–80, 1981–3, 1984–5, 1985–7, 1987–8, 1990–1
- *Palatinate*, October–December 1993

University of East Anglia
Union of Students
- Executive Committee 1985–90
- Student Union Services Management Committee 1981–3, 1980–8, 1991–2
- Union President Correspondence file
- *Alternative Prospectus*, 1982
- *Handbooks* 1981/1–1995/6
- Annual Report 1990–1
- *Concrete*, 1995
- *Broad View*, 1995

University of Edinburgh
Edinburgh Enterprise Centre
- *Annual Report*, 1990–1, 1991–2
- *Focus*, 8, 12, 15, 17, 20, 22

University of Glasgow
University of Glasgow Archives
- Senate files:
    50/2 (1967–80); 155/2/49 (1971–81) student representation
    155/2.50 (1976–85); 157/123 (1987–8); 255/1/145 (1987–93) SRC
    155/2/51 (1971–83); 157/140 (1950–84) students' unions
    157/85 (1978–84) mature students
    235/36 (1979–80); 255/141 (1972–92) accommodation
- Senate minutes 1975–6, 1992–3
- Court papers:
    113/2 (1972–84) general, SRC/University
    127/1/2 (1979–82); 174/1/89 (1987–8) students' unions
    174/1/88 (1977–88) SRC
    185/3 (1982–90) student health and welfare
    201/6/2 (1967–73) student participation

- SRC: DC/157/4/1/25 (Education Committee, representation, disabled students), DC 157/6/4 (grants and cuts)
- News cuttings:
  27/12 (1971–5); 242/2/59 (1977–84); 242/2/61 (1978–84); 242/2/62 students' unions and general
  27/24 (1971–7) (five envelopes) accommodation, SRC, incidents
  91/1 (1972/9) student finance
- *Report of the University Court*, 1964–5, 1965–6, 1967–8, 1969–70
- Principal's report, 1973–4, 1978–80, 1981–2, 1985–6, 1988–9, 1990–1, 1993–4
- HEQC, *Quality Audit Report*, 1993
Senate Office
- Joint Council, 1971–81
- Senate, 11 December 1969, 12 February 1970, 27 February 1970, 12 March 1970, 4 June 1970, 19 November 1970
- Ordinance No. 60, 4 February 1895 (Regulations for SRC)
- Ordinance No. 182, 23 May 1979 (Composition of the Court)
Accommodation Office
- *Code of Behaviour: Accommodation* (leaflet)
- *Student Accommodation Charter* (leaflet)
- *Living at Glasgow University!* (booklet)
- *Be safe, Be secure* (leaflet)
Glasgow University Union
- *Handbook*, 1994
- GUU diary
Queen Margaret Union
- QMU diary
Students' Representative Council
- *Constitution 1993–1994*
- *What is the SRC?* (leaflet)
- Student Advice Centre (various leaflets)
- *Welfare Handbook 1995*
- *Handbook*, 1994
- *Class Rep Guide*
- C. Sinclair and E. Borowski *Student Guide* (Pts 1–3). University of Glasgow: Enterprise in Higher Education project, 1993
- Scottish Higher Education Records of Achievement, *Personal Development Planning* and *Personal Development Planner*. University of Glasgow: Enterprise in Higher Education project
Student Volunteer Service
- *Annual Report 1992–93, 1995/96*
- *Placement Listing 1995/6*
- *Student Tutoring Programme Annual Report 1994/95*
- *Placements, Projects, Work Experience* (leaflet)
- *Student Tutoring Programme* (leaflet)
- Glasgow University Settlement, *60th Annual Report*, 1993

University of Hull
Archives, Brynmor Jones Library
- Report of the Committee on the Future of the College approved by Senate, Minute 126 of 16 January 1950. File: V.C. 100.

University of Humberside
Enterprise Unit
- 'Students and the Enterprise Project' (n.d.)
- 'Students and Enterprise Annual Report 1992–3', 1993
- *Your Views on Academic Issues: Getting them Heard* (leaflet)
- *You'll Get a Degree: So what?* (leaflet)
- 'Students and Tutoring Annual Report 1992–3', 1993
- *Student Tutoring* (leaflet)
Quality Unit
- *Academic Quality Assurance: Student Handbook*, 1993

University of Liverpool
University Archives and Records Centre
- Guild Council, Executive Committee, working parties, Community Service Committee, minutes and papers, 1969–81: A. 032/45, 50–1, 60, 78–9, 85–6, 88, A. 092/2
- *Guild Gazette, Guild and City Gazette, Liverpool Gazette*, 1969–81, 1994
  Sphinx, vol. 69, 1969–70
  University Senate minutes 1969–70 – 1973–4
  Report to the Court (Report of the Vice-Chancellor) 1969–70, 1970–1
Guild of Students
- Guild Council minutes and papers 1988–91
- Guild Constitution
- Guild publications: *Guide to Housing, Sport and Recreation Handbook* and other handbooks
Centre for Academic Practice (including Enterprise in Higher Education records)
- EHE: annual reports 1990–5
- Review of the Programme 1990–5
- *Networks* (EHE newletter)

Nene College of Higher Education
Students Union
- General Meetings, 1986–90
- General Management Committee, 1986–91, 1991–4
- Executive Committee Meetings, 1991–2, 1992–4
- Meetings with Directorate, 1990–4
  Link, 1977–8 [1980]
  Nene Scene, 1986–96
Library
- Northampton College of Technology, Students' Association *Year Book 1954–55*
- *Students Handbook 1970–1*
- *Handbook 1983/4*
Student Services
- Leaflets on individual student services
Central administration
- Charter
- *It's Your Course: Student Guide to Being Involved in Academic Quality*

University of North London (formerly North London Polytechnic)
Central administration
- *PNL Factfile*

- *UNL MIU Statistics*
- *Student Guide 1995*
- Guidance and Learner Autonomy Project, 'Current provision', 1994
- Academic Quality Council, 28 May 1993
- HEQC, *Quality Audit Report*, 1993
Students Union
- *Fuse* (newspaper), 9 February 1995
- *Fuse* (magazine), October 1995

Oxford Brookes University
Central administration
- *Students' Charter*
- *On Stream* (bulletin), 1993–6
Student Services
- Leaflets on individual student services
Educational Methods Unit
- *Teaching News*, 41, 1995 ('Student-centred university')

University of Pennsylvania
University Archives and Records Centre
- UPF 8.5 (misc. student government, volunteers, students general, 1960s–1980s) boxes 54 f.1; 201 f.3, 5; 202 f. 1–4, 6, 9; 204 f. 10
- UPS (student handbooks, societies, organization, late 1960s) 51.1, 51.5, 58 box 4
- UPA 4 (Meyerson papers) box 253 f. 6 (Open Expression Committee 1970–5); box 254, f. 4, 5, 11 (Undergraduate Affairs Committee 1970s); box 284, f. 25–6 (handicapped, 1970s); box 348, f. 7–9, 17, 21; box 349, f. 1, 6, 36 (University life, student affairs 1970s)
- UPA 8 (Office of the Secretary, Student Life Committee, governance, 1970s), boxes 272, 274
- Hackney files, 1980s: boxes 129, 285 (handicapped), 184–7, 309, 533 (University life, students, Undergraduate Assembly)
- *Daily Pennsylvanian*, 1968–9, 1994–5
- *Almanac*, 3 December 1991 (guidelines on open expression); 10 May 1994 (minority permanence at Penn); 31 January 1995 (Student Judicial Charter); 7 February 1995 (consensual sexual relations); 28 March 1995 (Self-Study for Middle States Association); 18 April 1995 (firearms on campus)
Office of the Provost
- *21st Century Project for the Student Experience* (collection of historical material as part of planning), including:
- SCUE Report on Undergraduate Education, 1966
- Office of the Provost, 'A Candid Evaluation of the University', 1969
- Task Force on Governance, 1970
- SCUE Report on Undergraduate Education, 1971
- Conference on Undergraduate Education (inc. Gerald Robinson, 'Residential Life'), 1971
- 'The Advancement of Undergraduate Education: A [students'] Reply'
- Report on University Life by the Joint Subcommittee of the Committee on Faculty Affairs and Committee on Student Affairs, 1973
- Anita Sama, 'Watching Good Things Grow: four of Pennsylvania's 233 Years as a New Alumna Saw Them', 1973

- 'Undergraduate Education at the University of Pennsylvania. A report prepared for the Middle States Assocation of Colleges and Secondary Schools', 1974
- Task Force on University Governance, 1979
- *Almanac* summary of SCUE White Paper on Undergraduate Education, 1985
- SCUE, 'The 1990 White Paper on Undergraduate Education'
- *Almanac*, 16 October 1990, Report of the President's Committee on University Life
- Vice Provost for University Life, 'Residential Planning for the 21st Century', 1992
- SCUE, 'A Response to the Vice-Provost's Report on Residential Planning', 1993
- *Almanac*, 19 April 1994, 'Report of Faculty Senate Committee on Students and Educational Policy, Enriching the Intellectual and Social Life of Penn Undergraduates'

Undergraduate Assembly

- Anon. (230pp. typescript, title page missing, probably about 1987) 'Undergraduate and University Life, Education, and Community Service'
- Committee on the Goals of Higher Education of the College of Arts and Sciences, 'The Causes of Student Unrest and the Proper Response of the Universities to that Unrest', 1969
- Politics and Education Collective, 'The Case for Student Rights', 1972
- Student Affairs Committee, two papers on faculty–student interaction, 1984
- UA High Rise Committee, *Examination of the High Rise Experience* (a reduced version), 1987
- UA Report on Undergraduate Social Planning, 1989
- The Undergraduate Assembly Year 1990: 'Outlook on Student Life, 1986'
- The Undergraduate Assembly 1995: 'Evaluation of Progress, 1990'
- Student Task Force on Academic Integrity, 1993
- *Almanac*, 30 March 1993, 'The Code of Academic Integrity'
- UA, 'What Has the Undergraduate Assembly Accomplished this Year?', 1995
- *Daily Pennsylvanian*, 4 April 1995, 'Residential Living Officials Grapple with Continual Vandalism on Campus'
- 'Project 2000: A Five-year Plan for the Undergraduate Experience at Penn', 1995

Program for Student-Community Involvement

- *The Community Connection* (newsletter), 1994–5

Center for Community Partnerships

- Leaflets
- Extensive files on community partnerships and 'service learning' at Penn and other universities, projects, courses, newspaper and other cuttings, articles by Ira Harkavy (Director) and others, including material on Penn's work with the West Philadelphia Improvement Corps (WEPIC), and national work with schools, reflected in files of *Universities and Community Schools*, published by the Center.

Pennsylvania State University

University Archives

- PSR Inventory (history: University Student Advisory Board)
- PSR Inventory (history: position of Vice-President for Student Affairs)
- E.A. Walker [Pres] Student Activism 1963–1986 Boxes 1 and 2 (collection of file material, cuttings and personal notes)
- AX 0356/1 University health services
- AX 0356/36; AX 1357/40 Office of Student Activities, Annual Reports 1977–8, 1978–9

- Box 1423/20–21 Activist movement
- Box 1427 Organization of Student Government Associations
- Box 1428 Office of Student Affairs, Division of Greek Life
- Box USG 1970–2, 1973–4, 1976–7
- USG Congress 1977/8–1981/2 (5 vols)
- USG Department of Minority Affairs, *Collegian* articles, 1987–8
- GVF Women – general, Women – protests
- GVF Office of Student Affairs Research, 'Needs Assessment of Penn State Students 1982'
- *Student Handbook*, 1967–8, 1976–7
- *Daily Collegian*, 1983–4, 1988–9, 1995
- *Weekly Collegian*, 1993–4

Office for Disability Services
- Leaflets on specific services

Offices of Student Affairs and Student Life
- Annual Report, Student Life *1993–4*
- Student Affairs, *Policies and Rules for Student Organizations 1994–95*
- Escort Service, leaflet
- Offices of Unions and Student Life, *Penn State Student Organization Directory 1994–1995*

Undergraduate Student Government
- USG Congress 1986/7–1993/4 (8 vols)
- *Finding Common Ground*, Vol. 1 (coalition of environmental and other campaign groups)

University of Plymouth (formerly Plymouth Polytechnic, Polytechnic South West, including amalgamation with Rolle College, Exmouth)
Central Administration
- Academic Board 1965/74–1992/3 (42 vols)
- Faculty boards: Plymouth Business School 1980/2–1985/6 (4 vols); Technology 1987–8; Science 1980–1, 1981–4, 1986–7; Social Science, 1987–8
- *Spectrum*, 16, 1975
- *Plymouth Polytechnic Ten Years On 1970–1980*
- *inTouch*, 4, 1992 (inc. G. Buckton, 'Early Days at Rolle')
- *The Bulletin*, November 1993 (inc. M. Horton, 'The Customer's Perspective)
- *Ethos*, 3, 1994 (inc. C. Harris, 'Student representatives')
- *Code of Conduct and General Regulations for Students*, 1990
- *Articles of Government*, Polytechnic South West
- *Act of Incorporation*, HMSO, 1993
- Academic Board Constitution [1993]
- Constitution and Management Structure 1993
- *Code on Sexual Harassment* (n.d.)
- *Student Handbook 1995/96*

Enterprise in Higher Education
- Programme Progress Report 1992–3
- Programme 48: Community Action report 1993

Student Services
- Student Services Committee 1980–7
- Students' Union Consultative Committee 1983–92
- Students' Union Site Executive 1992–3

– An Institutional Policy for Student Support 1989
– Leaflets on individual student services
Students' Union
– Executive Committee 1982/3–1992/3 (10 vols)
– EC Sub-committees 1992–3
– General Meetings 1984/5–1992/3 (7 vols)
– (Second) Welfare Report [1992]
– *Extension*, 1–25, 1970–2; 1–28, 1972–3
– *Fly*, 1–24, 1973–4; Emergency issue, 12 November 1974; unnumbered 1975–6; 1–30, 1977–8
– *4 Site* (newspaper) [1993]
– *Pact* (newspaper of Plymouth Area Students' Association), 19 October 1978
– Devon and Somerset Students Assocation bulletin [1980–1]
– *The Academic Rep System: Have Your Say* (n.d.)
– *Mature Students Handbook* (n.d.)
– *Be in Control for 93–94: Academic Handbook*
– *Handbook 92, U.P.S.U. Handbook 93, Student Handbook* (1994)
– *Clubs and Societies Handbook* [1994]
– M. McGrory and S. Fearnside, *Jeanz, Beanz and the Meanz* [1994]
Students Union (Exmouth site)
– Rolle College Students Union:
    General Meetings 1962–79
    Council 1980–3
    file: The Constitution
    Scratch, 27 October 1986

University of Portsmouth
Students Union
– *The Student Survival Guide* (joint publication, Students Union and University Student Services)
– *Information and Advice Centre* (leaflet)

Queen Margaret College, Edinburgh (formerly Edinburgh College of Domestic Science)
Central Administration
– Governing Body 1970–83 (9 vols)
– Academic Council 1972–9
– Annual report 1990/1
– *Prospectus*, 1965/66, 1969/70, 1972/73, 1975/76, 1979/80, 1986/87
– *Queen Margaret College 1875–1975*
Library
– *A Second Chance to Learn: Opportunities for Mature Students*, 1987
– Membership of the Academic Council and Its Committees, 1987
– *Student Handbook* 1978/79, 1983/84, 1990/91
The Departments
– Student/Staff Consultative Committee, BA degree in Applied Consumer Studies, committee composition, meetings, memoranda, 1986–91
– Student/Staff Consultative Committee, Communication Studies, Course Document, 'Channels of Communication open to Students', committee composition, meetings, 1983–5

Students' Association
- Executive Committee 1962–70, 1992–3
- Student/Staff Committees (miscellaneous), Physiotherapy, Podiatry and Radiography, Dietetics and Nutrition, Occupational Therapy, Speech Pathology and Therapy, Health and Nursing, 1990s
- *Freshers Handbook, Alternative Reading Matter 1982–3*

Sheffield Hallam University (formerly Sheffield City Polytechnic)
Union of Students
- Union of Students, Sheffield City Polytechnic, Course Rep. Handbook and information and training pack, 1991
- Union of Students, Course Rep. Handbook and information and training pack, 1994–5

University of Sheffield
Students' Union
- SUSU/Gallup, 'Final tabulations and introduction' (report); Social Surveys (Gallup Poll), 1989
- SUSU (1993) 'Report on student hardship', 1993
- P. Gerrard 'Student lifestyle survey' (report), 1993a
- P. Gerrard 'Student lifestyle group interviews' (report), 1993b

University of Strathclyde
Students' Association
- Council and Executive Committee 1974–80, 1988–9, 1994–5
- President's Report to Council, 26 October 1992
- R. Adams and B. Johnston, *Staff–Student Committees. Being a Student Representative* (joint SA and University publication), 1994
- *Membership Services*, 1994
- *How to Get Elected on to the Students Representative Council* (leaflet)
- *How to Get Elected on to the Students' Union Executive* (leaflet)
- *Developing an Opportunity Profile*
- *Welfare Volunteers* (leaflet)
- Training Programme: Executive Training 1995 course programme
- M. Day, Workshop session: Representation and feedback, 1995
- Sports Union President, 7th Report to SRC, 1995
- Mature Students Association, leaflet (programme for 1995–6)
- Students' Association diary
- *It's a Jungle Out There* (Welfare handbook) [1995]
- *Bullseye: Handbook '95/'96*
- *CRUST – University of Strathclyde – A Guide to Student Life 1964–65*
- *CRUST* (1980) (inc. 'Cactus – Student Community Action at Strathclyde')
- *CACTUS, Project Handbook 1993–1994*
- *Strathclyde Telegraph*, 1978–91, 15 September 1992 (McLean) September 1994–May 1995

Student Community Action Development Unit (SCADU), London
- Annual Report 1991–3
- Review 1993–5
- New Volunteers' Induction Pack

- Guides, leaflets on events, activities
- *SCA News* and other publications
- SCA Groups Database
- Student Community Action Network Committee publications

University of Sunderland
Students Union
- *Student Representatives Handbook 1993–1994*

University of Sussex
Students Union
- *Handbook 1994/5*
- *Alternative Prospectus 94/95*
- Welfare Centre, *Moving Off Campus* pack, and leaflets
- Student Community Action: Link-Up, *Handbook* and leaflets
- Enterprise in Higher Education, *Briefing*, 9, 1995

University of Wales Swansea
Swansea Student Community Action
- *Making the Difference! Swansea Student Community Action Annual Report 1994–95*
- *Not Such a Trivial Pursuit . . . Project Handbook 1995–96*
- *Volunteer Induction Pack*
- *'Fun Talks': A Fun Day of Skills and Training for SSCA Volunteers Working with Children*
- *Learning with a Student Tutor: The Pilot Year*
- Leaflets on specific projects
- *Mature Students Society* (leaflet)
Central Administration
- *Student Charter 1995–96*

Swansea Institute of Higher Education
Academic Quality Unit
- 'Monitoring and Evaluation for 1994/5, Part-time Employment Feedback'
Students' Union
- Course Representatives' Feedback analysis, 1995/6
- Foreword to SU Accounts (Report of the Officers) 1990/1, 1991/2, 1992/3, 1993/4, 1994/5,
- Financial Statements for the year ended 31st August 1995
- Analysis of Societies for the year ended 31st August 1994
- D.A. Parker (n.d.) Long hot summer for students (article)

University of Teesside (including Constantine College, and formerly Teesside Polytechnic)
Central Administration
- Students' union records:
    Constantine College Students' Union, Executive Committee, General Meetings 1966–8, 1968–71
    Teesside Polytechnic Students' Union General Meetings, Executive Committee, Council 1971–90 (16 vols)
    Cleveland Students' Union (temporary name) 1977–8
    file: Welfare: Disabled Students 1978–86

- *Tease*, 1993
- *Franchised Student's Handbook 93–4*
- Constantine College of Technology/Teesside Polytechnic Staff/Student Liaison Committee 1968–85
- Academic Board 1970–93 (6 vols)
- Academic Board University and Student Support Committee 1993 (including draft charter)
- Department of Student Services, *Student Handbook 93/94*
- *Universe*, 1993

University of Wolverhampton
Students' Union
- Advice Unit, *Welfare Handbook*
- *Putting Students First: UWSU Info Service* (series of six leaflets)
- *Fix*, 2 [1994]

Bibliography

Abercrombie, M.L.J. (1966) Educating for change, *Universities Quarterly*, 21(1).

Abrahamowicz, D. (1988) College involvement, perceptions, and satisfaction: a study of membership in student organizations, *Journal of College Student Development*, 29(3).

Adams, W. (1969) L.S.E. and the new militancy, *British Universities Annual*, 1969.

Adelman, C. and Gibbs, I. (1979) A study of student choice in the context of institutional change: final report. Reading, Bulmershe College of Higher Education.

Adler, C. (1974) The student revolt: a special case of a youth culture. In C.W. Gordon (ed.), *Uses of the Sociology of Education*. Chicago: National Society for the Study of Education.

Aiken, M. (1984) What has Community Action got to do with students?, *Talking Point* (Association of Community Workers), 52.

Albrow, M.C. (1966) The influence of accommodation upon 64 Reading University students – an *ex post facto* experimental study, *British Journal of Sociology*, 17(4).

Altbach, P.G. (1979) From revolution to apathy – American student activism in the 1970s, *Higher Education*, 8(6).

Altbach, P.G. (1992) Student movements and associations. In B.R. Clark and G.R. Neave (eds), *Encyclopedia of Higher Education*, Vol. 3. Oxford: Pergamon Press.

Altbach, P.G. (1993) Students: interests, culture and activism. In A. Levine (ed.), *Higher Learning in America 1980–2000*. Baltimore, MD: Johns Hopkins University Press.

Altbach, P.G. and Cohen, R. (1990) American student activism: the post-sixties transformation, *Journal of Higher Education*, 61(1).

American Association of University Professors (1970) Student participation in college and university government. In *Policy Documents and Reports*. Washington, DC: AAUP.

American Council on Education (1984) *Rates of College Participation 1969, 1974, and 1981*. Washington, DC: ACE.

Andersen, C.J. (1990) *Enrollment by Age: Distinguishing the Numbers from the Rates*. Washington, DC: American Council on Education.

Anderson, C.W. (1993) *Prescribing the Life of the Mind*. Madison: Wisconsin University Press.

Andrews, A. with Bagnall, N., Cox, E. and Gill, P. (1970) Student grants – fair or unfair?, *Sunday Telegraph*, 11 October.

Annan, Lord (1975) The university in Britain. In M.D. Stephens and G.W. Roderick (eds), *Universities for a Changing World*. Newton Abbot: David and Charles.

Antcliffe, K.A. (1972) A Local Education Authority view. In Association of Colleges of Further and Higher Education, *Student Unions.* London: ACFHE.

Appleton, S.N. [1987] *The National Union of Students: A Contributor to Educational Policy Making?* London: NUS.

Arblaster, A. (1979) Students and power in higher education. In S. Armstrong (ed.), *Decade of Change.* Guildford: Society for Research into Higher Education.

Arlitt, A.A. (1938) *The Adolescent.* New York: McGraw-Hill.

Armstrong, S. (1979) Introduction. In S. Armstrong (ed.), *Decade of Change.* Guildford: Society for Research into Higher Education.

Armstrong, S. and McMurdo, M. (1979) The student movement of the late sixties. In S. Armstrong (ed.), *Decade of Change.* Guildford: Society for Research into Higher Education.

Ashby, E. (1951) A note on an alternative to halls of residence, *Universities Quarterly,* 5(2).

Ashby, E. (1965) *. . . and Scholars: Oration Delivered at the London School of Economics and Political Science . . . 1964.* London: LSE.

Ashby, E. (1968) The case for ivory towers. In A.D. Henderson (ed.), *Higher Education in Tomorrow's World.* Ann Arbor: University of Michigan.

Ashby, E. (1970) *Masters and Scholars: Reflections on the Rights and Responsibilities of Students.* London: Oxford University Press.

Ashby, E. (1973) Is the university a community? In E. Ashby, C. Carter, J.A. Perkins and J.S. Watson (eds), *The University on Trial.* Christchurch, New Zealand: University of Canterbury.

Ashby, E. (Lord) (1977) A hippocratic oath for the academic profession. In G.R. Urban (ed.), *Hazards of Learning: An International Symposium on the Crisis of the University.* London: Temple Smith.

Ashby, E. and Anderson, M. (1970) *The Rise of the Student Estate in Britain.* London: Macmillan.

Association of University Teachers [1963a] *The Chances of Getting a Place in a University* (leaflet). London: AUT.

Association of University Teachers [1963b] *Why We Need More Student Places in Universities* (leaflet). London: AUT.

Association of University Teachers (1965) *University Government and Organisation.* London: AUT.

Astin, A.W. (1980) Summary of effects [of college on beliefs, attitudes, and knowledge]. In H.F. Owens, C.H. Witten and W.R. Bailey (eds), *College Student Personnel Administration.* Springfield, IL: Charles C. Thomas.

Astin, A.W. (1991) The changing American college student: implications for educational policy and practice, *Higher Education,* 22(2).

Astin, A.W. (1993) *Higher Education and the Concept of Community* (with four responses). Urbana-Champaign: University of Illinois.

Astin, A.W., Astin, H.S., Bayer, A.E. and Bisconti, A.S. (1975) *The Power of Protest.* San Francisco: Jossey-Bass.

Avorn, J.L. with [others] of the staff of the *Columbia Daily Spectator* (1969) *University in Revolt: A History of the Columbia Crisis.* London: Macdonald.

Aylmer, G.E. (1958) University government – but by whom?, *Universities Quarterly,* 13(1).

Bagnall, N. with Cox, E. and Gill, P. (1970) Student affluence – in squalor?, *Sunday Telegraph,* 4 October.

Baird, L.L. (1990) The undergraduate experience: commonalities and differences among colleges, *Research in Higher Education,* 31(3).

Baker, D. and Ford, B. (1968) How much student participation?, *Universities Quarterly,* 22(4).

Baker, P. (1982) *Report on Student Housing.* London: National Union of Students.

Barnett, R. (1990a) *Changing Patterns of Course Review.* London: Council for National Academic Awards.

Barnett, R. (1990b) *The Idea of Higher Education.* Buckingham: Society for Research into Higher Education and Open University Press.

Barnett, R. (1991) Break-up of a happy marriage?, *Times Higher Education Supplement,* 15 March.

Barnett, R. (ed.) (1994) *Academic Community: Discourse or Discord?* London: Jessica Kingsley.

Barr, A. (1972) *Student Community Action.* London: Bedford Square Press.

Barzun, J. (1968) *The American University: How It Runs and Where It Is Going.* New York: Harper and Row.

Barzun, J. (1991) *Begin Here: The Forgotten Conditions of Teaching and Learning.* Chicago: University of Chicago Press.

Bates, J. and Ibbotson, C. (1994) *The World of UCL Union 1893–1993.* London: University College London Union.

Bearman, J. and Kilgore, J. (1993) *1993–94 National Members' Survey and Resource Guide.* Providence, RI: Brown University, Campus Compact.

Beckett, F. (1994) Rebel, rebel . . . , *The Guardian Education,* 1 February.

Beeler, K.D. (1979) New forms of student activism: lobbying, trusteeing, and collective bargaining, *Journal of College Student Personnel,* 20.

Beeler, K.D. (1985) American college student activism in the mid-1980s, *NASPA Journal,* 22.

Begg, T. (1994) *The Excellent Women: The Origins and History of Queen Margaret College.* Edinburgh: John Donald.

Bell, D.A., Dunning-Davies, J., Martin, A.G. and Stephenson, F.W. (1972) A survey of student representation on university senates, *Universities Quarterly,* 27(1).

Bellah, R.N., Madsen, R.N., Sullivan, W.M., Swidler, A. and Tipton, S.M. (1985) *Habits of the Heart: Individualism and Commitment in American Life.* San Francisco: University of California Press.

Bellot, H.H. (1929) *University College London 1826–1926.* London: University of London Press.

Beloff, M. (1968) The myth of student power, *British Universities Annual,* 1968.

Beloff, M. (1977) Can the university be conceived as a model of democracy? In G.R. Urban (ed.), *Hazards of Learning: An International Symposium on the Crisis of the University.* London: Temple Smith.

Belsey, J. and MacLeod, D. (1993) Revolting students revisited, *The Guardian,* 7 October.

Berry, M. (1995) The experience of being a woman student, *British Journal of Guidance and Counselling,* 23(2).

Beswick, D.G. (1982) *The Changing Student Population in Australia from the Seventies to the Eighties.* Melbourne: University of Melbourne, Centre for the Study of Higher Education.

Bevan, J. (1996) *30 Years of SSCA.* Swansea: Swansea Student Community Action.

Beveridge, Lord (1960) *The London School of Economics and its Problems, 1919–1937.* London: Allen & Unwin.

Bezilla, M. (1985) *Penn State: An Illustrated History.* University Park, PA: Pennsylvania State University Press.

Biggs, D.A. (1976) Recent research on British students: a brief analysis, *Research in Education*, 15.

Birnbaum, N. (1973) Students, professors, and philosopher kings. In C. Kaysen (ed.), *Content and Context: Essays on College Education*. New York: McGraw-Hill.

Bjorklund, Stefan (1995) A University constitution for disputation, *Studies of Higher Education and Research* (Stockholm), 4.

Blackstone, T. *et al.* (1970) *Students in Conflict: L.S.E. in 1967*. London: Weidenfeld and Nicolson.

Blakey, M. (1994) Student accommodation. In S. Haselgrove (ed.), *The Student Experience*. Buckingham: Society for Research into Higher Education and Open University Press.

Bloom, A. (1987) *The Closing of the American Mind: How Higher Education Has Failed Democracy and Impoverished the Souls of Today's Students*. New York: Simon and Schuster.

Bloustein, E.J. (1968) The new student and his role in American colleges, *Liberal Education*, October.

Bolton, C.D. and Kammeyer, K.C.W. (1967) *The University Student: A Study of Student Behavior and Values*. New Haven, CT: College and University Press.

Bonner, T.N. (1986) The unintended revolution in America's colleges since 1940, *Change*, 18(5).

Booth, C. (1993) Paid work and student performance, *On Stream* (Oxford Brookes University), 1 November.

Boseley, S. (1986) Easing the strains and sprains and growing pains, *The Guardian*, 5 September.

Bottomore, T.B. (1968) Students observed, *Universities Quarterly*, 22(4).

Bourner, T. and Hamed, M. (1987) *Entry Qualifications and Degree Performance: Summary Report*. London: Council for National Academic Awards.

Bourner, T., with Reynolds, A., Hamed, M. and Barnett, R. (1991) *Part-time Students and their Experience of Higher Education*. Buckingham: Society for Research into Higher Education and Open University Press.

Bowles, W.D. (1968) Student participation in academic governance, *Educational Record*, 49(3).

Boyer, E.L. (1987) *College: The Undergraduate Experience in America*. New York: Harper and Row.

Boys, C.J. (1984) *Inside a University*. Uxbridge: Brunel University, Expectations of Higher Education project.

Boys, C.J. and Kogan, M. (1984) *Commentary on Three Studies of Higher Education (The Providers)*. Uxbridge: Brunel University, Expectations of Higher Education project.

Brennan, J.L. and Percy, K.A. (1976) What do students want? An analysis of staff and student perceptions in British higher education. In A. Bonboir (ed.), *Proceedings of 2nd Congress of EARDHE*, Louvain-la-Neuve, Vol. 1.

Brierley, S. (1995) Interview on 'a student-centred university', *Teaching News* (Oxford Brookes University), 41.

Bright, M. (1996) March of the moderates, *The Guardian Education*, 30 January.

Brighton Polytechnic (1985) Documentation for the CNAA Quinquennial Review Visit 1 and 2 May 1985 (including A Statement by the Students' Union).

Brothers, J. and Hatch, S. (eds) (1971) *Residence and Student Life: A Sociological Inquiry into Residence in Higher Education*. London: Tavistock.

Burnhill, P. and McPherson, A. (1983) The Scottish university and undergraduate expectations, *Universities Quarterly*, 37(3).

Bushnell, J.H. (1962) Student culture at Vassar. In N. Sanford (ed.), *The American College.* New York: John Wiley.

Cage, M.C. (1993) The post-baby boomers arrive on campus, *Chronicle of Higher Education,* 30 June.

Cage, M.C. (1994) Beyond the B.A.: a record number of students, especially women, plan to seek graduate degrees, *Chronicle of Higher Education,* 26 January.

Caine, S. (1969) *British Universities: Purpose and Prospects.* London: Bodley Head.

Campbell, D. (1966) Student accommodation, *British Universities Annual,* 1966.

Carey, J.C., Stanley, D'L.A. and Biggers, J. (1988) Peak alert time and rapport between residence hall roommates, *Journal of College Student Development,* 29(3).

Carnegie Commission on Higher Education (1974) *A Digest of Reports.* New York: McGraw-Hill.

Carnegie Foundation for the Advancement of Teaching (1982) *The Control of the Campus: A Report on the Governance of Higher Education.* Princeton, NJ: CFAT.

Carnegie Foundation for the Advancement of Teaching (1986) Part-timers: myths and realities, *Change,* 18(4).

Carnegie Foundation for the Advancement of Teaching (1987) *College: the Undergraduate Experience in America.* Princeton, NJ: CFAT.

Carnegie Foundation for the Advancement of Teaching (1990) *Campus Life: In Search of Community.* Princeton, NJ: CFAT.

Carter, D.J. (1988) *Racial and Ethnic Trends in College Participation: 1976 to 1988.* Washington, DC: American Council on Education.

Cartledge, J. (1972) Community concern (review of Barr), *Universities Quarterly,* 27(1).

Cassidy, M. (1964) Architecture and the sociology of university life, *Universities Quarterly,* 18(4).

Cauthery, P. (1973) *Student Health.* London: Priory Press.

Change (1972) *Inside Academe: Culture in Crisis.* New Rochelle, NY: *Change.*

Charlton, D.G. (1954) University entry for adult students, *Universities Quarterly,* 8(4).

Charlton, D.J. (1995) Students on the night shift (letter), *The Guardian,* 18 November.

Cheltenham and Gloucester College of Higher Education, Enterprise in Higher Education Unit [1994] *EHE and Student Empowerment.* Cheltenham: CGHE.

Chickering, A.W. (1974) *Commuting versus Resident Students: Overcoming the Educational Inequities of Living off Campus.* San Francisco: Jossey-Bass.

Clark, B. and Trow, M. (1966) The organizational context. In T.H. Newcomb and E.K. Wilson (eds), *College Peer Groups: Problems and Prospects for Research.* Chicago: Aldine Publishing.

Clarke, C.F.O. (1970) *The Meaning of an Academic Community.* Enstone, Oxon: Ditchley Foundation.

Cobban, A.B. (1988) *The Medieval English Universities: Oxford and Cambridge to c.1500.* Aldershot: Scolar Press.

Cohen, L. (1970) Sixth-form pupils and their views of higher education, *Journal of Curriculum Studies,* 2(1).

Collins, M. (1959–60) Health, family and teaching, *Universities Quarterly,* 14(1).

Columbia University (1968) *Fact Finding Commission Appointed to Investigate the Disturbances at Columbia University in April and May 1968.* New York: Random House.

Committee of Enquiry into the Governance of the University of London (1972) *Final Report* (Murray Report). London: University of London.

Committee of Principals (Scottish Centrally-funded Colleges) (1991) *Performance Indicators: Report of Working Party.*

Committee of Vice-Chancellors and Principals and National Union of Students (1968) *Joint Statement*, 7 October.

Committee on Higher Education (1963) *Report* (Robbins Report), Cmnd 2154. London: HMSO.

Committee on Higher Education (1963) Appendices Two (A) and (B) *Students and their Education*, Cmnd 2154-II and 2154-II-1. London: HMSO.

Coomber, R. and Harrison, W.C. (1992) *Course Evaluation and Monitoring*. London: University of Greenwich.

Cooper, R.M. and Fisher, M.B. (1982) *The Vision of a Contemporary University: A Case Study of Expansion and Development in American Higher Education, 1950–1975*. Tampa: University Presses of Florida.

Cope, R. and Hannah, W. (1975) *Revolving College Doors: The Causes and Consequences of Dropping Out, Stopping Out, and Transferring*. New York: John Wiley.

Cornwell, T. (1995) Comfort factor wins students, *Times Higher Education Supplement*, 15 September.

Costin, F., Greenough, W.T. and Menges, R.J. (1971) Student ratings of college teaching: reliability, validity and usefulness, *Review of Educational Research*, 41(5).

Council for National Academic Awards (1969) *Quality Assurance Systems: Issues for Consideration*, Development Services Briefing 16. London: CNAA.

Coventry University [1993] *Strategic Plan 1994/95–1998/99*. Coventry: Coventry University.

Cowley, W.H. and Waller, W. (1979) A study of student life. The appraisal of student traditions as a field of research, *Journal of Higher Education*, 6(3). First published in 1935.

Cross, K.P. (1980) Our changing students and their impact on colleges: prospects for a true learning society. In H.F. Owens, C.H. Witten and W.R. Bailey (eds), *College Student Personnel Administration*. Springfield IL: Charles C. Thomas.

Crouch, C. (1968) Three approaches to student participation. In Fabian Society *Students Today*. London: Fabian Society.

Crouch, C. (1972) Britain. In M.S. Archer (ed.), *Students, University and Society: A Comparative Sociological Review*. London: Heinemann.

Crouch, C. (1992) Citizenship and community. In C. Crouch and A. Heath (eds), *Social Research and Social Reform: Essays in Honour of A.H. Halsey*. Oxford: Clarendon Press.

Curry, J.A. and Waldron, P. (1983) What's in what's out, *Daily Collegian*, 6 September.

Damrosch, D. (1995) *We Scholars: Changing the Culture of the University*. Cambridge, MA: Harvard University Press.

Davey, B. (1992) The Student Charter Project Report. University of Kent at Canterbury: Enterprise Kent.

Davies, D.J. (1949) Work and the universities, *Universities Quarterly*, 4(1).

Davies, L. (1990) *Experience-based Learning within the Curriculum: A Synthesis Study*. London: Council for National Academic Awards.

Davis, R.G. (1988) Back to the '60s, *Change*, 20(6).

Day, M. (1994) Developing Work with Course Representatives. Paper presented to Research and Welfare Staff Annual Conference, National Union of Students.

Deacon, R. (1994) Student life and expectations, *Higher Education Review*, 27(1).

DeCoster, D.A. and Mable, P. (eds) (1981) *Understanding Today's Students*. San Francisco: Jossey-Bass.

de Jonghe, E. (1973) The student and mass higher education, *Higher Education*, 2(2).

Department for Education (1993) *The Charter for Higher Education*. London: DFE.

Department for Education (1994) *Higher Education in the 1990s.* London: DFE.

Department of Education and Science (1978) *Special Educational Needs* (Warnock Report), Cmnd. 7212. London: HMSO.

Department of Education and Science (1991) *Performance Indicators in Higher Education January–April 1990: A Report by HMI.* London: DES.

DeVane, W.C. (1965) *Higher Education in Twentieth-century America.* Cambridge, MA: Harvard University Press.

Dole, A.A. (1970) Stability of reasons for going to college, *Journal of Educational Research,* 63(8).

Donaldson, L. (1995) Generation of the missing 'X', *The Guardian Society,* 26 April.

Driver, C. (1971) *The Exploding University.* Indianapolis, IN: Bobbs-Merrill.

Drummond, D., Gaukroger, A. and Lowe, R. (1993) Writing a university history: problems and possibilities, *History of Education Society Bulletin,* 51.

Duke, C. (1992) *The Learning University: Towards a New Paradigm?* Buckingham: Society for Research into Higher Education and Open University Press.

Dunn, R.S. and Lloyd, M.F. (eds) (1990) *A Pennsylvania Album: Undergraduate Essays on the 250th Anniversary of the University of Pennsylvania.* Philadelphia: University of Pennsylvania.

Eddy, E.E. (1977) What happened to student values?, *Educational Record,* 58(1).

Eight Scottish University Student Bodies (1985) *The Case for Student Unionism.*

El-Khawas, E.H. (1977) Putting the student consumer issue in perspective, *Educational Record,* 58(2).

Entwistle, N.J. and Wilson, J. (1970) Personality, study methods and academic performance, *Universities Quarterly,* 24(2).

Entwistle, N.J. and Wilson, J. (1977) *Degrees of Excellence: The Academic Achievement Game.* London: Hodder & Stoughton.

Evans, N. (1992) Experiential learning as learning to effect. In R. Barnett (ed.), *Learning to Effect.* Buckingham: Society for Research into Higher Education and Open University Press.

Farago, J.M. (1982) When they bought in, did we sell out? David Riesman on the student as consumer, *Journal of Higher Education,* 53(6).

Farber, J. (1969) *The Student as Nigger.* New York: Contact Books.

Farrell, D.M. (1979) College student subcultures and institutional goal preferences – a longitudinal analysis. Unpublished EdD dissertation, University of California, Los Angeles.

Fashing, J. and Deutsch, S.E. (1971) *Academics in Retreat.* Albuquerque: University of New Mexico Press.

Fass, R.A. (1986) In loco parentis revisited?, *Change,* 18(1).

Fisher, S. (1988) Cracking under pressure, *Times Higher Education Supplement,* 4 March.

Fisk, T. (1967) University discipline – the student viewpoint, *British Universities Annual,* 1967.

Fisk, T. (1968) Consecrated obstruction, *Universities Quarterly,* 22(4).

Fisk, T. (1969) The nature and causes of student unrest. In B. Crick and W.A. Robson (eds), *Protest and Discontent.* Harmondsworth: Penguin.

Flacks, R. (1972) The liberated generation. In S.M. Clark and J.P. Clark (eds), *Youth in Modern Society.* New York: Holt, Rinehart and Winston.

Flather, P. (1980) The mixed marriage that was born of meritocracy, *Times Higher Education Supplement,* 26 September.

Fletcher, L. (1972) Restless students: a modern phenomenon?', *Universities Quarterly,* 26(4).

Foote, C. and Associates (1968) *The Culture of the University: Governance and Education*. San Francisco: Jossey-Bass.

Francis, L.J. (1982) *Youth in Transit: A Profile of 16–25 Year Olds*. Aldershot: Gower.

Frankel, C. (1968) *Education and the Barricades*. New York: W.W. Norton.

Freedman, M.B. (1967) *The College Experience*. San Francisco: Jossey-Bass.

Friedson, E. (ed.) (1955) *Student Government, Student Leaders and the American College*. Philadelphia: United States National Student Association.

Frost, S.B. (1984) *McGill University. For the Advancement of Learning, Vol 2: 1895–1971*. Kingston: McGill-Queen's University Press.

Frye, N. (1969) The university and personal life: student anarchism and the educational contract. In W.R. Niblett (ed.), *Higher Education: Demand and Response*. London: Tavistock.

Fulton, J.S. (1962) The shape of universities. In W.R. Niblett (ed.), *Higher Education: Demand and Response*. London: Faber and Faber.

Fulton, J. (1964a) *Experiment in Higher Education*. London: Tavistock.

Fulton, J. (1964b) New universities in perspective. In D. Daiches (ed.), *The Idea of a New University: An Experiment in Sussex*. London: André Deutsch.

Furnham, A.F. (1993) The adjustment of foreign students, *Higher Education Review*, 26(1).

Gamson, Z.F. (1984) The undergraduate experience, *AAHE Bulletin*, 37(1).

Gardner, J.W. (1968) Agenda for the colleges and universities. In A.C. Eurich (ed.), *Campus 1980*. New York: Delacorte Press.

Garner, U. (1970) Knowledge for what?, *Journal of Higher Education*, 41(4).

Garrett, A. (1995) Poachers turned landlords, *Observer*, 17 September.

Geiger, R.L. (1993) *Research and Relevant Knowledge: American Research Universities since World War II*. New York: Oxford University Press.

Genereux, R.L. and McLeod, B.A. (1995) Circumstances surrounding cheating: a questionnaire study of college students, *Research in Higher Education*, 36(6).

Gibbs, G. and Lucas, L. (1994) Does student performance suffer in large classes?, *Teaching News* (Oxford Brookes University), 37.

Gibbs, I. (1984) *The Diversified Colleges: The Student Perspective* (Combined Colleges Research Group, Final Report).

Goddard, D.R. and Koons, L.C. (1973) A profile of the University of Pennsylvania. In D. Riesman and V.A. Stadtman (eds), *Academic Transformation: Seventeen Institutions under Pressure*. New York: McGraw-Hill.

Goldsen, R.K., Rosenberg, M., Williams, R.M. Jr. and Suchman, E.A. (1960) *What College Students Think*. Princeton, NJ: Van Nostrand.

Gordon, A. and Williams, G. (1977) Attitudes of fifth and sixth formers to school, work and higher education (research report). Lancaster: University of Lancaster.

Gowenlock, B. (1962) Contribution to discussion on 'departmentalism and community'. In W.R. Niblett (ed.), *The Expanding University*. London: Faber and Faber.

Grant, G. and Riesman, D. (1978) *The Perpetual Dream: Reform and Experiment in the American College*. Chicago: Chicago University Press.

Green, K. and Astin, A.W. (1985) The mood on campus: more conservative or just more materialistic?, *Educational Record*, 66(1).

Green, V.H.H. (1969) *The Universities*. Harmondsworth: Penguin.

Greenall, S. (1971) Student views on wastage, *Universities Quarterly*, 25(2).

Greene, M. (1970) The spectrum of disenchantment. In R.L. Hart and J.G. Saylor (eds), *Student Unrest: Threat or Promise?* Washington, DC: Association for Supervision and Curriculum Development.

Griffiths, S. (1988) The acceptable face of capitalism, *Times Higher Education Supplement*, 3 June.

Griffiths, S. (1990) Bedroom farce will run and run, *Times Higher Education Supplement*, 14 September.

Gross, A. and Shlomchik, M. (eds) (1980) *A Report on the First Intercollegiate Conference*. Philadelphia: Ivy Association for College Research and Communication.

Habermas, J. (1968) *Toward a Rational Society: Student Protest, Science and Politics*. Boston: Beacon Press.

Hall, S. (1961) The new student, *Universities Quarterly*, 15(2).

Halsey, A.H. and Marks, S. (1968) British student politics, *Daedalus*, 97(1).

Harcleroad, F.F. (1971) Assessment of colleges and universities. In F.F. Harcleroad and J.H. Cornell (eds), *Assessment of Colleges and Universities*. Iowa City: American College Testing Program.

Harrison, D. and McKay, R. (1996) Hard-up students skip class to work in sweatshops, *Observer*, 24 March.

Harvey, L. and Burrows, A. (1992) Empowering students, *The New Academic*, 1(3).

Haselgrove, S. (ed.) (1994) *The Student Experience*. Buckingham: Society for Research into Higher Education and Open University Press.

Hatch, S. (1968) *Student Residence: A Discussion of the Literature*. London: Society for Research into Higher Education.

Hatch, S. (1971) Student culture and the impact of institutions. In J. Brothers and S. Hatch (eds), *Residence and Student Life: A Sociological Inquiry into Residence in Higher Education*. London: Tavistock.

Hatch, S. (1972) Change and dissent in the universities: an examination of the sources of protest. In H.J. Butcher and E. Rudd (eds), *Contemporary Problems in Higher Education: An Account of Research*. London: McGraw-Hill.

Hawes, L.C. and Trux IV, H.R. (1974) Student participation in the university decision-making process, *Journal of Higher Education*, 45(2).

Hayden, T. (1967) Student social action: from liberation to community. In M. Cohen and D. Hale (eds), *The New Student Left: An Anthology*. Boston: Beacon Press.

Herrman, I.M. (1969) *Students and Universities*. Enstone, Oxon: Ditchley Foundation.

Hexter, H. (1990) *Students Who Work: A Profile*. Washington, DC: American Council on Education.

Heywood, J. (1971) A report on student wastage, *Universities Quarterly*, 25(2).

Higher Education (1973) Special issue on 'The implications of mass higher education', *Higher Education*, 2(2).

Higher Education (1991) Special issue on 'Approaches to learning and perceptions of the learning environment', *Higher Education*, 22(3).

Higher Education Digest (1995a) Supplement: The role of students in quality assurance, *Higher Education Digest*, 21.

Higher Education Digest (1995b) Supplement: Students in UK higher education 1994/5, *Higher Education Digest*, 23.

Higher Education Funding Council for England (1993) *Assessors' Handbook*. Bristol: HEFC.

Higher Education Quality Council (1993) *Notes for the Guidance of Auditors*. London: HEQC.

Higher Education Quality Council (1994a) *Guidelines on Quality Assurance*. London: HEQC.

Higher Education Quality Council (1994b) *Learning from Audit*. London: HEQC.

Higher Education Quality Council (1994c) *Choosing to Change: Extending Access, Choice and Mobility in Higher Education. The Report of the HFQC CAT Development Project* (Robertson Report). London: HEQC.

Hodges, L. (1995) Politics proves a fresher turn-off, *Times Higher Education Supplement*, 20 January.

Hodgkinson, H.L. (1968) Students and an intellectual community, *Educational Record*, 49(4).

Hodgkinson, H.L. (1971) Student participation in governance. In W.B. Martin, H.L. Hodgkinson and P.K. Cross (eds), *Education Task Force Papers Prepared for the White House Conference on Youth.* Berkeley: University of California, Berkeley, Center for Research and Development in Higher Education.

Hoggart, R. (1979) 1968–1978: the student movement and its effects on universities. In S. Armstrong (ed.), *Decade of Change.* Guildford: Society for Research into Higher Education.

Hoggart, S. (1970) Student power without being militant, *The Guardian*, 24 November.

Hollinshead, B. and Griffith, J. (1990) *Mature Students: Marketing and Admissions Policy.* London: Council for National Academic Awards.

Holman, R. (1972) Students and community action, *Universities Quarterly*, 26(2).

Home Universities Conference 1961 [1962] *Report of Proceedings.* London: Association of Universities of the British Commonwealth.

Hookham, M. (1964) Student affairs, *British Universities Annual*, 1964.

Hookham, M. (1966) Student affairs, *British Universities Annual*, 1966.

Hookham, M. (1967) Student matters, *British Universities Annual*, 1967.

Hore, T. and West, L.H.T. (eds) (1980) *Mature Age Students in Australian Higher Education.* Clayton, Victoria: Monash University Higher Education Advisory and Research Unit.

Horowitz, H.L. (1987) *Campus Life: Undergraduate Cultures from the End of the Eighteenth Century to the Present.* New York: Knopf.

Horowitz, I.L. and Friedland, W.H. (1970) *The Knowledge Factory: Student Power and Academic Politics in America.* Carbondale: Southern Illinois University Press.

House of Commons Select Committee on Education and Science (1969a) *Student Relations*, Vol. 1: *Report*, HC 449–i, Session 1968–69. London: HMSO.

House of Commons Select Committee on Education and Science (1969b) *Student Relations*, Vol. 2: *Full Committee, Evidence and Appendices*, HC 449–ii, Session 1968–69. London: HMSO.

House of Commons Select Committee on Education and Science (1969c) *Student Relations*, Vol. 7: *Documents*, HC 449–vii, Session 1968–69. London: HMSO.

Hull IV, W.F. (1978) *Foreign Students in the United States of America: Coping Behavior within the Educational Environment.* New York: Praeger.

Hunter, T. (1995) Facing the university financial challenge, *Guardian*, 9 December.

Hutt, M. (1964) Undergraduates and their problems. In D. Daiches (ed.), *The Idea of a New University: An Experiment in Sussex.* London: André Deutsch.

Insley, J. (1995) Bachelor of debts, *Observer*, 17 September.

Jacks, D. (1973) Student representation (summary of a paper), *Higher Education*, 2(2).

Jacks, D. (1975) *Student Politics and Higher Education.* London: Lawrence and Wishart.

Jacoby, B. (1989) *The Student as Commuter. Developing a Comprehensive Institutional Response* (ASHE-ERIC Report 7). Washington, DC: George Washington University.

James, T.E. (1960) The age of majority, *American Journal of Legal History*, 4.

Jeffery, G.B. (1950) *The Unity of Knowledge: Some Reflections on the Universities of Cambridge and London.* London: Cambridge University Press.

Jencks, C. and Riesman, D. (1968) *The Academic Revolution.* Garden City, NY: Doubleday.

Jencks, C. and Riesman, D. (1972) The war between the generations. In S.M. Clark and J.P. Clark (eds), *Youth in Modern Society.* New York: Holt, Rinehart and Winston.

Johnson, E.L. (1971) *From Riot to Reason.* Urbana: University of Illinois Press.

Johnson, R.W. (1988) Dreaming a revolution, *The Guardian,* 15 January.

Johnson, S.H. (1994) Presentation to conference on careers, University of Glasgow, 28 November.

Johnston, R. (1971) Student culture and student power. In H.L. Hodgkinson and L.R. Meeth (eds), *Power and Authority: Transformation of Campus Governance.* San Francisco: Jossey-Bass.

Jones, C. (1996) Hard-hit young just say no to life of pay as you learn, *The Guardian,* 20 January.

Jones, H.A. and Williams, K.E. (1979) *Adult Students and Higher Education.* Leicester: Advisory Council for Adult and Continuing Education.

Kapp, G.J. (1979) College extracurricular activities: who participates and what are the benefits? Unpublished PhD dissertation, University of California, Los Angeles.

Katz, F.M. and Arbib, P.S. (1971) The ideal student – role definitions by students and staff, *Universities Quarterly,* 25(3).

Katz, F.M. and Katz, C.N. (1967) Occupational aspirations of university students, *Australian Journal of Higher Education,* 3(1).

Katz, F.M. and Katz, C.N. (1968) Students' definition of the objectives of a university education, *Australian Journal of Higher Education,* 3(2).

Katz, J. and Sanford, N. (1969) The new student power and needed educational reforms. In H.W. Bernard (ed.), *Readings in Adolescent Development.* Scranton, PA: International Textbook Co.

Kelley, B.M. (1974) *Yale: A History.* New Haven, CT: Yale University Press.

Kendall, B.B. and McDonnell, K.G.T. (1960) The student population of Queen Mary College, 1934–59, *East London Papers,* 3(1).

Kendall, M. [1966] The location of student residence in London and Sussex. In Society for Research into Higher Education, *Student Residence – Research Aspects.* London: SRHE.

Keylock, B. (1975) A week in the life of a university undergraduate, *Higher Education Bulletin,* 3(2).

Kirkland, J. and Jepson, M. (1984) *The Role of the Careers Adviser.* Uxbridge: Brunel University, Expectations of Higher Education project.

Kitzinger, U. (1991) Higher education: an international dimension, *Oxford Review of Education,* 17(1).

Kogan, M. and Boys, C.J. (1984) *Expectations of Higher Education: A Synopsis and Commentary on Its Main Findings.* Uxbridge: Brunel University, Expectations of Higher Education project.

Kristol, I. (1965) What's bugging the students?' In *Atlantic Monthly, The Troubled Campus.* Boston: Little, Brown and Co.

Kuh, G.D., Bean, J.P., Bradley, R.K., Coomes, M.D. and Hunter, D.E. (1986) Changes in research on college students published in selected journals between 1969 and 1983, *Review of Higher Education,* 9(2).

Kunen, J.S. (1972) Campus protest: an inside perspective. In S.M. Clark and J.P. Clark (eds), *Youth in Modern Society.* New York: Holt, Rinehart and Winston.

La Belle, T.J. (1974) Youth as sociocultural systems in American society. In C.W. Gordon (ed.), *Uses of the Sociology of Education*. Chicago: National Society for the Study of Education.

Lasch, C. (1978) *The Culture of Narcissism: American Life in an Age of Diminishing Expectations*. New York: W.W. Norton.

Lauter, P. and Howe, F. (1971) *The Conspiracy of the Young*. New York: World Publishing Co.

Lee, C.B.T. (1970) *The Campus Scene, 1900–1970: Changing Styles of Undergraduate Life*. New York: David McKay.

Leslie, D.W. (1969) Student Unrest on the American University Campus: A Bibliography. State College, PA: Pennsylvania State University, Center for the Study of Higher Education.

Leslie, W.B. (1992) *Gentlemen and Scholars: College Community in the 'Age of the University,' 1865–1917*. University Park, PA: Pennsylvania State University Press.

Levi, E.H. (1969) *Point of View: Talks on Education*. Chicago: University of Chicago Press.

Levine, A. (1980) *When Dreams and Heroes Died: A Portrait of Today's College Student*. San Francisco: Jossey-Bass.

Levine, A. and Hirsch, D. (1991) Undergraduates in transition: a new wave of activism on American college campus, *Higher Education*, 22(2).

Levine, A. and Wilson, K.R. (1979) Student activism in the 1970s: transformation not decline, *Higher Education*, 8(6).

Lewis, I. (1984) *The Student Experience of Higher Education*. London: Croom Helm.

Lipset, S.M. (1972) *Rebellion in the University: A History of Student Activism in America*. London: Routledge & Kegan Paul.

Lipset, S.M. (1975) The American university – 1964–1974: from activism to austerity. In P. Seabury (ed.), *Universities in the Western World*. New York: Free Press.

Livingstone, R. (1948) *Some Thoughts on University Education*. London: Cambridge University Press.

Lloyd-Jones, E. (1989) Foreword. In D.C. Roberts (ed.), *Designing Campus Activities to Foster a Sense of Community*. San Francisco: Jossey-Bass.

Long, S. (1982) Educational disenchantment and the university student, *Higher Education*, 11(2).

Lord Chancellor's Office (1967) *Report of the Committee on the Age of Majority* (Latey Report), Cmnd. 3342, Session 1966–67. London: HMSO.

Lucas, C.J., Kelvin, R.P. and Ojha, A.B. (1966) Mental health and student wastage, *British Journal of Psychiatry*, 112.

McCartan, A.-M. (1988) Students who work. Are they paying too high a price?, *Change*, 20(5).

McCarthy, P. and Humphrey, R. (1995) Debt: the reality of student life, *Higher Education Quarterly*, 49(1).

McConnell, T.R. (1971) *The Redistribution of Power in Higher Education*. Berkeley: University of California, Berkeley, Center for Research and Development in Higher Education.

McConnell, T.R. and Edelstein, S. (1977) *Campus Governance at Berkeley: A Study in Jurisdictions*. Berkeley: University of California, Berkeley, Center for Research and Development in Higher Education.

McDowell, L. (1991) *Course Evaluation: Using Students' Experiences of Learning and Teaching*. Newcastle upon Tyne: Newcastle Polytechnic.

McGrath, E.J. (1970) *Should Students Share the Power? A Study of their Role in College and University Governance*. Philadelphia: Temple University Press.

McHardy, A. (1995) The caring campus, *The Guardian Education*, 19 September.

Maclay, I. (1968) A random sample of university undergraduates, *Universities Quarterly*, 23(1).

McLean, J. (1992) It weren't like this when I were a lad . . . , *Strathclyde Telegraph*, 15 September.

MacLeod, D. (1994) University swots worry employers, *The Guardian*, 22 August.

MacLeod, D. (1995) Taxing time, *The Guardian Education*, 28 November.

McLintock, M.E. (1974) *University of Lancaster: Quest for Innovation*. Lancaster: University of Lancaster.

McNay, I. (1994) The future student experience. In S. Haselgrove (ed.), *The Student Experience*. Buckingham: Society for Research into Higher Education and Open University Press.

MacRae, D.G. (1967) The culture of a generation: students and others. In W. Laqueur and G.L. Mosse (eds), *Education and Social Structure in the Twentieth Century*. New York: Harper and Row.

MacRae, D.G. (1977) Students in orbit. In G.R. Urban (ed.), *Hazards of Learning: An International Symposium on the Crisis of the University*. London: Temple Smith.

Maitland-Jones, J.F. (1971) What do students expect from the university? In J.H.M. Scott (ed.), *University Independence: The Main Questions*. London: Rex Collings.

Malleson, N. (1958) Student performance at University College London, 1948–1951, *Universities Quarterly*, 12(3).

Malleson, N. (1959) University student, 1953. I. Profile, *Universities Quarterly*, 13(3).

Malleson, N. (1959–60) University student, 1953. II. Schooling, *Universities Quarterly*, 14(1).

Malleson, N. (1960a) University student, 1953. III. Men and women, hours of study, *Universities Quarterly*, 14(2).

Malleson, N. (1960b) University student, 1953. IV. Different sorts of students, *Universities Quarterly*, 15(1).

Malleson, N. (1963) Memorandum on 'Student wastage in British universities'. In Committee on Higher Education, *Higher Education. Evidence, Part 2: Documentary Evidence*, London: HMSO.

Malleson, N. (1975) Student personal problems and courses. In North East London Polytechnic, *What Has Happened to the Students?* London: NELPRESS.

Mann, P.H. and Mills, G. (1961) Living and learning at Redbrick: a sample survey at Sheffield University, *Universities Quarterly*, 16(1).

Marks, J. and Cox, C. (1979) Students, staff and academic government. Ideas and consequences. In S. Armstrong (ed.), *Decade of Change*. Guildford: Society for Research into Higher Education.

Marris, P. (1964) *The Experience of Higher Education*. London: Routledge & Kegan Paul.

Mathews, D. (1993) Why students hate politics, *Chronicle of Higher Education*, 7 July.

Mead, M. (1972) *Culture and Commitment: A Study of the Generation Gap*. London: Bodley Head. First published in 1970.

Meyerson, S. (ed.) (1975) *Adolescence: The Crisis of Adjustment*. London: Allen & Unwin.

Milani, T. and Johnston, J.W. (eds) (1992) *The College Union in the Year 2000*. San Francisco: Jossey-Bass.

Miller, G.W. (1968) Students' needs and counselling, *Universities Quarterly*, 22(4).

Miller, G.W. (1970) *Success, Failure and Wastage in Higher Education*. London: Harrap.

Millett, J.D. (1962) *The Academic Community*. New York: McGraw-Hill.

Ministry of Education (1960a) *The Youth Service in England and Wales* (Albermarle Report), Cmnd. 929, Session 1959–60. London: HMSO.

Ministry of Education (1960b) *Grants to Students. Report of the Committee Appointed by the Minister of Education and the Secretary of State for Scotland* (Anderson Report), Cmnd. 1051, Session 1959–60. London: HMSO.

Minogue, K.R. (1973) *The Concept of a University.* London: Weidenfeld and Nicolson.

Moberly, W. (1949) *The Crisis in the University.* London: SCM Press.

Moffatt, M. (1991) College life: undergraduate culture and higher education, *Journal of Higher Education,* 62(1).

Molloy, S. and Carroll, V. (1991) Progress and performance in higher education: a report on performance monitoring of 'standard' and 'non-standard' entrants to undergraduate courses (CNAA project). Bradford: Bradford and Ilkley Community College.

Moodie, G. (1979) Students and academic government. In S. Armstrong (ed.), *Decade of Change.* Guildford: Society for Research into Higher Education.

Morrill, R.L. and Mount, C.E. Jr (1986) In loco parentis revisited?, *Change,* 18(1).

Morris, W.S. (1947) A freshmen's conference: introduction to the university, *Times Education Supplement,* 27 September.

Mott, J. and Goldie, N. (1971) The social characteristics of militant and anti-militant students, *Universities Quarterly,* 26(1).

Mountford, J. (1957) Success and failure at the university, *Universities Quarterly,* 11(3).

Muller, L.C. and Muller, O.G. (1960) *College for Coeds.* New York: Pitman.

National Commission on Education (1993) *Learning to Succeed.* London: Heinemann.

National Union of Students (1963) Memorandum submitted to the Committee on Higher Education, and oral evidence *Higher Education. Evidence – Part One. Vol. A, Written and Oral Evidence.* London: HMSO.

National Union of Students (1966) *Student Participation in College Government.* London: NUS.

National Union of Students (1967) *Mixed Visiting in Colleges* (leaflet). London: NUS.

National Union of Students (1973) *Student Representation Survey.* London: NUS.

National Union of Students (1978) *Disabled Students in Halls of Residence: Provision for Students with Locomotive Disorders.* London: NUS.

National Union of Students (1981) *Survey of Provision for Students with Locomotive Disorders in Halls of Residence.* London: NUS.

National Union of Students (1992) *NUS Student Charter.* London: NUS.

National Union of Students [1994] Student Charters in Higher Education: Briefing. London: NUS.

National Union of Students and National Bureau for Handicapped Students (1981) *IYDB – Guidance Notes to Students Unions.* London: NUS.

Nelkin, D. (1972) *The University and Military Research: Moral Politics at M.I.T.* Ithaca, NY: Cornell University Press.

Newman, F. (1985) *Higher Education and the American Resurgence.* Princeton, NJ: Carnegie Foundation for the Advancement of Teaching.

Niblett, W.R. (1990) An absence of outrage: cultural change and values in British higher education 1930–1990, *Reflections on Higher Education,* 2(2).

Nicholls, A. and Simon, K. (1995) A whole new ball game, *The Guardian Education,* 21, February.

Nicholls, R. and Crawley, M. (1993) Increasing the effectiveness of the course representative system. Report of a project jointly undertaken by Enterprise in Higher Education and the Students Union at the University of Greenwich, December 1992 – March 1993. London: University of Greenwich.

Nisbet, R. (1971) *The Degradation of the Academic Dogma: The University in America, 1945–1970*. New York: Basic Books.

North East London Polytechnic (1973) Report of the Academic Board Working Party on Facilities for Disabled Students. London: NELP.

North East London Polytechnic (1975) *What Has Happened to the Students?* London: NELPRESS.

Nowicka, H. (1995) 'Soft target' students a magnet for muggers, *Observer*, 8 October.

Nuffield Foundation Group for Research and Innovation in Higher Education (1973–4) *Newsletter*, nos 1–5.

Oakeshott, M. (1989) The universities, *Cambridge Journal*, II (1948–9), reprinted in T. Fuller (ed.), *The Voice of Liberal Learning: Michael Oakeshott on Education*. New Haven, CT: Yale University Press.

Observer (1996) News item on term-time jobs, 7 January.

Ogilvie, R.M. (1962) The role of the teacher. In W.R. Niblett (ed.), *The Expanding University*. London: Faber and Faber.

Oliver, R. (1979) How far have we come since 1968? What lies ahead? In S. Armstrong (ed.), *Decade of Change*. Guildford: Society for Research into Higher Education.

Opacic, S. (1996) The students' experience of franchising. In M. Abramson, J. Bird and A. Stennett (eds), *Further and Higher Education Partnerships*. Buckingham: Society for Research into Higher Education and Open University Press.

Organization for Economic Co-operation and Development (1987) *Universities under Scrutiny*. Paris: OECD.

Orrick, W.H. (1969) *Shut it Down! A College in Crisis. San Francisco State College October, 1968 – April, 1969*. Washington, DC: US Government Printing Office.

Otten, C.M. (1970) *University Authority and the Student: The Berkeley Experience*. Berkeley: University of California Press.

Ottinger, C. (1991) *College Going, Persistence, and Completion Patterns in Higher Education: What do we Know?* Washington, DC: American Council on Education.

Otuya, E. and Mitchell, A. (1994) *Today's College Students: Varied Characteristics by Sector*. Washington, DC: American Council on Education.

Overseas Student Trust (1987) *The Next Steps: Overseas Student Policy*. London: OST.

Oxtoby, M. (1968) Are students wasting their time?, *Universities Quarterly*, 22(4).

Oxtoby, M. and Smith, B.M. (1970) Students entering Sussex and Essex universities in 1966: some similarities and differences, II, *Research in Education*, 3.

Palmer, P.J. (1987) Community, conflict, and ways of knowing, *Change*, 19(5).

Parker, D.A. (1996) Winter chill for penniless students, *South Wales Evening Post*, 30 January.

Parnell, D. (1990) *Dateline 2000: The New Higher Education Agenda*. Washington, DC: Community College Press.

PCAS Microcomputer Statistics Service (1993) 1993 applications (students indicating disability), 4 November.

Penn, J.R. and Franks, R.G. (1982) Student consumerism in an era of conservative politics, *NASPA Journal*, 19.

Pennsylvania Campus Compact [1994] *Inventory of Student Community Service Activities*. Harrisburg, PA: PCC.

Percy, K. (1985) Adult learners in higher education. In C. Titmus (ed.), *Widening the Field: Continuing Education in Higher Education*. Guildford: Society for Research into Higher Education.

Percy, K.A. and Salter, F.W. (1976) Student and staff perceptions and 'the pursuit of excellence' in British higher education, *Higher Education*, 5(4).

Philip, H. and others (1964) *The University and the Community.* Sydney: I. Novak.
Phillips, R. (1974) *Student Community Action: Report of the Pilot Programme of the NUS (UK) Student Community Action Project 1971–1974.* London: National Union of Students.
Phillips, V. (1989) Students: partners, clients or consumers? In Sir Christopher Ball and H. Eggins (eds), *Education into the 1990s: New Dimensions.* Milton Keynes: Society for Research into Higher Education and Open University Press.
Pilkington, P. (1994) Student financial support. In S. Haselgrove (ed.), *The Student Experience.* Buckingham: Society for Research into Higher Education and Open University Press.
Platt, E. (1994) The glittering prizes, *The Guardian Education,* 15 February.
Polk, K. (1972) Student protest in the UK and the US. In T. Burgess (ed.), *The Shape of Higher Education.* London: Cornmarket Press.
Pomery, C. (1982) Bending the rod of iron, *Times Higher Education Supplement,* 30 July.
Porter, H. (1994) Best years of their lives?, *The Guardian Education,* 16 November.
Potter, P. (1965) Student discontent and campus reform. In O.A. Knorr and W.J. Minter (eds), *Order and Freedom on the Campus: The Rights and Responsibilities of Faculty and Students.* Boulder, CO: Western Interstate Commission for Higher Education.
Powell, A. (1951) *A Question of Upbringing.* London: Heinemann.
Powney, J. (1994) Peer review of CNAA courses. Unpublished PhD thesis, University of East Anglia.
Powney, J. and Coyle, P. (1990) Student participation in quality assurance (project report). Preston: Lancashire Polytechnic.
Ragheb, M.G. and McKinney, J. (1993) Campus recreation and perceived academic stress, *Journal of College Student Development,* 34(1).
Read, J.C. (1954) Psychiatry and the undergraduate, *Universities Quarterly,* 9(1).
Redwood, F. (1995) When freshers freak, *The Guardian Education,* 7 November.
Rees, A.B. (1979) 'In loco parentis' and student discipline in private higher education. Unpublished PhD dissertation, State University of New York at Buffalo.
Reeves, M. (1969) Academic values in an age of revolution. In S. Sterling (ed.), *Reflections on Student Protest.* London: SCM Press.
Reid, A.S. (1976) *Furman University: Toward a New Identity 1925–1975.* Durham, NC: Duke University Press.
Rhodes, F.A. (1990) *The National Union of Students.* Coventry: Student Union Senior Officers' Conference, c/o Warwick University Students' Union.
Richards, H. and Thomson, A. (1996) Loan bill survives exodus, *Times Higher Education Supplement,* 19 January.
Richards, M. (1987) Long-term mission of Enterprise, *Times Higher Education Supplement,* 11 December.
Richardson, J.T.E. (1994) A British evaluation of the course experience questionnaire, *Studies in Higher Education,* 19(1).
Richling, J. (1971) 70 per cent, *Universities Quarterly,* 25(2).
Riesman, D. (1978) Spoilt American heirs turn to great cathedrals of learning, *Times Higher Education Supplement,* 5 May.
Riesman, D. (1980) *On Higher Education: The Academic Enterprise in an Era of Rising Student Consumerism.* San Francisco: Jossey-Bass.
Riesman, D. and Stadtman, V.A. (eds) (1973) *Academic Transformation: Seventeen Institutions under Pressure.* New York: McGraw-Hill.
Robbins, Lord (1969) Present discontents of the student age group (address 1968).

In House of Commons Select Committee on Education and Science, *Student Relations*, Vol. 7: *Documents*, HC 449–vii, Session 1968–69. London: HMSO.

Roberts, D. and Higgins, T. (1992) *Higher Education: The Student Experience*. Leeds, HEIST.

Rooney, A. (1993) Oxford: an American perspective, *Vade Mecum* (Oxford), 111.

Ross, M.G. (1976) *The University: The Anatomy of Academe*. New York: McGraw-Hill.

Rowe, A.P. (1960) Red brick and whitewash, *Universities Quarterly*, 14(3).

Rowlands, C. (1978) Why students are turning their backs on the university challenge, *Daily Mail*, 7 September.

Rudolph, F. (1966) Neglect of students as a historical tradition. In L.E. Dennis and J.F. Kauffman (eds), *The College and the Student*. Washington, DC: American Council on Education.

Ryle, A. (1966) Student health services, *Universities Quarterly*, 21(1).

Ryle, A. (1969) *Student Casualties*. London: Allen Lane.

Ryle, A. (1971) Student health and student wastage, *Universities Quarterly*, 25(2).

Sampson, E.E. (1970) Student activism and the decade of protest. In E.E. Sampson, H.A. Korn and Associates, *Student Activism and Protest*. San Francisco: Jossey-Bass.

Sanders, C. (1992) When the locals wish students would leave old Durham town, *Times Higher Education Supplement*, 18 December.

Scherer, J. (1969) *Students in Residence: A Survey of American Studies*. Slough: National Foundation for Educational Research.

Schlesinger, S.H. (1979) Student lobbies: a new voice in the politics of higher education. Unpublished PhD dissertation, University of California, Los Angeles.

Schwab, J.J. (1969) *College Curriculum and Student Protest*. Chicago: University of Chicago Press.

Scottish Higher Education Funding Council (1993) *Quality Assessors' Handbook*. Edinburgh: SHEFC.

Scottish Union of Students (1963) Memorandum to the Committee on Higher Education, and oral evidence, in *Higher Education. Evidence – Part One*. Vol. C. London: HMSO.

Searle, J.R. (1971) *The Campus War: A Sympathetic Look at the University in Agony*. New York: World Publishing.

Segall, J.P. and Pickett, R.M. (eds) (1979) *Student Political Involvement in the 1970s*. Port Washington, NY: Kennikatt Press.

Seidel, H. (1979) The image of the university as given by students, *CRE – Information*, 46.

Sen, A. (1970) *Problems of Overseas Students and Nurses*. Slough: National Foundation for Educational Research.

Serow, R.C. (1991) Students and voluntarism: looking into the motives of community service participants, *American Educational Research Journal*, 28(3).

Shark, A.R., Brouder, K. and Associates (1976) *Students and Collective Bargaining*. Washington, DC: National Student Educational Fund.

Shea, C. (1994) New protest: students use hunger strikes to push campus demands, *Chronicle of Higher Education*, 25 May.

Shipman, M.D. (1969) *Participation and Staff–Student Relations. A Seven-Year Study of Social Changes in an Expanding College of Education*. London: Society for Research into Higher Education.

Siegel, R. (1967) The college commodity. In M. Cohen and D. Hale (eds), *The New Student Left*. Boston: Beacon Press.

Silver, H. (1965) Salaries for students?, *Universities Quarterly*, 19(4).

Silver, H. (1983) Higher education: the contenders. In N. Phillipson (ed.), *Universities, Society, and the Future.* Edinburgh: Edinburgh University Press.

Silver, H. (1987) From great expectations to bleak house, *Higher Education Quarterly,* 41(3).

Silver, H. (1990) *A Higher Education: The Council for National Academic Awards and British Higher Education 1964–1989.* London: Falmer.

Silver, H. (1992) *Student Feedback: Issues and Experience.* London: Council for National Academic Awards.

Silver, H. and Brennan, J. (1988) *A Liberal Vocationalism.* London: Methuen.

Silver, H. and Silver P. (1991) *Expectations of Higher Education: Some Historical Pointers.* Uxbridge: Brunel University, Expectations of Higher Education project.

Silver, P. and Silver, H. (1990) Students with disabilities in higher education: a project report. Oxford: Oxford Polytechnic.

Silverman, L.M. (1990) Women at Penn in the 1950s. In R.S. Dunn and M.F. Lloyd (eds), *A Pennsylvania Album: Undergraduate Essays on the 250th Anniversary of the University of Pennsylvania.* Philadelphia: University of Pennsylvania.

Simon, B. (1943) *A Student's View of the Universities.* London: Longmans, Green.

Simon, B. (1987) The student movement in England and Wales during the 1930s, *History of Education,* 16(3).

Sinclair, C. (1993) Networks of an articulate new breed, *Times Higher Education Supplement,* 30 April.

Slee, P. (1994) Enterprise in Higher Education 1989/93: Programme Evaluation. Durham: University of Durham.

Slipman, S. (1979) A student point of view. In S. Armstrong (ed.), *Decade of Change.* Guildford: Society for Research into Higher Education.

Sloman, A. (1970) British universities and their students. In J. Straw, A. Sloman and P. Doty, *Universities: Boundaries of Change.* London: Panther.

Smith, C. (1968) *Adolescence.* London: Longmans.

Smith, D.M. and Saunders, M.R. (1991) *Other Routes: Part-time Higher Education Policy.* Buckingham: Society for Research into Higher Education and Open University Press.

Society for Research into Higher Education [1966] *Student Residence – Research Aspects.* London: SRHE.

Soffer, R.N. (1992) Authority in the university: Balliol, Newnham and the new mythology. In R. Porter (ed.), *Myths of the English.* London: Polity Press.

Sparrow, J. (1970) Why do the young look like this?, *Sunday Times,* 6 September.

Stadtman, V.A. (1980) *Academic Adaptations: Higher Education Prepares for the 1980s and 1990s.* San Francisco: Jossey-Bass.

Stage, F.K. (1990) Research on college students: commonality, difference, and direction, *Review of Higher Education,* 13(3).

Stamm, M.J. (1972) The American college campus: a question of survival, *Universities Quarterly,* 26(2).

Stark, J.S. and associates (1977) *The Many Faces of Educational Consumerism.* Lexington, MA: D.C. Heath.

Startup, R. (1972a) Is the university a community?, *Higher Education Review,* 5(1).

Startup, R. (1972b) Why go to university?, *Universities Quarterly,* 26(3).

Startup, R. (1974) Why students wish to reform university government, *Research in Education,* 11.

Stedman Jones, G. (1969) The meaning of the student revolt. In A. Cockburn and R. Blackburn (eds), *Student Power: Problems, Diagnosis, Action.* Harmondsworth: Penguin.

Stern, F. (1971) Reflections on the international student movement. In T. Green (ed.), *Educational Planning in Perspective.* Guildford: Futures, IPC Business Press.

Still, R.J. (1954) The prevention of psychological illness among students, *Universities Quarterly,* 9(1).

Stone, L. (1983) Social control and intellectual excellence: Oxbridge and Edinburgh 1560–1983. In N. Phillipson (ed.), *Universities, Society, and the Future.* Edinburgh: Edinburgh University Press.

Straw, J. (1968) Participation in practice. In Fabian Society, *Students Today.* London: Fabian Society.

Straw, J. (1970) Student participation in higher education: education for democracy and technology. In J. Straw, A. Sloman and P. Doty (eds), *Universities: Boundaries of Change.* London: Panther.

Sunday Times (1970) Insight: on the Cambridge riot trial: four reasonable doubts, 12 July.

Swirsky, S. (1971) Four decades of activism. In P.G. Altbach, R.S. Laufer and S. McVey (eds), *Academic Supermarkets: A Critical Study of a Multiversity.* San Francisco: Jossey-Bass.

Symonds, K. (1995) Bite-sized chunks stick in the throat, *Times Higher Education Supplement,* 21 April.

Tajfel, H. and Dawson, J.L. (eds) *Disappointed Guests.* Oxford: Oxford University Press.

Taylor, H. (1969) *Students without Teachers: The Crisis in the University.* New York: Avon Books.

Taylor, W. (1965) Student culture and residence, *Universities Quarterly,* 19(4).

Terenzini, P.T. and Pascarella, E.T. (1984) Freshman attrition and the residential context, *Review of Higher Education,* 7(2).

Terenzini, P.T., Pascarella, E.T. and Lorang, W.G. (1982) An assessment of the academic and social influences on freshman year educational outcomes, *Review of Higher Education,* 5(2).

The Guardian/Gallup (1993–4) *Graduate Facts: Careers Research Project,* 3 vols. London: *The Guardian.*

The Guardian (1969) The unrest among students (interviews, British and American academics), 13 September.

Theus, K.T. (1988) Campus-based community service: new populism or 'smoke and mirrors?', *Change,* 20(5).

Thoday, D. (1957) How undergraduates work, *Universities Quarterly,* 11(2).

Thomas, N.L. (1991) The new *in loco parentis, Change,* 23(5).

Thorn, N.J. (1991) Revolutionaries and reformists: a history of the National Union of Students (UK), 1968–88. Unpublished MPhil thesis, University of Warwick.

Tight, M. (1982) *Part-time Degree Level Study in the United Kingdom.* Leicester: Advisory Council for Adult and Continuing Education.

Times Higher Education Supplement (1991) Student culture in decline, 20 September.

Times Higher Education Supplement (1993) Time to grow up, 5 November.

Tinto, V. (1975) Dropout from higher education: a theoretical synthesis of recent research, *Review of Educational Research,* 45.

Toombs, W. and Tierney, W.G. (1991) *Meeting the Mandate: Renewing the College and Departmental Curriculum* (ASHE-ERIC Higher Education Report No. 6). Washington, DC: George Washington University.

Townsend, B.K., Newell, L.J. and Wiese, M.D. (1992) *Creating Distinctiveness: Lessons from Uncommon Colleges and Universities* (ASHE-ERIC Higher Education Report No. 6). Washington, DC: George Washington University.

Trent Polytechnic (1988) Student participation in course monitoring and review (report of a working party of Academic Review Sub-Committee). Nottingham: Trent Polytechnic.

Trollope, A. (1906) *Barchester Towers*. London: Dent. First published in 1857.

Trow, M. (1966) The undergraduate dilemma in large state universities, *Universities Quarterly*, 21(1).

Trow, M. (1972) *The Expansion and Transformation of Higher Education*. Morristown, NJ: General Learning Press.

Truscot, B. (1945) *Redbrick and These Vital Days*. London: Faber and Faber.

Truscot, B. (1951) *Red Brick University*. Harmondsworth: Penguin. (First published in 1943.)

Tudor, H. (1988) *St Cuthbert's Society 1888–1988*. Durham: St Cuthbert's Society.

Tussman, J. (1969) *Experiment at Berkeley*. New York: Oxford University Press.

Tysome, T. (1995) Alarm over student suicides, *Times Higher Education Supplement*, 3 November.

Universities Quarterly (1954) Symposium on 'health and the student', 9(1).

University of Birmingham (1972) *Report of the Review Body Appointed by the Council of the University of Birmingham* (Grimond Report). Birmingham: University of Birmingham.

University of California at Berkeley (1968) *Education at Berkeley: Report of the Select Committee on Education* (Muscatine Report). Berkeley: University of California Press.

University Grants Committee (1948) *University Development from 1935 to 1947*. London: HMSO.

University Grants Committee (1953) *University Development. Report on the Years 1947 to 1952*. London: HMSO.

University Grants Committee (1958) *University Development 1952–1957*. London: HMSO.

University Grants Committee (1963) *University Development 1957–1962*. London: HMSO.

University of Oxford (1966) *Report of Commission of Inquiry* (Franks Report), Vol. 1. Oxford: Clarendon Press.

University of Oxford (1972) *Report of the Committee on Co-residence* (supplement to *University Gazette*), 102, May.

University of Warwick Union of Students (1968) The Development of the University 1968–1998 (a report by the Students' Representative Council). Warwick: UWUS.

University of York (1969) The role of students in the government of the university: report of a staff/student working party. In House of Commons Select Committee on Education and Science, *Student Relations*, Vol. 7: *Documents*, HC 449–vii, Session 1968–69. London: HMSO.

Vellela, T. (1988) *New Voices: Student Activism in the '80s and '90s*. Boston: South End Press.

Verger, J. (1983) Université et communauté au Moyen Age, *CRE-Information*, 62.

Veysey, L.R. (1970) *The Emergence of the American University*. Chicago: University of Chicago Press.

Wallace, S. (1987) Silent majority pushed into the cold, *Times Higher Education Supplement*, 25 September.

Wallerstein, I. (1969) *University in Turmoil: The Politics of Change*. New York: Atheneum.

Wallerstein, I and Starr, P. (eds) *The University Crisis Reader. Vol. One: The Liberal University under Attack*. New York: Random House.

Walton, C.C. and Bolman, F. den (1979) *Disorders in Higher Education*. New York: Prentice Hall.

Warner, G. (1985) *Conquering by Degrees: Glasgow University Union. A Centenary History 1885–1985*. Glasgow: GUU.

Warr, P.B. (1964) Attitudes and behaviour in a hall of residence, *Universities Quarterly*, 19(1).

Watkins, B.T. (1993) Getting a jump on jobs: students in 'co-op' programs work in professions related to their majors, *Chronicle of Higher Education*, 24 November.

Weinberg, I. and Walker, K.N. (1969) Student politics and political systems: towards a typology, *American Journal of Sociology*, 75(1).

Weinstein, N. (1995) Interviewed on 'a student-centred university', *Teaching News* (Oxford Brookes University), 41.

Whitburn, J., Mealing, M. and Cox, C. (1976) *People in Polytechnics: A Survey of Polytechnic Staff and Students 1972–3*. Guildford: Society for Research into Higher Education.

Whitworth, T.A. [1971] *Yellow Sandstone and Mellow Brick: An Account of Hatfield*. Durham: The College.

Wilcox, J.R. and Ebbs, S.L. (1992) *The Leadership Compass: Values and Ethics in Higher Education* (ASHE-ERIC Higher Education Report No. 1). Washington, DC: George Washington University.

Williams, B. (1968) *Protest, Reform and Revolution*. London: Birkbeck College.

Williams, D.T. Jr (1971) Students assess their colleges and universities: historical backgrounds. In F.F. Harcleroad and J.H. Cornell (eds), *Assessment of Colleges and Universities*. Iowa City: American Testing Program.

Williams, G. and Gordon, A. (1975) 16 and 19 year olds: attitudes to education, *Higher Education Bulletin*, 4(1).

Wilson, B. (1968) Youth culture, the universities and student unrest, *British Universities Annual*, 1968.

Wilson, B. [1970] *The Youth Culture and the Universities*. London: Faber and Faber.

Wilson, C.H. [1970] Principal's report 1969–70. In *Report of Council*. Glasgow: University of Glasgow.

Wilson, L. (1966) Is the student becoming the 'forgotten man'? In L.E. Dennis and J.F. Kauffman (eds), *The College and the Student*. Washington, DC: American Council on Education.

Winfrey, J.K. and Feder, D.D. (1965) Noninstructional services, *Review of Educational Research*, 35(4).

Wingfield, C.J. (1970) Campus conflict and institutional maintenance: an agenda for public administration, *Public Administration Review*, 30(2).

Wood, B. (1994) Living in hall: how was it for you?, *Teaching News* (Oxford Brookes University), 37.

Wood, J.L. (1974) *The Sources of American Student Activism*. Lexington, MA: D.C. Heath.

Woodley, A., Thompson, M. and Cowan, J. (1992) *Factors Affecting Non-completion Rates in Scottish Universities*. Milton Keynes: Open University, Student Research Centre.

Woolas, P. (1984) Why student will revolt, *Observer*, 18 November.

Wright, P. (1992) Learning through Enterprise: the Enterprise in Higher Education initiative. In R. Barnett (ed.), *Learning to Effect*. Buckingham: Society for Research into Higher Education and Open University Press.

Yankelovich, D. (1972) *The Changing Values on Campus: Political and Personal Attitudes of Today's College Students*. New York: Washington Square Press.

Yonge, G.D. (1965) Students, *Review of Educational Research*, 25(4).

Younge, Pat (1995) Figure it out, *Times Higher Education Supplement*, 7 April.

Zweig, F. (1963) *The Student in an Age of Anxiety: A Survey of Oxford and Manchester Students*. London: Heinemann.

Index

The Society for Research into Higher Education

The Society for Research into Higher Education exists to stimulate and coordinate research into all aspects of higher education. It aims to improve the quality of higher education through the encouragement of debate and publication on issues of policy, on the organization and management of higher education institutions, and on the curriculum and teaching methods.

The Society's income is derived from subscriptions, sales of its books and journals, conference fees and grants. It receives no subsidies, and is wholly independent. Its individual members include teachers, researchers, managers and students. Its corporate members are institutions of higher education, research institutes, professional, industrial and governmental bodies. Members are not only from the UK, but from elsewhere in Europe, from America, Canada and Australasia, and it regards its international work as among its most important activities.

Under the imprint *SRHE & Open University Press*, the Society is a specialist publisher of research, having some 60 titles in print. The Editorial Board of the Society's Imprint seeks authoritative research or study in the above fields. It offers competitive royalties, a highly recognizable format in both hardback and paperback and the world-wide reputation of the Open University Press.

The Society also publishes *Studies in Higher Education* (three times a year), which is mainly concerned with academic issues, *Higher Education Quarterly* (formerly *Universities Quarterly*), mainly concerned with policy issues, *Research into Higher Education Abstracts* (three times a year), and *SRHE News* (four times a year).

The Society holds a major annual conference in December, jointly with an institution of higher education. In 1994 the topic was 'The Student Experience' at the University of York. In 1995 it was 'The Changing University' at Heriot-Watt University in Edinburgh and in 1996, 'Working in Higher Education' at Cardiff Institute of Higher Education. Conferences in 1997 include 'Beyond the First Degree' at the University of Warwick.

The Society's committees, study groups and branches are run by the members. The groups at present include:

Teacher Education Study Group
Continuing Education Group
Staff Development Group
Excellence in Teaching and Learning

Benefits to members

Individual

Individual members receive:

- *SRHE News*, the Society's publications list, conference details and other material included in mailings.
- Greatly reduced rates for *Studies in Higher Education* and *Higher Education Quarterly*.
- A 35 per cent discount on all SRHE & Open University Press publications.
- Free copies of the Proceedings – commissioned papers on the theme of the Annual Conference.
- Free copies of *Research into Higher Education Abstracts*.
- Reduced rates for conferences.
- Extensive contacts and scope for facilitating initiatives.
- Reduced reciprocal memberships.
- Free copies of the *Register of Members' Research Interests*.

Corporate

Corporate members receive:

- All benefits of individual members, plus
- Free copies of *Studies in Higher Education*.
- Unlimited copies of the Society's publications at reduced rates.
- Special rates for its members, e.g. to the Annual Conference.
- The right to submit application for the Society's research grants.

Membership details: SRHE, 3 Devonshire Street, London WIN 2BA, UK. Tel: 0171 637 2766. Fax: 0171 637 2781
Catalogue: SRHE & Open University Press, Celtic Court, 22 Ballmoor, Buckingham MK18 1XW. Tel: (01280) 823388.